E.E. Cummings

Complete Poems

1904-1962

E. E. Cummings

Complete
Poems
1904-1962

REVISED, CORRECTED, AND EXPANDED EDITION
CONTAINING ALL THE PUBLISHED POETRY

EDITED BY GEORGE J. FIRMAGE

LIVERIGHT • *New York*

Library of Congress Cataloging-in-Publication Data

Cummings, E. E. (Edward Estlin), 1894–1962.
[Poems]
Complete poems, 1904–1962/E. E. Cummings : edited by George J. Firmage.—Rev., corr., and expanded ed. containing all the published poetry.
p. cm.
Includes bibliographical references and index.
I. Firmage, George James. II. Title.
PS3505.U334A17 1991
811'.52—dc20
91–29158

ISBN: 978-0-87140-710-8

Liveright Publishing Coporation
500 Fifth Avenue, New York, N.Y. 10110
www.wwnorton.com

W. W. Norton & Company Ltd.
Castle House, 75/76 Wells Street, London W1T 3QT

1 2 3 4 5 6 7 8 9 0

EDITOR'S NOTE

This revised, corrected, and expanded edition of E. E. Cummings's *Complete Poems* brings together, for the very first time, all of the poems published or designated for publication by the poet in his lifetime. In addition, 164 unpublished poems, issued in 1983 under the title *Etcetera*, and edited by Professor Richard S. Kennedy and the undersigned, have also been included.

The first American edition of *Complete Poems* was, of necessity, based only on printed sources. Unfortunately, many of these contain errors that can be traced back to the original typesetter's misreadings of the poet's manuscripts. For this new edition, the texts and order of all the poems are based entirely on the original manuscripts of Cummings's works which are now in the collections of the Houghton Library, Harvard University; the Clifton Waller Barrett Library, University of Virginia; the University of Texas Humanities Research Center; and the Beinecke Rare Book and Manuscript Library, Yale University. The cooperation and assistance of the foregoing institutions is gratefully acknowledged.

Between the poet's individual "booksofpoems" and the unpublished works from *Etcetera*, the reader will find a group of thirty-six "Uncollected Poems." Published between 1910 and 1962 in a variety of periodicals, an anthology of work by Cummings and his Harvard classmates, a volume of translations by the poet's friend D. Jon Grossman, and a book of photographs by Cummings's wife to which he contributed the text, these poems represent all of his published work not hitherto available in book form.

"Uncollected Poems" includes the poet's translation of Louis Aragon's *Le Front Rouge* with the French original *en face*. According to Cummings's account of his visit to the Soviet Union (*Eimi,* 1933), the translation was undertaken at the request of the Russian Revolutionary Literature Bureau as "a friendly gesture of farewell." The translator was quick to point out that Aragon's political beliefs were not his own; but "The Red Front" was not without interest as a poem, and its author and Cummings had been friends during the 1920s in Paris. Most important, the translation is excellent and one of the few mature examples we have of this phase of E. E. Cummings's art.

George James Firmage

CONTENTS

CHIMNEYS

& [AND] (1925)

is 5 (1926)

ONE

TWO

THREE

FOUR

FIVE

W [ViVa] (1931)

No Thanks (1935 Manuscript)

New Poems [from Collected Poems] (1938)

50 Poems (1940)

1 x 1 [One Times One] (1944)

1

XAIPE (1950)

95 Poems (1958)

73 Poems (1963)

Uncollected Poems (1910–1962)

Etcetera: The Unpublished Poems (1983)

The Harvard Years, 1911–16

Appendices

A. From the Poet's First Collection, 1904–5

B. From the Cambridge Latin School Years, 1908–11

C. Translations from Horace, 1913

Index of First Lines

E.E. Cummings

Complete Poems

1904-1962

Tulips & Chimneys

Tulips

EPITHALAMION

I.

Thou aged unreluctant earth who dost
with quivering continual thighs invite
the thrilling rain the slender paramour
to toy with thy extraordinary lust,
(the sinuous rain which rising from thy bed
steals to his wife the sky and hour by hour
wholly renews her pale flesh with delight)
—immortally whence are the high gods fled?

Speak elm eloquent pandar with thy nod
significant to the ecstatic earth
in token of his coming whom her soul
burns to embrace—and didst thou know the god
from but the imprint of whose cloven feet
the shrieking dryad sought her leafy goal,
at the mere echo of whose shining mirth
the furious hearts of mountains ceased to beat?

Wind beautifully who wanderest
over smooth pages of forgotten joy
proving the peaceful theorems of the flowers
—didst e'er depart upon more exquisite quest?
and did thy fortunate fingers sometime dwell
(within a greener shadow of secret bowers)
among the curves of that delicious boy
whose serious grace one goddess loved too well?

Chryselephantine Zeus Olympian
sceptred colossus of the Pheidian soul
whose eagle frights creation,in whose palm
Nike presents the crown sweetest to man,
whose lilied robe the sun's white hands emboss,
betwixt whose absolute feet anoint with calm
of intent stars circling the acerb pole
poises,smiling,the diadumenos

in whose young chiseled eyes the people saw
their once again victorious Pantarkes
(whose grace the prince of artists made him bold
to imitate between the feet of awe),
thunderer whose omnipotent brow showers
its curls of unendured eternal gold
over the infinite breast in bright degrees,
whose pillow is the graces and the hours,

father of gods and men whose subtle throne
twain sphinxes bear each with a writhing youth
caught to her brazen breasts,whose foot-stool tells
how fought the looser of the warlike zone
of her that brought forth tall Hippolytus,
lord on whose pedestal the deep expels
(over Selene's car closing uncouth)
of Helios the sweet wheels tremulous—

are there no kings in Argos,that the song
is silent,of the steep unspeaking tower
within whose brightening strictness Danae
saw the night severed and the glowing throng
descend,felt on her flesh the amorous strain
of gradual hands and yielding to that fee
her eager body's unimmortal flower
knew in the darkness a more burning rain?

2.

And still the mad magnificent herald Spring
assembles beauty from forgetfulness
with the wild trump of April:witchery
of sound and odour drives the wingless thing
man forth into bright air,for now the red
leaps in the maple's cheek,and suddenly
by shining hordes in sweet unserious dress
ascends the golden crocus from the dead.

On dappled dawn forth rides the pungent sun
with hooded day preening upon his hand
followed by gay untimid final flowers
(which dressed in various tremulous armor stun
the eyes of ragged earth who sees them pass)
while hunted from his kingdom winter cowers,
seeing green armies steadily expand
hearing the spear-song of the marching grass.

A silver sudden parody of snow
tickles the air to golden tears,and hark!
the flicker's laughing yet,while on the hills
the pines deepen to whispers primeval and throw
backward their foreheads to the barbarous bright
sky,and suddenly from the valley thrills
the unimaginable upward lark
and drowns the earth and passes into light

(slowly in life's serene perpetual round
a pale world gathers comfort to her soul,
hope richly scattered by the abundant sun
invades the new mosaic of the ground
—let but the incurious curtaining dusk be drawn
surpassing nets are sedulously spun
to snare the brutal dew,—the authentic scroll
of fairie hands and vanishing with dawn).

Spring,that omits no mention of desire
in every curved and curling thing,yet holds
continuous intercourse—through skies and trees
the lilac's smoke the poppy's pompous fire
the pansy's purple patience and the grave
frailty of daises—by what rare unease
revealed of teasingly transparent folds—
with man's poor soul superlatively brave.

Surely from robes of particoloured peace
with mouth flower-faint and undiscovered eyes
and dim slow perfect body amorous
(whiter than lilies which are born and cease
for being whiter than this world)exhales
the hovering high perfume curious
of that one month for whom the whole year dies,
risen at length from palpitating veils.

O still miraculous May!O shining girl
of time untarnished!O small intimate
gently primeval hands,frivolous feet
divine!O singular and breathless pearl!
O indefinable frail ultimate pose!
O visible beatitude sweet sweet
intolerable!silence immaculate
of god's evasive audible great rose!

3.

Lover,lead forth thy love unto that bed
prepared by whitest hands of waiting years,
curtained with wordless worship absolute,
unto the certain altar at whose head
stands that clear candle whose expecting breath
exults upon the tongue of flame half-mute,
(haste ere some thrush with silver several tears
complete the perfumed paraphrase of death).

Now is the time when all occasional things
close into silence,only one tree,one
svelte translation of eternity
unto the pale meaning of heaven clings,
(whose million leaves in winsome indolence
simmer upon thinking twilight momently)
as down the oblivious west's numerous dun
magnificence conquers magnificence.

In heaven's intolerable athanor
inimitably tortured the base day
utters at length her soft intrinsic hour,
and from those tenuous fires which more and more
sink and are lost the divine alchemist,
the magus of creation,lifts a flower—
whence is the world's insufferable clay
clothed with incognizable amethyst.

Lady at whose imperishable smile
the amazed doves flicker upon sunny wings
as if in terror of eternity,
(or seeming that they would mistrust a while
the moving of beauteous dead mouths throughout
that very proud transparent company
of quivering ghosts-of-love which scarcely sings
drifting in slow diaphanous faint rout),

queen in the inconceivable embrace
of whose tremendous hair that blossom stands
whereof is most desire,yet less than those
twain perfect roses whose ambrosial grace,
goddess,thy crippled thunder-forging groom
or the loud lord of skipping maenads knows,—
having Discordia's apple in thy hands,
which the scared shepherd gave thee for his doom—

O thou within the chancel of whose charms
the tall boy god of everlasting war
received the shuddering sacrament of sleep,
betwixt whose cool incorrigible arms
impaled upon delicious mystery,
with gaunt limbs reeking of the whispered deep,
deliberate groping ocean fondled o'er
the warm long flower of unchastity,

imperial Cytherea,from frail foam
sprung with irrevocable nakedness
to strike the young world into smoking song—
as the first star perfects the sensual dome
of darkness,and the sweet strong final bird
transcends the sight,O thou to whom belong
the hearts of lovers!—I beseech thee bless
thy suppliant singer and his wandering word.

OF NICOLETTE

dreaming in marble all the castle lay
like some gigantic ghost-flower born of night
blossoming in white towers to the moon,
soft sighed the passionate darkness to the tune
of tiny troubadours,and(phantom-white)
dumb-blooming boughs let fall their glorious snows,
and the unearthly sweetness of a rose
swam upward from the troubled heart of May;

a Winged Passion woke and one by one
there fell upon the night,like angel's tears,
the syllables of that mysterious prayer,
and as an opening lily drowsy-fair
(when from her couch of poppy petals peers
the sleepy morning)gently draws apart
her curtains,and lays bare her trembling heart,
with beads of dew made jewels by the sun,

so one high shining tower(which as a glass
turned light to flame and blazed with snowy fire)
unfolding,gave the moon a nymphlike face,
a form whose snowy symmetry of grace
haunted the limbs as music haunts the lyre,
a creature of white hands,who letting fall
a thread of lustre from the castle wall
glided,a drop of radiance,to the grass—

shunning the sudden moonbeam's treacherous snare
she sought the harbouring dark,and(catching up
her delicate silk)all white,with shining feet,
went forth into the dew:right wildly beat
her heart at every kiss of daisy-cup,
and from her cheek the beauteous colour went
with every bough that reverently bent
to touch the yellow wonder of her hair.

SONGS

I

(thee will i praise between those rivers whose
white voices pass upon forgetting(fail
me not)whose courseless waters are a gloat
of silver;o'er whose night three willows wail,
a slender dimness in the unshapeful hour
making dear moan in tones of stroked flower;
let not thy lust one threaded moment lose:
haste)the very shadowy sheep float
free upon terrific pastures pale,

whose tall mysterious shepherd lifts a cheek
teartroubled to the momentary wind
with guiding smile,lips wisely minced for blown
kisses,condemnatory fingers thinned
of pity—so he stands counting the moved
myriads wonderfully loved,
(hasten,it is the moment which shall seek
all blossoms that do learn,scents of not known
musics in whose careful eyes are dinned;

and the people of perfect darkness fills
his mind who will their hungering whispers hear
with weepings soundless,saying of "alas
we were chaste on earth we ghosts:hark to the sheer
cadence of our grey flesh in the gloom!
and still to be immortal is our doom;
but a rain frailly raging whom the hills
sink into and their sunsets,it shall pass.
Our feet tread sleepless meadows sweet with fear")

then be with me:unseriously seem
by the perusing greenness of thy thought
my golden soul fabulously to glue
in a superior terror;be thy taut
flesh silver,like the currency of faint
cities eternal—ere the sinless taint
of thy long sinful arms about me dream
shall my love wholly taste thee as a new
wine from steep hills by darkness softly brought—

(be with me in the sacred witchery
of almostness which May makes follow soon
on the sweet heels of passed afterday,
clothe thy soul's coming merely,with a croon
of mingling robes musically revealed
in rareness:let thy twain eyes deeply wield
a noise of petals falling silently
through the far-spaced possible nearaway
from huge trees drenched by a rounding moon)

II

when life is quite through with
and leaves say alas,
much is to do
for the swallow,that closes
a flight in the blue;

when love's had his tears out,
perhaps shall pass
a million years
(while a bee dozes
on the poppies,the dears;

when all's done and said,and
under the grass
lies her head
by oaks and roses
deliberated.)

III

Always before your voice my soul
half-beautiful and wholly droll
is as some smooth and awkward foal,
whereof young moons begin
the newness of his skin,

so of my stupid sincere youth
the exquisite failure uncouth
discovers a trembling and smooth
Unstrength,against the strong
silences of your song;

or as a single lamb whose sheen
of full unsheared fleece is mean
beside its lovelier friends,between
your thoughts more white than wool
My thought is sorrowful:

but my heart smote in trembling thirds
of anguish quivers to your words,
As to a flight of thirty birds
shakes with a thickening fright
the sudden fooled light.

it is the autumn of a year:
When through the thin air stooped with fear,
across the harvest whitely peer
empty of surprise
death's faultless eyes

(whose hand my folded soul shall know
while on faint hills do frailly go
The peaceful terrors of the snow,
and before your dead face
which sleeps,a dream shall pass)

and these my days their sounds and flowers
Fall in a pride of petaled hours,
like flowers at the feet of mowers
whose bodies strong with love
through meadows hugely move.

yet what am i that such and such
mysteries very simply touch
me,whose heart-wholeness overmuch
Expects of your hair pale,
a terror musical?

while in an earthless hour my fond
soul seriously yearns beyond
this fern of sunset frond on frond
opening in a rare
Slowness of gloried air...

The flute of morning stilled in noon—
noon the implacable bassoon—
now Twilight seeks the thrill of moon,
washed with a wild and thin
despair of violin

IV

Thy fingers make early flowers of
all things.
thy hair mostly the hours love:
a smoothness which
sings,saying
(though love be a day)
do not fear,we will go amaying.

thy whitest feet crisply are straying.
Always
thy moist eyes are at kisses playing,
whose strangeness much
says;singing
(though love be a day)
for which girl art thou flowers bringing?

To be thy lips is a sweet thing
and small.
Death,Thee i call rich beyond wishing
if this thou catch,
else missing.
(though love be a day
and life be nothing,it shall not stop kissing).

V

All in green went my love riding
on a great horse of gold
into the silver dawn.

four lean hounds crouched low and smiling
the merry deer ran before.

Fleeter be they than dappled dreams
the swift sweet deer
the red rare deer.

Four red roebuck at a white water
the cruel bugle sang before.

Horn at hip went my love riding
riding the echo down
into the silver dawn.

four lean hounds crouched low and smiling
the level meadows ran before.

Softer be they than slippered sleep
the lean lithe deer
the fleet flown deer.

Four fleet does at a gold valley
the famished arrow sang before.

Bow at belt went my love riding
riding the mountain down
into the silver dawn.

four lean hounds crouched low and smiling
the sheer peaks ran before.

Paler be they than daunting death
the sleek slim deer
the tall tense deer.

Four tall stags at a green mountain
the lucky hunter sang before.

All in green went my love riding
on a great horse of gold
into the silver dawn.

four lean hounds crouched low and smiling
my heart fell dead before.

VI

Where's Madge then,
Madge and her men?
buried with
Alice in her hair,
(but if you ask the rain
he'll not tell where.)

beauty makes terms
with time and his worms,
when loveliness
says sweetly Yes
to wind and cold;
and how much earth
is Madge worth?
Inquire of the flower that sways in the autumn
she will never guess.
but i know

VII

Doll's boy 's asleep
under a stile
he sees eight and twenty
ladies in a line

the first lady
says to nine ladies
his lips drink water
but his heart drinks wine

the tenth lady
says to nine ladies
they must chain his foot
for his wrist 's too fine

the nineteenth
says to nine ladies
you take his mouth
for his eyes are mine.

Doll's boy 's asleep
under the stile
for every mile the feet go
the heart goes nine

VIII

cruelly,love
walk the autumn long;
the last flower in whose hair,
thy lips are cold with songs

for which is
first to wither,to pass?
shallowness of sunlight
falls and,cruelly,
across the grass
Comes the
moon

love,walk the
autumn
love,for the last
flower in the hair withers;
thy hair is acold with
dreams,
love thou art frail

—walk the longness of autumn
smile dustily to the people,
for winter
who crookedly care.

IX

when god lets my body be

From each brave eye shall sprout a tree
fruit that dangles therefrom

the purpled world will dance upon
Between my lips which did sing

a rose shall beget the spring
that maidens whom passion wastes

will lay between their little breasts
My strong fingers beneath the snow

Into strenuous birds shall go
my love walking in the grass

their wings will touch with her face
and all the while shall my heart be

With the bulge and nuzzle of the sea

PUELLA MEA

Harun Omar and Master Hafiz
keep your dead beautiful ladies.
Mine is a little lovelier
than any of your ladies were.

In her perfectest array
my lady,moving in the day,
is a little stranger thing
than crisp Sheba with her king
in the morning wandering.
    Through the young and awkward hours
my lady perfectly moving,
through the new world scarce astir
my fragile lady wandering
in whose perishable poise
is the mystery of Spring
(with her beauty more than snow
dexterous and fugitive
my very frail lady drifting
distinctly,moving like a myth
in the uncertain morning,with
April feet like sudden flowers
and all her body filled with May)
—moving in the unskilful day
my lady utterly alive,
to me is a more curious thing
(a thing more nimble and complete)
than ever to Judea's king
were the shapely sharp cunning
and withal delirious feet
of the Princess Salomé
carefully dancing in the noise
of Herod's silence,long ago.

If she a little turn her head
i know that i am wholly dead:
nor ever did on such a throat
the lips of Tristram slowly dote,
La beale Isoud whose leman was.
And if my lady look at me
(with her eyes which like two elves
incredibly amuse themselves)
with a look of faerie,

perhaps a little suddenly
(as sometimes the improbable
beauty of my lady will)
—at her glance my spirit shies
rearing(as in the miracle
of a lady who had eyes
which the king's horses might not kill.)
    But should my lady smile,it were
a flower of so pure surprise
(it were so very new a flower,
a flower so frail,a flower so glad)
as trembling used to yield with dew
when the world was young and new
(a flower such as the world had
in Springtime when the world was mad
and Launcelot spoke to Guenever,
a flower which most heavy hung
with silence when the world was young
and Diarmuid looked in Grania's eyes.)
    But should my lady's beauty play
at not speaking(sometimes as
it will)the silence of her face
doth immediately make
in my heart so great a noise,
as in the sharp and thirsty blood
of Paris would not all the Troys
of Helen's beauty:never did
Lord Jason(in impossible things
victorious impossibly)
so wholly burn,to undertake
Medea's rescuing eyes;nor he
when swooned the white egyptian day
who with Egypt's body lay.

Lovely as those ladies were
mine is a little lovelier.

And if she speaks in her frail way,
it is wholly to bewitch
my smallest thought with a most swift
radiance wherein slowly drift
murmurous things divinely bright;
it is foolingly to smite
my spirit with the lithe free twitch
of scintillant space,with the cool writhe

of gloom truly which syncopate
some sunbeam's skilful fingerings;
it is utterly to lull
with foliate inscrutable
sweetness my soul obedient;
it is to stroke my being with
numbing forests frolicsome,
fleetly mystical,aroam
with keen creatures of idiom
(beings alert and innocent
very deftly upon which
indolent miracles impinge)
—it is distinctly to confute
my reason with the deep caress
of every most shy thing and mute,
it is to quell me with the twinge
of all living intense things.

    Never my soul so fortunate
is(past the luck of all dead men
and loving)as invisibly when
upon her palpable solitude
a furtive occult fragrance steals,
a gesture of immaculate
perfume—whereby(with fear aglow)
my soul is wont wholly to know
the poignant instantaneous fern
whose scrupulous enchanted fronds
toward all things intrinsic yearn,
the immanent subliminal
fern of her delicious voice
(of her voice which always dwells
beside the vivid magical
impetuous and utter ponds
of dream;and very secret food
its leaves inimitable find
beyond the white authentic springs,
beyond the sweet instinctive wells,
which make to flourish the minute
spontaneous meadow of her mind)
—the vocal fern,always which feels
the keen ecstatic actual tread
(and thereto perfectly responds)
of all things exquisite and dead,
all living things and beautiful.

(Caliph and king their ladies had
to love them and to make them glad,
when the world was young and mad,
in the city of Bagdad—
mine is a little lovelier
than any of those ladies were.)

Her body is most beauteous,
being for all things amorous
fashioned very curiously
of roses and of ivory.
The immaculate crisp head
is such as only certain dead
and careful painters love to use
for their youngest angels(whose
praising bodies in a row
between slow glories fleetly go.)
Upon a keen and lovely throat
the strangeness of her face doth float,
which in eyes and lips consists
—always upon the mouth there trysts
curvingly a fragile smile
which like a flower lieth(while
within the eyes is dimly heard
a wistful and precarious bird.)
Springing from fragrant shoulders small,
ardent,and perfectly withal
smooth to stroke and sweet to see
as a supple and young tree,
her slim lascivious arms alight
in skilful wrists which hint at flight
—my lady's very singular
and slenderest hands moreover are
(which as lilies smile and quail)
of all things perfect the most frail.

(Whoso rideth in the tale
of Chaucer knoweth many a pair
of companions blithe and fair;
who to walk with Master Gower
in Confessio doth prefer
shall not lack for beauty there,
nor he that will amaying go
with my lord Boccaccio—
whoso knocketh at the door

of Marie and of Maleore
findeth of ladies goodly store
whose beauty did in nothing err.
If to me there shall appear
than a rose more sweetly known,
more silently than a flower,
my lady naked in her hair—
i for those ladies nothing care
nor any lady dead and gone.)

Each tapering breast is firm and smooth
that in a lovely fashion doth
from my lady's body grow;
as morning may a lily know,
her petaled flesh doth entertain
the adroit blood's mysterious skein
(but like some passionate earlier
flower,the snow will oft utter,
whereof the year has perfect bliss—
for each breast a blossom is,
which being a little while caressed
its fragrance makes the lover blest.)
Her waist is a most tiny hinge
of flesh,a winsome thing and strange;
apt in my hand warmly to lie
it is a throbbing neck whereby
to grasp the belly's ample vase
(that urgent urn which doth amass
for whoso drinks,a dizzier wine
than should the grapes of heaven combine
with earth's madness)—'tis a gate
unto a palace intricate
(whereof the luscious pillars rise
which are her large and shapely thighs)
in whose dome the trembling bliss
of a kingdom wholly is.
    Beneath her thighs such legs are seen
as were the pride of the world's queen:
each is a verb,miraculous
inflected oral devious,
beneath the body's breathing noun
(moreover the delicious frown
of the grave great sensual knees
well might any monarch please.)
Each ankle is divinely shy;

as if for fear you would espy
the little distinct foot(if whose
very minuteness doth abuse
reason,why then the artificer
did most exquisitely err.)

When the world was like a song
heard behind a golden door,
poet and sage and caliph had
to love them and to make them glad
ladies with lithe eyes and long
(when the world was like a flower
Omar Hafiz and Harun
loved their ladies in the moon)
—fashioned very curiously
of roses and of ivory
if naked she appears to me
my flesh is an enchanted tree;
with her lips' most frail parting
my body hears the cry of Spring,
and with their frailest syllable
its leaves go crisp with miracle.

Love!—maker of my lady,
in that always beyond this
poem or any poem she
of whose body words are afraid
perfectly beautiful is,
forgive these words which i have made.
And never boast your dead beauties,
you greatest lovers in the world!
who with Grania strangely fled,
who with Egypt went to bed,
whom white-thighed Semiramis
put up her mouth to wholly kiss—
never boast your dead beauties,
mine being unto me sweeter
(of whose shy delicious glance
things which never more shall be,
perfect things of faerie,
are intense inhabitants;
in whose warm superlative
body do distinctly live
all sweet cities passed away—
in her flesh at break of day

are the smells of Nineveh,
in her eyes when day is gone
are the cries of Babylon.)
Diarmuid Paris and Solomon,
Omar Harun and Master Hafiz,
to me your ladies are all one—
keep your dead beautiful ladies.

Eater of all things lovely—Time!
upon whose watering lips the world
poises a moment(futile,proud,
a costly morsel of sweet tears)
gesticulates,and disappears—
of all dainties which do crowd
gaily upon oblivion
sweeter than any there is one;
to touch it is the fear of rhyme—
in life's very fragile hour
(when the world was like a tale
made of laughter and of dew,
was a flight,a flower,a flame,
was a tendril fleetly curled
upon frailness)used to stroll
(very slowly)one or two
ladies like flowers made,
softly used to wholly move
slender ladies made of dream
(in the lazy world and new
sweetly used to laugh and love
ladies with crisp eyes and frail,
in the city of Bagdad.)

Keep your dead beautiful ladies
Harun Omar and Master Hafiz.

CHANSONS INNOCENTES

I

in Just-
spring   when the world is mud-
luscious the little
lame balloonman

whistles   far   and wee

and eddieandbill come
running from marbles and
piracies and it's
spring

when the world is puddle-wonderful

the queer
old balloonman whistles
far   and   wee
and bettyandisbel come dancing

from hop-scotch and jump-rope and

it's
spring
and
    the

        goat-footed

balloonMan   whistles
far
and
wee

II

hist   whist
little ghostthings
tip-toe
twinkle-toe

little twitchy
witches and tingling
goblins
hob-a-nob   hob-a-nob

little hoppy happy
toad in tweeds
tweeds
little itchy mousies

with scuttling
eyes   rustle and run   and
hidehidehide
whisk

whisk   look out for the old woman
with the wart on her nose
what she'll do to yer
nobody knows

for she knows the devil   ooch
the devil   ouch
the devil
ach   the great

green
dancing
devil
devil

devil
devil

     wheeEEE

III

little tree
little silent Christmas tree
you are so little
you are more like a flower

who found you in the green forest
and were you very sorry to come away?
see   i will comfort you
because you smell so sweetly

i will kiss your cool bark
and hug you safe and tight
just as your mother would,
only don't be afraid

look   the spangles
that sleep all the year in a dark box
dreaming of being taken out and allowed to shine,
the balls the chains red and gold the fluffy threads,

put up your little arms
and i'll give them all to you to hold
every finger shall have its ring
and there won't be a single place dark or unhappy

then when you're quite dressed
you'll stand in the window for everyone to see
and how they'll stare!
oh but you'll be very proud

and my little sister and i will take hands
and looking up at our beautiful tree
we'll dance and sing
"Noel Noel"

IV

why did you go
little fourpaws?
you forgot to shut
your big eyes.

where did you go?
like little kittens
are all the leaves
which open in the rain.

little kittens who
are called spring,
is what we stroke
maybe asleep?

do you know?or maybe did
something go away
ever so quietly
when we weren't looking.

V

Tumbling-hair
                picker of buttercups
                              violets
dandelions
And the big bullying daisies
                        through the field wonderful
with eyes a little sorry
Another comes
                also picking flowers

ORIENTALE

I

i spoke to thee
with a smile and thou didst not
answer
thy mouth is as
a chord of crimson music
                              Come hither

O thou,is life not a smile?

i spoke to thee with
a song and thou
didst not listen
thine eyes are as a vase
of divine silence
                    Come hither
O thou,is life not a song?

i spoke
to thee with a soul and
thou didst not wonder
thy face is as a dream locked
in white fragrance
                        Come hither
O thou,is life not love?

i speak to
thee with a sword
and thou art silent
thy breast is as a tomb
softer than flowers
                          Come hither
O thou,is love not death?

II

my love
thy hair is one kingdom
    the king whereof is darkness
thy forehead is a flight of flowers

thy head is a quick forest
    filled with sleeping birds
thy breasts are swarms of white bees
    upon the bough of thy body
thy body to me is April
in whose armpits is the approach of spring

thy thighs are white horses yoked to a chariot
    of kings
they are the striking of a good minstrel
between them is always a pleasant song

my love
thy head is a casket
    of the cool jewel of thy mind
the hair of thy head is one warrior
    innocent of defeat
thy hair upon thy shoulders is an army
    with victory and with trumpets

thy legs are the trees of dreaming
whose fruit is the very eatage of forgetfulness

thy lips are satraps in scarlet
    in whose kiss is the combining of kings
thy wrists
are holy
    which are the keepers of the keys of thy blood
thy feet upon thy ankles are flowers in vases
    of silver

in thy beauty is the dilemma of flutes

    thy eyes are the betrayal
of bells comprehended through incense

34

III

listen
beloved
i dreamed
    it appeared that you thought to
    escape me and became a great
    lily atilt on
    insolent
    waters   but i was aware of
    fragrance and i came riding upon
    a horse of porphyry   into the
    waters i rode down the red
    horse shrieking   from splintering
    foam caught you clutched you upon my
    mouth
listen
beloved
    i dreamed   in my dream you had
    desire to thwart me and became
    a little bird and hid
    in a tree of tall marble
    from a great way i distinguished
    singing and i came
    riding upon a scarlet sunset
    trampling the night   easily
    from the shocked impossible
    tower i caught
    you strained you
    broke you upon my blood
listen
    beloved i dreamed
    i thought you would have deceived
    me and became a star in the kingdom
    of heaven
    through day and space i saw you close
    your eyes   and i came riding
    upon a thousand crimson years arched with agony
    i reined them in tottering before
    the throne and as
    they shied at the automaton moon from
    the transplendent hand of sombre god
    i picked you
as an apple is picked by the little peasants for their girls

IV

unto thee i
burn incense
the bowl crackles
upon the gloom arise purple pencils

fluent spires of fragrance
the bowl
seethes
a flutter of stars

a turbulence of forms
delightful with indefinable flowering,
the air is
deep with desirable flowers

i think
thou lovest incense
for in the ambiguous faint aspirings
the indolent frail ascensions,

of thy smile rises the immaculate
sorrow
of thy low
hair flutter the level litanies

unto thee i burn
incense,over the dim smoke
straining my lips are vague with
ecstasy my palpitating breasts inhale the

slow
supple
flower
of thy beauty,my heart discovers thee

unto
whom i
burn
olbanum

V

lean candles hunger in
the silence a
brown god
smiles between greentwittering

smokes   from broken eyes
a sound
of strangling breasts and bestial
grovelling

hands rasps the purple
dark-
ness
a

worshipper
prostrate within twitching shadow
lolls

sobbing

with lust

VI

I.

the emperor
sleeps in a palace of porphyry
which was a million years building
he takes the air in a howdah
of jasper beneath saffron
umbrellas
upon an elephant
twelve feet high
behind whose ear
sits always a crowned
king twir-
ling an
ankus of
ebony
the fountains of the emperor's
palace run sunlight and
moonlight and the emperor's
elephant is a thousand years old

the harem of
the emperor
is carpeted with
gold cloth
from the
ceiling(one
diamond timid
with nesting incense)
fifty
marble
pillars
slipped from immeasurable
height,fall,fifty,silent

in the incense is tangled a cool moon

there are thrice-three-hundred
doors carven of chalcedony and
before every door a naked
eunuch watches
on their heads turbans of a hundred
colours
in their hands scimitars like windy torches
each
is
blacker than oblivion

the ladies
of the emperor's
harem are queens
of all the earth and the rings
upon their hands are from mines
a mile deep
but the body of
the queen of queens is
more transparent
than water,she is softer than birds

2.

when the emperor is very
amorous he reclines upon
the couch of couches and
beckons   with
the little
finger of his left
hand
then the
thrice-three-hundredth
door is opened by the tallest
eunuch and the queen
of queens comes
forth
ankles
musical with large pearls
kingdoms in her ears

at the feet of
the emperor a cithern-
player squats with
quiveringgold
body
behind
the emperor ten
elected warriors with
bodies of lazy jade
and twitching
eyelids
finger
their
unquiet
spears

the queen of queens is dancing

her subtle
body weaving
insinuating upon the gold cloth
incessantly creates patterns of sudden
lust
her
stealing body ex-
pending gathering pouring upon itself   stiffenS
to a
white thorn
of desire

the taut neck of the citharede wags
in the dust the ghastly warriors
amber with lust breathe
together   the emperor,exerting
himself among his pillows throws
jewels at the queen of queens and
white money upon her nakedness
he
nods
            and all
depart through the bruised air aflutter with pearls

3.

they are
alone
he beckons,she rises she
stands
a moment
in the passion of the fifty
pillars
listening

while the queens of all the
earth writhe upon deep rugs

AMORES

I

your little voice
                    Over the wires came leaping
and i felt suddenly
dizzy
            With the jostling and shouting of merry flowers
wee skipping high-heeled flames
courtesied before my eyes
                                or twinkling over to my side
Looked up
with impertinently exquisite faces
floating hands were laid upon me
I was whirled and tossed into delicious dancing
up
Up
with the pale important
                            stars and the Humorous
                                                        moon
dear girl
How i was crazy how i cried when i heard
                                        over time
and tide and death
leaping
Sweetly
        your voice

II

in the rain-
darkness,   the sunset
being sheathed i sit and
think of you

the holy
city which is your face
your little cheeks the streets
of smiles

your eyes half-
thrush
half-angel and your drowsy
lips where float flowers of kiss

and
there is the sweet shy pirouette
your hair
and then

your dancesong
soul.   rarely-beloved
a single star is
uttered,and i

think
        of you

III

there is a
moon sole
in the blue
night

     amorous of waters
tremulous,
blinded with silence the
undulous heaven yearns where

in tense starlessness
anoint with ardor
the yellow lover

stands in the dumb dark
svelte
and
urgent

     (again
love i slowly
gather
of thy languorous mouth the

thrilling
flower)

IV

consider O
woman this
my body.
for it has

lain
with empty arms
upon the giddy hills
to dream of you,

approve these
firm unsated
eyes
which have beheld

night's speechless carnival
the painting
of the dark
with meteors

streaming from playful
immortal hands
the bursting
of the wafted stars

(in time to come you shall
remember of this night amazing
ecstasies   slowly,
in the glutted

heart fleet
flowerterrible
memories
shall

rise,slowly
return upon the
                    red elected lips

scaleless visions)

V

as is the sea marvelous
from god's
hands which sent her forth
to sleep upon the world

and the earth withers
the moon crumbles
one by one
stars flutter into dust

but the sea
does not change
and she goes forth out of hands and
she returns into hands

and is with sleep....

love,
    the breaking

of your
       soul
       upon
my lips

VI

into the smiting
sky tense
with
blend

ing
the
tree   leaps
           a stiffened exquisite

i
wait the sweet
annihilation of swift
flesh

i make me stern against
your charming strength

O haste
       annihilator
drawing into you my enchanting
leaves

VII

if i believe
in death be sure
of this
it is

because you have loved me,
moon and sunset
stars and flowers
gold crescendo and silver muting

of seatides
i trusted not,
          one night
when in my fingers

drooped your shining body
when my heart
sang between your perfect
breasts

darkness and beauty of stars
was on my mouth petals danced
against my eyes
and down

the singing reaches of
my soul
spoke
the green-

greeting pale-
departing irrevocable
sea
i knew thee death.

          and when
i have offered up each fragrant
night,when all my days
shall have before a certain

face become
white
perfume
only,

      from the ashes
then
thou wilt rise and thou
wilt come to her and brush

the mischief from her eyes and fold
her
mouth the new
flower with

thy unimaginable
wings,where dwells the breath
of all persisting stars

VIII

the glory is fallen out of
the sky the last immortal
leaf
is

dead and the gold
year
a formal spasm
in the

dust
this is the passing of all shining things
therefore we also
blandly

into receptive
earth,O let
us
descend

take
shimmering wind
these fragile splendors from
us crumple them hide

them in thy breath drive
them in nothingness
for we
would sleep

this is the passing of all shining things
no lingering no backward-
wondering be unto
us O

soul,but straight
glad feet fearruining
and glorygirded
faces

lead us
into the
serious
steep

darkness

IX

i like
to think that on
the flower you gave me when we
loved

      the far-
departed mouth sweetly-saluted
lingers.
        if one marvel

seeing the hunger of my
lips for a dead thing,
i shall instruct
him silently with becoming

steps to seek
your face   and i
entreat,by certain foolish perfect
hours

      dead too,
if that he come receive
him as your lover sumptuously
being

kind
      because i trust him to
your grace,and for
in his own land

he is called death.

X

after five
times the poem
of thy remembrance
surprises with refrain

of unreasoning summer
that by responding
ways cloaked with renewal
my body turns toward

thee
again   for the stars have been
finished in the nobler trees and
the language of leaves repeats

eventual perfection
while east deserves of dawn.
i lie at length,breathing
with shut eyes

the sweet earth where thou liest

XI

O Distinct
Lady of my unkempt adoration
if i have made
a fragile certain

song under the window of your soul
it is not like any songs
(the singers the others
they have been faithful

to many things and which
die
i have been sometimes true
to Nothing and which lives

they were fond of the handsome
moon   never spoke ill of the
pretty stars   and to
the serene the complicated

and the obvious
they were faithful
and which i despise,
frankly

admitting i have been true
only to the noise of worms.
in the eligible day
under the unaccountable sun)

Distinct Lady
swiftly take
my fragile certain song
that we may watch together

how behind the doomed
exact smile of life's
placid obscure palpable
carnival where to a normal

melody of probable violins dance
the square virtues and the oblong sins
perfectly
gesticulate the accurate

strenuous lips of incorruptible
Nothing   under the ample
sun,under the insufficient
day under the noise of worms

LA GUERRE

I

Humanity i love you
because you would rather black the boots of
success than enquire whose soul dangles from his
watch-chain which would be embarrassing for both

parties and because you
unflinchingly applaud all
songs containing the words country home and
mother when sung at the old howard

Humanity i love you because
when you're hard up you pawn your
intelligence to buy a drink and when
you're flush pride keeps

you from the pawn shop and
because you are continually committing
nuisances but more
especially in your own house

Humanity i love you because you
are perpetually putting the secret of
life in your pants and forgetting
it's there and sitting down

on it
and because you are
forever making poems in the lap
of death Humanity

i hate you

II

earth like a tipsy
biddy with an old mop punching
underneath
conventions exposes

hidden obscenities
nudging
into neglected sentiments brings
to light dusty

heroisms
and
finally colliding with the most
expensive furniture upsets

a
crucifix which smashes into several
pieces and is hurriedly picked up and
thrown on the ash-heap

where
lies
          what was once the discobolus of
one

Myron

III

the bigness of cannon
is skilful,

but i have seen
death's clever enormous voice
which hides in a fragility
of poppies....

i say that sometimes
on these long talkative animals
are laid fists of huger silence.

I have seen all the silence
filled with vivid noiseless boys

at Roupy
i have seen
between barrages,

the night utter ripe unspeaking girls.

IV

little ladies more
than dead exactly dance
in my head,precisely
dance where danced la guerre.

Mimi à
la voix fragile
qui chatouille Des
Italiens

the putain with the ivory throat
Marie Louise Lallemand
n'est–ce pas que je suis belle
chéri? les anglais m'aiment
tous,les américains
aussi...."bon dos,bon cul de Paris"(Marie
Vierge
Priez
Pour
Nous)

with the
long lips of
Lucienne which dangle
the old men and hot
men se promènent
doucement le soir(ladies

accurately dead les anglais
sont gentils et les américains
aussi,ils payent bien les américains dance

exactly in my brain voulez–
vous coucher avec
moi? Non? pourquoi?)

ladies skilfully
dead precisely dance
where has danced la
guerre j'm'appelle
Manon,cinq rue Henri Monnier
voulez-vous coucher avec moi?
te ferai Mimi
te ferai Minette,
dead exactly dance
si vous voulez
chatouiller
mon lézard ladies suddenly
j'm'en fous des nègres

                            (in the twilight of Paris
Marie Louise with queenly
legs cinq rue Henri
Monnier a little love
begs,Mimi with the body
like une boîte à joujoux,want nice sleep?
toutes les petites femmes exactes
qui dansent toujours in my
head dis-donc,Paris

ta gorge mystérieuse
pourquoi se promène-t-elle,pourquoi
éclate ta voix
fragile couleur de pivoine?)
                                with the

long lips of Lucienne which
dangle the old men and hot men
precisely dance in my head
ladies carefully dead

V

O sweet spontaneous
earth how often have
the
doting

      fingers of
prurient philosophers pinched
and
poked

thee
,has the naughty thumb
of science prodded
thy

     beauty   .how
often have religions taken
thee upon their scraggy knees
squeezing and

buffeting thee that thou mightest conceive
gods
     (but
true

to the incomparable
couch of death thy
rhythmic
lover

     thou answerest

them only with

       spring)

IMPRESSIONS

I

Lady of Silence
from the winsome cage of
thy body
rose
    through the sensible
night
a
quick bird

(tenderly upon
the dark's prodigious face
thy
voice
    scattering perfume-gifted
wings
suddenly escorts
with feet
sun-sheer

the smarting beauty of dawn)

II

the sky a silver
dissonance by the correct
fingers of April
resolved

        into a
clutter of trite jewels

now like a moth with stumbling

wings flutters and flops along the
grass collides with trees and
houses and finally,
butts into the river

III

writhe and
gape of tortured

  perspective
  rasp and graze of splintered

normality
         crackle and
         sag
  of planes   clamors of
  collision
  collapse   As

peacefully,
lifted
into the awful beauty
              of sunset

              the young city
putting off dimension with a blush
enters
the becoming garden of her agony

IV

the hills
like poets' put on
purple thought against
the

magnificent clamor of
                            day
tortured
in gold,which presently

crumpled
collapses
exhaling a red soul into the dark

so
duneyed master
enter
the sweet gates

                        of my heart and
take
the
rose,

which perfect
is
With killing hands

V

stinging
gold swarms
upon the spires
silver

    chants the litanies the
great bells are ringing with rose
the lewd fat bells
                and a tall

wind
is dragging
the
sea

with

dream

-S

VI

the
    sky
          was
can   dy lu
minous
            edible
spry
      pinks shy
lemons
greens   coo   l choc
olate
s.

  un   der,
  a   lo
co
mo
     tive   s   pout
                    ing
                     vi
                      o
                      lets

VII

i was considering how
within night's loose
sack a star's
nibbling in-

fin
-i-
tes-
i
-mal-
ly devours

darkness the
hungry star
which
will e

-ven
tu-
al
-ly jiggle
the bait of
dawn and be jerked

into

eternity. when over my head a
shooting
star
Bur   s

          (t
               into a stale shriek
like an alarm-clock)

VIII

between green
                    mountains
sings the flinger
of

fire   beyond red rivers
of fair perpetual
feet the
sinuous

        riot

the
flashing
bacchant.

partedpetaled
mouth,face
delirious.   indivisible
grace

        of dancing

IX

the hours rise up putting off stars and it is
dawn
into the street of the sky light walks scattering poems

on earth a candle is
extinguished   the city
wakes
with a song upon her
mouth having death in her eyes

and it is dawn
the world
goes forth to murder dreams....

i see in the street where strong
men are digging bread
and i see the brutal faces of
people contented hideous hopeless cruel happy

and it is day,

in the mirror
i see a frail
man
dreaming
dreams
dreams in the mirror

and it
is dusk   on earth

a candle is lighted
and it is dark.
the people are in their houses
the frail man is in his bed
the city

sleeps with death upon her mouth having a song in her eyes
the hours descend,
putting on stars....

in the street of the sky night walks scattering poems

X

i will wade out
     till my thighs are steeped in burning flowers
I will take the sun in my mouth
and leap into the ripe air
    Alive
      with closed eyes
to dash against darkness
      in the sleeping curves of my body
Shall enter fingers of smooth mastery
with chasteness of sea-girls
     Will i complete the mystery
     of my flesh
I will rise
   After a thousand years
lipping
flowers
   And set my teeth in the silver of the moon

PORTRAITS

I

of my
soul a street is:
prettinesses Pic-
abian tricktrickclickflick-er
garnished
of stark Picasso
throttling trees

hither
my soul
repairs herself with
prisms of sharp mind
and Matisse rhythms
to juggle Kandinsky gold-fish

away from the gripping gigantic
muscles of Cézanne's
logic,
      oho.
       a street
there is

where strange birds   purr

II

being
twelve
who hast merely
gonorrhea

            Oldeyed
child,to
ambitious weeness
of boots

tiny
add
death
 what

shall?

III

as usual i did not find him in cafes,the more dissolute atmosphere
of a street superimposing a numbing imperfectness upon such peregri-
nations as twilight spontaneously by inevitable tiredness of flang-
ing shop-girls impersonally affords furnished a soft first clue to
his innumerable whereabouts   violet logic of annihilation demon-
strating from woolworthian pinnacle a capable millennium of faces
meshing with my curiously instant appreciation exposed his hiber-
native contours,
aimiable immensity impeccably extending the courtesy of five o'clock
became the omen of his presence   it was spring by the way in the
soiled canary-cage of largest existence

(when he would extemporise the innovation of muscularity upon the
most crimson assistance of my comforter a click of deciding glory
inflicted to the negative silence that primeval exposure whose elec-
tric solidity remembers some accurately profuse scratchings in a
recently discovered cave,   the carouse of geometrical putrescence
whereto my invariably commendable room has been forever subject his
Earliest word wheeled out on the sunny dump of oblivion)

a tiny dust finely arising at the integration of my soul i coughed

,naturally

IV

the skinny voice

of the leatherfaced
woman with the crimson
nose and coquettishly-
cocked bonnet

having ceased   the

captain
announces that as three
dimes seven nickels and ten
pennies have been deposited upon

the drum   there is need

of just twenty five cents
dear friends
to make it an even
dollar   whereupon

the Divine Average who was

attracted by the inspired
sister's howling moves
off
will anyone tell him why he should

blow two bits for the coming of Christ Jesus

?
??
???
!

nix,kid

V

Babylon slim
-ness of
evenslicing
eyes are chisels

scarlet Goes
with her
whitehot
face,gashed

by hair's blue cold

jolts of
lovecrazed abrupt

flesh split "Pretty
Baby"
to
numb rhythm before christ

VI

the dress was a suspicious madder,importing the cruelty of roses.
The exciting simplicity of her hipless body,pausing to invent im-
perceptible bulgings of the pretended breasts,forked in surpris-
able unliving eyes chopped by a swollen inanity of picture hat.

the arms hung ugly.,the hands sharp and impertinently dead.

expression began with the early cessation of her skirt.   flesh-
less melody of the,keenly lascivious legs.   painful ankles large
acute brutal feet propped on irrelevantly ferocious heels.

Her gasping slippery body moved with the hideous spontaneity
of a solemn mechanism.   beneath her drab tempo of hasteful futility
lived brilliantly the enormous rhythm of absurdity.

skin like the poisonous fragility of ice newly formed upon an old
pool.   Her nose was small,exact,stupid.   mouth normal,large,unclever.
hair genuinely artificial,unpleasantly tremendous.

under flat lusts of light her nice concupiscence appeared round-
ed.

if she were alive,death was amusing

VII

of evident invisibles
exquisite the hovering

at the dark portals

of hurt girl eyes

sincere with wonder

a poise a wounding
a beautiful suppression

the accurate boy mouth

now droops the faun head

now the intimate flower dreams

of parted lips
dim upon the syrinx

VIII

the
nimble
heat
had

long on a certain
taut precarious
holiday
frighteningly

performed
and
at tremont and bromfield i
paused a moment because

on the frying
curb the
quiet face
lay

which had been dorothy
and once
permitted
me for

twenty
iron
men
her common purple

soul
the absurd eyelids sulked
enormous
sobs puckered the foolish

breasts the
droll
mouth
wilted

and not old,harry,a
woman in the crowd
whinnied and a man squeezing her
waist said

the cop 's rung for the
wagon but as i was
lifting the horror
of her toylike

head and vainly
tried to
catch one funny
hand opening the hard great

eyes to noone in particular she
gasped almost
loudly
i'm

so
drunG

k,dear

IX

ta
ppin
g
toe

hip
popot
amus Back

gen
teel-ly
lugu-
bri ous

                    eyes
LOOPTHELOOP

as

fathandsbangrag

X

it's just like a coffin's
inside when you die,
pretentious and
shiny and
not too wide
                    dear god

there's a portrait
over the door very notable of
the sultan's nose pullable and rosy
flanked by the scrumptious magdalene
of whoisit and madame
something by gainsborough
                              just the playthings
                        for dust   n'est-ce pas

      effendi drifts between
      tables like an old leaf
      between toadstools
he is the cheerfulest of men
      his peaked head smoulders
      like a new turd in April
      his legs are brittle and small
      his feet large and fragile
his queer hands twitter before him,like foolish
      butterflies
he is the most courteous of men

should you remark the walls have been repapered

he will nod
            like buddha
            or answer modestly
i am dying

so let us come in together and
drink coffee covered with froth
half-mud
and not too
sweet?

XI

between nose-red gross
walls   sprawling with tipsy
tables the abominable
floor belches smoky

laughter into the filigree
frame of a microscopic
stage whose jouncing curtain.   ,rises
upon one startling doll

undressed in unripe green with
nauseous spiderlegs
and excremental
hair and the eyes of the mother of

god who spits seeds of dead
song about home and love from her
transfigured face a queer
pulp of ecstasy

while in the battered
bodies the odd unlovely
souls struggle   slowly   and   writhe
like caught.brave:flies;

XII

i walked the boulevard

i saw a dirty child
skating on noisy wheels of joy

pathetic dress fluttering

behind her a mothermonster
with red grumbling face

cluttered in pursuit

pleasantly elephantine

while nearby the father

a thick cheerful man

with majestic bulbous lips
and forlorn piggish hands

joked to a girlish whore

with busy rhythmic mouth
and silly purple eyelids

of how she was with child

XIII

5
derbies-with-men-in-them smoke Helmar
cigarettes   2
play backgammon,3 watch

a has gold
teeth b pink
suspenders c
reads Atlantis

x and y play   b
cries "effendi" "Uh" "coffee"
"uh"   enter
paperboy,c

buys Bawstinamereekin,exit
paperboy   a finishes
Helmar   lights
another

       x and y
play,effendi approaches,sets
down coffee   withdraws
a and c discuss news in

turkish x and y play b spits
x and
y
play,b starts armenian record

                         pho
nographisrunn
ingd o w,   n   phonograph
                    stopS.

b swears in persian at phonograph
x wins   exeunt ax:by;c,
Goo dnightef fendi
....

five men in derbies

XIV

the young
man sitting
in Dick Mid's Place
said to Death

teach me of her
Thy yonder servant who
in Thy very house silently
sits looking beyond the

kissing and the striving of
that old man who at her
redstone mouth renews his
childhood

and He
said
"willingly
for the tale is short

it was
i think yourself delivered into
both my hands herself to
always keep"

always?
the young
man sitting in Dick Mid's
Place

asked
"always"
Death
said

"then as i recollect her
girlhood was by the kindly
lips and body fatherly of a
romantic tired business man

somewhat tweaked and dinted
then
did my servant
become of the company of those

ladies with faces painteaten
and bodies lightly
desperate certainly wherefrom
departed is youth's indispensable

illusion"

XV

one April dusk the
sallow street-lamps were turning
snowy against a west of robin's egg blue when
i entered a mad street whose

mouth dripped with slavver of
spring
chased two flights of squirrel-stairs into
a mid-victorian attic which is known as
Ο ΠΑΡΘΕΝΩΝ
                        and having ordered
yaoorti from
Nicho'
settled my feet on the

ceiling inhaling six divine inches
of Haremina   in
the thick of the snick-
er of cards and smack of back-

gammon boards i was aware of an entirely
dirty circle of habitués their
faces like cigarettebutts, chewed
with disdain,   led by a Jumpy

Tramp who played each
card as if it were a thunderbolt red-
hot   peeling
off huge slabs of a fuzzy

language with the aid of an exclamatory
tooth-pick
And who may that
be i said exhaling into

eternity as Nicho' laid
before me bread
more downy than street-lamps
upon an almostclean

plate
"Achilles"
said
Nicho'

"and did you perhaps wish also shishkabob?"

XVI

between the breasts
of bestial
Marj lie large
men who praise

Marj's cleancornered strokable
body   these men's
fingers toss trunks
shuffle sacks spin kegs they

curl
loving
around
beers

        the world has
these men's hands but their
bodies big and boozing
belong to

Marj
the greenslim purse of whose
face opens
on a fatgold

grin
hooray
hoorah for the large
men who lie

between the breasts
of bestial Marj
for the strong men
who

sleep between the legs of Lil

XVII

but the other
day i was passing a certain
gate,   rain
fell(as it will

in spring)
ropes
of silver gliding from sunny
thunder into freshness

as if god's flowers were
pulling upon bells of
gold   i looked
up

and
thought to myself   Death
and will You with
elaborate fingers possibly touch

the pink hollyhock existence whose
pansy eyes look from morning till
night into the street
unchangingly   the always

old lady always sitting in her
gentle window like
a reminiscence
partaken

softly   at whose gate smile
always the chosen
flowers of reminding

XVIII

inthe,exquisite;

morning   sure   lyHer eye s exactly sit,ata little roundtable
among otherlittle roundtables   Her,eyes   count   slow(ly

obstre peroustimidi ties surElyfl)oat   iNg,the

ofpieces ofof sunligh tof fa l l in gof throughof treesOf.

(Fields Elysian

the like,a)slEEping neck a breathing a   ,lies
(slo wlythe wom an pa)ris her
flesh:wakes
                in little streets

while exactlygir lisHlegs;play;ing;nake;D
and

chairs wait under the trees

Fields slowly Elysian in
a firmcool-Ness   taxis, s.QuirM

and,   b etw ee nch air st ott er s thesillyold
WomanSellingBalloonS

In theex qui site

morning,
        her sureLyeye s sit-ex actly her sitsat a surely!little,
roundtable amongother;littleexactly round.   tables,

Her
    .eyes

XIX

the rose
is dying the
lips of an old man murder

the petals
hush
mysteriously
invisible mourners move
with prose faces and sobbing,garments
The symbol of the rose

motionless
with grieving feet and
wings
mounts

against the margins of steep song
a stallion sweetness   ,the

lips of an old man murder

the petals.

XX

spring omnipotent goddess thou dost
inveigle into crossing sidewalks the
unwary june-bug and the frivolous angleworm
thou dost persuade to serenade his
lady the musical tom-cat,thou stuffest
the parks with overgrown pimply
cavaliers and gumchewing giggly
girls and not content
Spring,with this
thou hangest canary-birds in parlor windows

spring slattern of seasons you
have dirty legs and a muddy
petticoat,drowsy is your
mouth your eyes are sticky
with dreams and you have
a sloppy body
from being brought to bed of crocuses
When you sing in your whiskey-voice
                                  the grass
rises on the head of the earth
and all the trees are put on edge

spring,
of the jostle of
thy breasts and the slobber
of your thighs
i am so very
                glad that the soul inside me Hollers
for thou comest and your hands
are the snow
and thy fingers are the rain,
and i hear
the screech of dissonant
flowers,and most of all
i hear your stepping
                    freakish feet
                    feet incorrigible
ragging the world,

XXI

Buffalo Bill 's
defunct
     who used to
       ride a watersmooth-silver
               stallion
and break onetwothreefourfive pigeonsjustlikethat
                       Jesus

he was a handsome man
               and what i want to know is
how do you like your blueeyed boy
Mister Death

XXII

Cleopatra built
like a smooth arrow or
a fleet pillar is eaten
by yesterday

she was a silver tube of wise
lust whose arms and legs
like white squirming pipes
wiggle upon the perfumed roman

strength who how
furiously plays the hot
sweet horrible stops of
her

body
Cleopatra had a
body
it was

thick slim warm moist
built like an organ
and it
loved

he
was a roman   theirs was a
music sinuous globular
slippery intense witty huge

and its chords
brittle eager eternal luminous
firmly diminishing have swoopingly
fallen svelte sagging gone into the soaring silence

(put
your smallest
ear against yester-
day My Lady   hear

the purple trumpets
blow   horses of gold
delicately crouching beneath silver
youths   the leaneyed

Caesars borne neatly through enormous
twilight surrounded by their triumphs
and
     listen well

how the dainty destroyed
hero clamps the hearty sharp
column
of Egypt

       ,built like a fleet
pillar or a smooth
arrow
Cleopatra is eaten by

yester-
day)
       O i tell you out of
the minute incessant Was irrevocably

emanates a dignity of papyruscoloured
faces   superbly limp
the ostensible centuries
therefore let us be

a little uncouth and amorous in
memory of Cleopatra and of
Antony
and we will

confuse hotly our moreover irrevocable
bodies while the infinite processions
move like moths and like boys and
like incense and like sunlight

and like ships and like young girls and like
butterflies and like money
and like laughter
and like elephants

through our
single
brain   in memory of Cleopatra   while
easily

tremendously
floats
in the bright shouting street of time
her nakedness with its blue hair

(all is eaten by yester-
day
between the nibbling timid teethful hours
wilts the stern texture of Now

the arrow and the
pillar pursue curiously
a crumbling flight into the absolute stars
the gods are swallowed

even
Nile
the
kind black great god)

Cleopatra you
are eaten
by yester-
day

(and O My Lady Lady Of
Ladies you
who move beautifully in the winds
of my lust like a high troubling

ship upon the fragrant
unspeaking ignorant darkness of New
Lady whose kiss is
a procession of deep beasts

coming with keen ridiculous
silks coming with sharp languid perfumes
coming with the little profound gems and
the large laughing stones

a sinuous problem of colour
floating against
the clever deadly
heaven   i salute

you
whose body is
Egypt
whose hair is Nile)

put your ear
to the ground
there is a music
Lady

           the noiseless truth of swirling
worms
is
tomorrow

XXIII

Picasso
you give us Things
which
bulge:grunting lungs pumped full of sharp thick mind

you make us shrill
presents always
shut in the sumptuous screech of
simplicity

(out of the
black unbunged
Something gushes vaguely a squeak of planes
or

between squeals of
Nothing grabbed with circular shrieking tightness
solid screams whisper.)
Lumberman of The Distinct

your brain's
axe only chops hugest inherent
Trees of Ego,from
whose living and biggest

bodies lopped
of every
prettiness

you hew form truly

XXIV

conversation with my friend is particularly

to enjoy the composed sudden body atop which always quiv-
ers the electric Distinct face haughtily vital clinched
in a swoon of synopsis

despite a sadistic modesty his mind is seen frequently
fingering the exact beads of a faultless languor when
invisibly consult with some delicious image the a little
strolling lips and eyes inwardly crisping

for my friend,feeling is the sacred and agonizing prox-
imity to its desire of a doomed impetuous acute sentience
whose whitehot lips however suddenly approached may never
quite taste the wine which their nearness evaporates

to think is the slippery contours of a vase inexpressibly
fragile it is for the brain irrevocably frigid to touch a
merest shape which however slenderly by it caressed will
explode and spill the immediate imperceptible content

my friend's being,out of the spontaneous clumsy trivial
acrobatic edgeless gesture of existence,continually whit-
tles keen careful futile flowers

(isolating with perpetually meticulous concupiscence the
bright large undeniable disease of Life,himself occasion-
ally contrives an unreal precise intrinsic fragment of
actuality),

an orchid whose velocity is sculptural

XXV

my mind is
a big hunk of irrevocable nothing which touch and taste and smell
and hearing and sight keep hitting and chipping with sharp fatal
tools
in an agony of sensual chisels i perform squirms of chrome and ex-
ecute strides of cobalt
nevertheless i
feel that i cleverly am being altered that i slightly am becoming
something a little different,in fact
myself
Hereupon helpless i utter lilac shreiks and scarlet bellowings.

XXVI

the waddling
madam star
taps
taps.   "ready girls".   the

unspontaneous streets
make bright their eyes
a
blind irisher fiddles a

scotch jig in a stinking
joyman bar
a cockney is
buying whiskies for a turk

a waiter intones:bloo–moo–n
sirkusricky
platzburg
hoppytoad   yesmam.   the

furious taximan
p(ee)ps
on his whistle somebody
says here's luck

somebody else says down the hatch
the nigger smiles
the jew stands
beside his teddy-bears

the sailor shuffles the
night with fucking eyes
the great black preacher gargles jesus
the aesthete indulges

his soul for certain things which died
it is eighteen hundred
years....
exactly

   under the window
   under the window
   under the window walk

the unburied feet of
the little ladies more than dead

XXVII

her
flesh
Came
at

meassandca V
        ingint
                   oA
chute
     i had cement for her,
     merrily
we became each
other humped to tumbling

garble   when
a
minute
pulled the sluice

              emerging.

concrete

XXVIII

raise the shade
will youse dearie?
rain
wouldn't that

get yer goat but
we don't care do
we dearie we should
worry about the rain

huh
dearie?
yknow
i'm

sorry for awl the
poor girls that
gets up god
knows when every

day of their
lives
aint you,
                    oo–oo.   dearie

not so
hard dear

you're killing me

XXIX

somebody knew Lincoln somebody Xerxes

this man:a narrow thudding timeshaped face
plus innocuous winking hands,carefully
inhabits number 1 on something street

Spring comes
                    the lean and definite houses

are troubled.   A sharp blue day
fills with peacefully leaping air
the minute mind of the world.
The lean and

definite houses are
troubled.in the sunset their chimneys converse
angrily,their
roofs are nervous with the soft furious
light,and while fire-escapes and
roofs and chimneys and while roofs and fire-escapes and
chimneys and while chimneys and fire-escapes
and roofs are talking rapidly all together there happens
Something,and They

cease(and
one by one are turned suddenly and softly
into irresponsible toys.)
                    when this man with

the brittle legs winces
swiftly out of number 1 someThing
street and trickles carefully into the park
sits

Down.   pigeons circle
around and around and around the

irresponsible toys
circle wildly in the slow-ly-in creasing fragility
—.Dogs
bark
children
play
-ing
    Are

in the beautiful nonsense of twilight

and somebody Napoleon

POST IMPRESSIONS

I

windows go orange in the slowly.
town,   night
featherly swifts
the
      Dark on us
all;
      stories told returned

      gather

      the

Again:who
danc   ing
goes utter   ly

churning
witty,twitters

                  upon Our

(ta-te-ta
in a parenthesis!said the moon

)

II

beyond the brittle towns asleep
i look where stealing needles of foam
in the last light

thread the creeping shores

as out of dumb strong hands infinite

the erect deep upon me
in the last light
pours its eyeless miles

the chattering sunset ludicrously
dies,i hear only tidewings

in the last light
twitching at the world

III

the moon is hiding in
her hair.
The
lily
of heaven
full of all dreams,
draws down.

cover her briefness in singing
close her with intricate faint birds
by daisies and twilights
Deepen her,

Recite
upon her
flesh
the rain's

pearls singly-whispering.

IV

riverly is a flower
gone softly by tomb
rosily gods whiten
befall saith rain

anguish
and dream-send is
hushed
in

moan-loll where
night   gathers
morte carved smiles

cloud-gloss is at moon-cease
soon
verbal mist-flowers close
ghosts on prowl gorge

sly slim gods stare

V

any man is wonderful
and a formula
a bit of tobacco and gladness
plus little derricks of gesture

any skyscraper
bulges in the looseness of morning
but in twilight becomes
unutterably crisp

a thing,
which tightens
caught
in the hoisting light

any woman is smooth and ridiculous
a polite uproar of knuckling silent planes
a nudging bulb silkenly brutal
a devout flexion

VI

into the strenuous briefness
Life:
handorgans and April
darkness,friends

i charge laughing.
Into the hair-thin tints
of yellow dawn,
into the women-coloured twilight

i smilingly
glide.   I
into the big vermilion departure
swim,sayingly;

(Do you think?)the
i do,world
is probably made
of roses & hello:

(of solongs and,ashes)

VII

at the head of this street a gasping organ is waving moth-eaten
tunes.   a fattish hand turns the crank;the box spouts fairies,out
of it sour gnomes tumble clumsily,the little box is spilling ran-
cid elves upon neat sunlight into the flowerstricken air which is
filthy with agile swarming sonal creatures

—Children,stand with circular frightened faces glaring at the
shabby tiny smiling,man in whose hand the crank goes desperately,
round and round pointing to the queer monkey

(if you toss him a coin he will pick it cleverly from,the air and
stuff it seriously in,his minute pocket)Sometimes he does not
catch a piece of money and then his master will yell at him over
the music and jerk the little string and the monkey will sit,up,
and look at,you with his solemn blinky eyeswhichneversmile and
after he has caught a,penny or three,pennies he will be thrown a
peanut(which he will open skilfully with his,mouth carefully
holding,it,in his little toylike hand)and then he will stiff-ly
throw the shell away with a small bored gesture that makes the
children laugh.

But i don't,   the crank goes round desperate elves and hopeless
gnomes and frantic fairies gush clumsily from the battered box
fattish and mysterious the flowerstricken sunlight is thickening
dizzily is reeling gently the street and the children and the mon-
keyandtheorgan and the man are dancing slowly are tottering up
and down in a trembly mist of atrocious melody....tiniest dead
tunes crawl upon my face my hair is lousy with mutilated singing
microscopic things in my ears scramble faintly tickling putres-
cent atomies,
            and
                  i feel the jerk of the little string!the tiny
smiling shabby man is yelling over the music i understand him i
shove my round red hat back on my head i sit up and blink at you
with my solemn eyeswhichneversmile

yes,By god.
for i am they are pointing at the queer monkey with a little
oldish doll-like face and hairy arms like an ogre and rubbercolour-
ed hands and feet filled with quick fingers and a remarkable tail
which is allbyitself alive.(and he has a little red coat with i
have a real pocket in it and the round funny hat with a big feather
is tied under myhis chin.)   that climbs and cries and runs and
floats like a toy on the end of a string

VIII

i was sitting in mcsorley's.   outside it was New York and beauti-
fully snowing.

Inside snug and evil.   the slobbering walls filthily push witless
creases of screaming warmth chuck pillows are noise funnily swallows
swallowing revolvingly pompous a the swallowed mottle with smooth or
a but of rapidly goes gobs the and of flecks of and a chatter sobbings
intersect with which distinct disks of graceful oath,upsoarings the
break on   ceiling-flatness

the Bar.tinking luscious jigs dint of ripe silver with warmlyish
wetflat splurging smells waltz the glush of squirting taps plus slush
of foam knocked off and a faint piddle-of-drops she says I ploc spittle
what the lands thaz me kid in no sir hopping sawdust you kiddo he's a
palping wreaths of badly Yep cigars who jim him why gluey grins topple
together eyes pout gestures stickily point made glints squinting who's
a wink bum-nothing and money fuzzily mouths take big wobbly foot-steps
every goggle cent of it get out ears dribbles soft right old feller
belch the chap hic summore eh chuckles skulch....

and i was sitting in the din thinking drinking the ale,which never
lets you grow old blinking at the low ceiling my being pleasantly was
punctuated by the always retchings of a worthless lamp.

when With a minute terrif   iceffort one dirty squeal of soiling light
yanKing from bushy obscurity a bald greenish foetal head established
It suddenly upon the huge neck around whose unwashed sonorous muscle
the filth of a collar hung gently.

(spattered)by this instant of semiluminous nausea A vast wordless
nondescript genie of trunk trickled firmly in to one exactly-mutilated
ghost of a chair,

a;domeshaped interval of complete plasticity,shoulders,sprouted the
extraordinary arms through an angle of ridiculous velocity commenting
upon an unclean table,and,whose distended immense Both paws slowly
loved a dinted mug

gone Darkness   it was so near to me,i ask of shadow won't you have a
drink?

(the eternal perpetual question)

Inside snugandevil.   i was sitting in mcsorley's   It,did not answer.

outside.(it was New York and beautifully,snowing....

IX

at the ferocious phenomenon of 5 o'clock i find myself gently decompos-
ing in the mouth of New York.   Between its supple financial teeth delir-
iously sprouting from complacent gums,a morsel prettily wanders buoy-
ed on the murderous saliva of industry.   the morsel is i.

Vast cheeks enclose me.

a gigantic uvula with imperceptible gesticulations threatens the tubu-
lar downward blackness occasionally from which detaching itself bumps
clumsily into the throat A meticulous vulgarity:

a sodden fastidious normal explosion;a square murmur,a winsome flatu-
lence—

In the soft midst of the tongue sits the Woolworth building a serene
pastile-shaped insipid kinesis or frail swooping lozenge.   a ruglike
sentience whose papillae expertly drink the docile perpendicular taste
of this squirming cube of undiminished silence,supports while devour-
ing the firm tumult of exquisitely insecure sharp algebraic music.
For the first time in sorting from this vast nonchalant inward walk of
volume the flat minute gallop of careful hugeness i am conjugated by
the sensual mysticism of entire vertical being ,i am skilfully con-
strued by a delicately experimenting colossus whose irrefutable spiral
antics involve me with the soothings of plastic hypnotism   .i am ac-
curately parsed by this gorgeous rush of upward lips....

cleverly

perching on the sudden extremity of one immense tooth myself surveys
safely the complete important profane frantic inconsequential gastro-
nomic mystery of mysteries
                              ,life

Far below myself the lunging leer of horizontal large distinct ecstasy
wags and.rages   Laughters jostle grins nudge smiles push—.   deep into
the edgeless gloaming gladness hammers incessant putrid spikes of mad-
ness (at

Myself's height these various innocent ferocities are superseded by
the sole prostituted ferocity of silence,it is) still 5 o'clock

I stare only always into the tremendous canyon the

,tremendous canyon always only exhales a climbing dark exact walloping human noise of digestible millions whose rich slovenly obscene procession always floats through the thin amorous enormous only lips of the evening

And it is 5 o'clock

in the oblong air,from which a singular ribbon of common sunset is hanging,

snow speaks slowly

X

SNO

a white idea(Listen

drenches:earth's ugly)mind.
,Rinsing with exact death

the annual brain
                    clotted with loosely voices
look
look.   Skilfully

.fingered by(a parenthesis
the)pond on whoseswooning edge

black trees think

(hear little knives of flower
stropping sof a.   Thick silence)

blacktreesthink

tiny,angels sharpen:themselves

(on
    air)
don't speak
              A white idea,

drenching.   earth's brain detaches
clottingsand from a a nnual(ugliness
of)rinsed mind slowly:

from!the:A wending putrescence.   a.of,loosely

;voices

XI

i am going to utter a tree,Nobody
shall stop me

but first
earth   ,the reckless oral darkness
raging with thin impulse

i will have

a
  dream
  i
  think it shall be roses and
spring will bring her
worms rushing through loam.

(afterward i'll
climb
by tall careful muscles

into nervous and accurate silence....But   first

you)

press easily
at first,it will be leaves
and a little harder
for roses
only a little harder

last   we
on the groaning flame of neat huge
trudging kiss moistly climbing hideously with
large
minute
hips,O

       .press

worms rushing slowly through loam

Chimneys

SONNETS—REALITIES

I

the Cambridge ladies who live in furnished souls
are unbeautiful and have comfortable minds
(also,with the church's protestant blessings
daughters,unscented shapeless spirited)
they believe in Christ and Longfellow,both dead,
are invariably interested in so many things—
at the present writing one still finds
delighted fingers knitting for the is it Poles?
perhaps.   While permanent faces coyly bandy
scandal of Mrs. N and Professor D
....the Cambridge ladies do not care,above
Cambridge if sometimes in its box of
sky lavender and cornerless,the
moon rattles like a fragment of angry candy

II

when i am in Boston,i do not speak.
and i sit in the click of ivory balls....

noting flies,which jerk upon the weak
colour of table-cloths,the electric When
In Doubt Buy Of(but a roof hugs
whom)
          as the august evening mauls
Kneeland,and a waiter cleverly lugs
indigestible honeycake to men
....one perfectly smooth coffee
tasting of hellas,i drink,or sometimes two
remarking cries of paklavah meeah.
(Very occasionally three.)
and i gaze on the cindercoloured little ΜΕΓΑ
ΕΛΛΗΝΙΚΟΝ ΞΕΝΟΔΟΧΕΙΟΝ ΥΠΝΟΥ

III

goodby Betty,don't remember me
pencil your eyes dear and have a good time
with the tall tight boys at Tabari'
s,keep your teeth snowy,stick to beer and lime,
wear dark,and where your meeting breasts are round
have roses darling,it's all i ask of you—
but that when light fails and this sweet profound
Paris moves with lovers,two and two
bound for themselves,when passionately dusk
brings softly down the perfume of the world
(and just as smaller stars begin to husk
heaven)you,you exactly paled and curled

with mystic lips take twilight where i know:
proving to Death that Love is so and so.

IV

ladies and gentlemen this little girl
with the good teeth and small important breasts
(is it the Frolic or the Century whirl?
one's memory indignantly protests)
this little dancer with the tightened eyes
crisp ogling shoulders and the ripe quite too
large lips always clenched faintly,wishes you
with all her fragile might to not surmise
she dreamed one afternoon

                        ....or maybe read?

of a time when the beautiful most of her
(this here and This,do you get me?)
will maybe dance and maybe sing and be
absitively posolutely dead,
like Coney Island in winter

V

by god i want above fourteenth

fifth's deep purring biceps,the mystic screech
of Broadway,the trivial stink of rich

frail firm asinine life
                          (i pant

for what's below.   the singer.   Wall.   i want
the perpendicular lips the insane teeth
the vertical grin

                          give me the Square in spring,
the little barbarous Greenwich perfumed fake

And most,the futile fooling labyrinth
where noisy colours stroll....and the Baboon

sniggering insipidities while. i sit,sipping
singular anisettes as.   One opaque
big girl jiggles thickly hips to the kanoon

but Hassan chuckles seeing the Greeks breathe)

VI

when you rang at Dick Mid's Place
the madam was a bulb stuck in the door.
a fang of wincing gas showed how
hair,in two fists of shrill colour,
clutched the dull volume of her tumbling face
scribbled with a big grin. her sow-
eyes clicking mischief from thick lids.
the chunklike nose on which always the four
tablets of perspiration erectly sitting.
—If they knew you at Dick Mid's
the three trickling chins began to traipse
into the cheeks "eet smeestaire steevensun
kum een,dare ease Bet,an Leelee,an dee beeg wun"
her handless wrists did gooey severe shapes.

VII

a fragrant sag of fruit distinctly grouped.

I have not eaten peppers for a week.

On this street the houses immensely speak
(it is nine minutes past six)

the well-fed L's immaculate roar looped
straightens,into neatest distance....

A new curve of children gladly cricks
where a hurdy-gurdy accurately pants.

and pompous ancient jews obscurely twitch
through the bumping teem of Grand. a nudging froth
of faces clogs Second as Mrs. Somethingwich

(with flesh like an old toy balloon)

heavily swims to Strunsky's,

                    Monia's mouth
eats tangerines looking at the moon—

VIII

irreproachable ladies firmly lewd
on dangerous slabs of tilting din whose
mouths distinctly walk
                    your smiles accuse

the dusk with an untimid svelte subdued
magic
            while in your eyes there lives
a green egyptian noise. ladies with whom time

feeds especially his immense lips

On whose deep nakedness death most believes,
perpetual girls marching to love

whose bodies kiss me with the square crime
of life....Cecile,the oval shove
of hiding pleasure.   Alice,stinging quips
of flesh.   Loretta, cut the comedy
kid....

    Fran Mag Glad Dorothy

IX

nearer:breath of my breath:take not thy tingling
limbs from me:make my pain their crazy meal
letting thy tigers of smooth sweetness steal
slowly in dumb blossoms of new mingling:
deeper:blood of my blood:with upwardcringing
swiftness plunge these leopards of white dream
in the glad flesh of my fear:more neatly ream
this pith of darkness:carve an evilfringing
flower of madness on gritted lips
and on sprawled eyes squirming with light insane
chisel the killing flame that dizzily grips.

Querying greys between mouthed houses curl

thirstily.   Dead stars stink.   dawn.   Inane,

the poetic carcass of a girl

X

when thou hast taken thy last applause,and when
the final curtain strikes the world away,
leaving to shadowy silence and dismay
that stage which shall not know thy smile again,
lingering a little while i see thee then
ponder the tinsel part they let thee play;
i see the large lips vivid,the face grey,
and silent smileless eyes of Magdalen.
The lights have laughed their last;without,the street
darkling awaiteth her whose feet have trod
the silly souls of men to golden dust:
she pauses on the lintel of defeat,
her heart breaks in a smile—and she is Lust....

mine also,little painted poem of god

XI

god pity me whom(god distinctly has)
the weightless svelte drifting sexual feather
of your shall i say body?follows
truly through a dribbling moan of jazz

whose arched occasional steep youth swallows
curvingly the keenness of my hips;
or,your first twitch of crisp boy flesh dips
my height in a firm fragile stinging weather,

(breathless with sharp necessary lips)kid

female cracksman of the nifty,ruffian-rogue,
laughing body with wise breasts half-grown,
lisping flesh quick to thread the fattish drone
of I Want a Doll,
                          wispish–agile feet with slid
steps parting the tousle of saxophonic brogue.

XII

"kitty". sixteen,5′1″,white,prostitute.

ducking always the touch of must and shall,
whose slippery body is Death's littlest pal,

skilled in quick softness.   Unspontaneous.   cute.

the signal perfume of whose unrepute
focusses in the sweet slow animal
bottomless eyes importantly banal,

Kitty. a whore. Sixteen
                          you corking brute
amused from time to time by clever drolls
fearsomely who do keep their sunday flower.
The babybreasted broad "kitty" twice eight

—beer nothing,the lady'll have a whiskey-sour—

whose least amazing smile is the most great
common divisor of unequal souls.

XIII

it started when Bill's chip let on to
the bulls he'd bumped a bloke back in fifteen.
Then she came toward him on her knees across the locked
room.   he knocked her cold and beat it for Chicago.

Eddie was waiting for him,and they cleaned up a few
times—before she got the info
from a broad that knew Eddie in Topeka,went clean
daffy,and which was very silly hocked

the diamond he gave her.   Bill was put wise
that she was coming with his kid inside her.
He laughed.   She came.   he gave her a shove
and asked Eddie did he care to ride her?
....she exactly lay,looking hunks of love

in The Chair he kept talking about eyes

XIV

she sits dropping on a caret of clenched arms
a delicately elephantine face
(It is necessary to find Hassan's Place
by tiny streets shrugging with colour)
the mouth who sits between her cheeks
utters a thud of scarlet. always.   More
interesting,as i think,her charms
en repos....a fattish leg leaks
obscenely from the dress.   one nipple tries.
playfully to peek into the belly
whose deep squirm nibbles. another couches,
weary,upon a flabby mattress of jelly....
than when to the kanoon she totters,slouches,
with giggling hips and frozen eyes

XV

unnoticed woman from whose kind large flesh

i turn to the cruel-littleness of cold
(when battling street-lamps fail upon the gold
dawn,where teeth of slowturning streets mesh

in a frieze of smoking Face Bluish-old

and choked pat of going soles on flat
pavements with icy cries of this and that
stumbling in gloom,bad laughters,smiles unbold)

also,tomorrow the daily papers will feature
Peace and Good Will,and Mary with one lung
extended to the pumping Child,and " 'Twas

the night before Christmas when all through the house not a creature
was stirring,not even a mouse.   The stockings were hung
by the chimney with care in hopes that Saint Nicholas"

XVI

twentyseven bums give a prostitute the once
-over. fiftythree(and one would see if it could)

eyes say the breasts look very good:
firmlysquirmy with a slight jounce,

thirteen pants have a hunch

admit in threedimensional distress
these hips were made for Horizontal Business
(set on big legs nice to pinch

assiduously which justgraze
each other).   As the lady lazily struts
                                        (her
thickish flesh superior to the genuine daze
of unmarketable excitation,

whose careless movements carefully scatter

pink propaganda of annihilation

XVII

of this wilting wall the colour drub
souring sunbeams,of a foetal fragrance
to rickety unclosed blinds inslants
peregrinate,a cigar-stub
disintegrates,above,underdrawers club
the faintly sweating air with pinkness,
one pale dog behind a slopcaked shrub
painstakingly utters a slippery mess,
a star sleepily,feebly,scratches the sore
of morning.   But i am interested more
intricately in the delicate scorn
with which in a putrid window every day
almost leans a lady whose still-born
smile involves the comedy of decay,

XVIII

whereas by dark really released,the modern
flame of her indomitable body
uses a careful fierceness.   Her lips study
my head gripping for a decision:burn
the terrific fingers which grapple and joke
on my passionate anatomy
oh yes!   Large legs pinch,toes choke—
hair-thin strands of magic agony
....by day this lady in her limousine

oozes in fashionable traffic,just
a halfsmile (for society's sweet sake)
in the not too frail lips almost discussed;
between her and ourselves a nearly-opaque
perfume disinterestedly obscene.

XIX

my girl's tall with hard long eyes
as she stands,with her long hard hands keeping
silence on her dress,good for sleeping
is her long hard body filled with surprise
like a white shocking wire,when she smiles
a hard long smile it sometimes makes
gaily go clean through me tickling aches,
and the weak noise of her eyes easily files
my impatience to an edge—my girl's tall
and taut,with thin legs just like a vine
that's spent all of its life on a garden-wall,
and is going to die.   When we grimly go to bed
with these legs she begins to heave and twine
about me,and to kiss my face and head.

XX

Dick Mid's large bluish face without eyebrows

sits in the kitchen nights and chews a two–bit
cigar
      waiting for the bulls to pull his joint.
Jimmie was a dude.   Dark hair and nice hands.

with a little eye that rolled and made its point

Jimmie's sister worked for Dick.   And had some rows
over percent.   The gang got shot up twice,it
operated in the hundred ands

All the chips would kid Jimmie to give them a kiss
but Jimmie lived regular. stewed three times a week.
and slept twice a week with a big toothless girl
in Yonkers.
      Dick Mid's green large three teeth leak

smoke:remembering,two pink big lips curl....

how Jimmie was framed and got his

XXI

life boosts herself rapidly at me

through sagging debris of exploded day
the hulking perpendicular mammal
                                        a
grim epitome of chuckling flesh.
Weak thirsty fists of idiot futures bash

the bragging breasts,
                            puppy-faces to mouth
her ugly nipples squirming in pretty wrath,
gums skidding on slippery udders

                                      she
lifts an impertinent puerperal face
and with astute fatuous swallowed eyes
smiles,
        one grin very distinctly wobbles
from the thinning lips me hugely which embrace.
as in the hairy notching of clenched thighs

a friendless dingy female frenzy bubbles

SONNETS—UNREALITIES

I

and what were roses.   Perfume?for i do
forget....or mere Music mounting unsurely

twilight
          but here were something more maturely
childish,more beautiful almost than you.

Yet if not flower,tell me softly who

be these haunters of dreams always demurely
halfsmiling from cool faces,moving purely
with muted step,yet somewhat proudly too—

are they not ladies,ladies of my dream
justly touching roses their fingers whitely
live by?
          or better,
                              queens,queens laughing lightly
crowned with far colours,

                              thinking very much
of nothing and whom dawn loves most to touch

wishing by willows,bending upon streams?

II

when unto nights of autumn do complain
earth's ghastlier trees by whom Time measured is
when frost to dance maketh the sagest pane
of littler huts with peerless fantasies
or the unlovely longness of the year

droops with things dead athwart the narrowing hours
and hope(by cold espoused unto fear)
in dreadful corners hideously cowers—

i do excuse me,love,to Death and Time

storms and rough cold,wind's menace and leaf's grieving:
from the impressed fingers of sublime
Memory,of that loveliness receiving
the image my proud heart cherished as fair.

(The child-head poised with the serious hair)

III

a connotation of infinity
sharpens the temporal splendor of this night

when souls which have forgot frivolity
in lowliness,noting the fatal flight
of worlds whereto this earth's a hurled dream

down eager avenues of lifelessness

consider for how much themselves shall gleam,
in the poised radiance of perpetualness.
When what's in velvet beyond doomed thought

is like a woman amorous to be known;
and man,whose here is always worse than naught,
feels the tremendous yonder for his own—

on such a night the sea through her blind miles

of crumbling silence seriously smiles

IV

Thou in whose swordgreat story shine the deeds
of history her heroes,sounds the tread
of those vast armies of the marching dead,
with standards and the neighing of great steeds
moving to war across the smiling meads;
thou by whose page we break the precious bread
of dear communion with the past,and wed
to valor,battle with heroic breeds;

thou,Froissart,for that thou didst love the pen
while others wrote in steel,accept all praise
of after ages,and of hungering days
for whom the old glories move,the old trumpets cry;
who gavest as one of those immortal men
his life that his fair city might not die.

V

when my sensational moments are no more
unjoyously bullied of vilest mind

and sweet uncaring earth by thoughtful war
heaped wholly with high wilt of human rind—
when over hate has triumphed darkly love

and the small spiritual cry of spring
utters a striving flower,
                    just where strove
the droll god-beasts

                  do thou distinctly bring
thy footstep,and the rushing of thy deep
hair and the smiting smile didst love to use
in other days (drawing my Mes from sleep
whose stranger dreams thy strangeness must abuse....)

Time being not for us,purple roses were
sweeter to thee
                perchance to me deeper.

VI

god gloats upon Her stunning flesh.   Upon
the reachings of Her green body among
unseen things,things obscene (Whose fingers young

the caving ages curiously con)

—but the lunge of Her hunger softly flung
over the gasping shores
                              leaves his smile wan,
and his blood stopped hears in the frail anon

the shovings and the lovings of Her tongue.

god Is The Sea.   All terrors of his being
quake before this its hideous Work most old
Whose battening gesture prophecies a freeing

of ghostly chaos
                    in this dangerous night
through moaned space god worships God—

                                        (behold!
where chaste stars writhe captured in brightening fright)

VII

O Thou to whom the musical white spring

offers her lily inextinguishable,
taught by thy tremulous grace bravely to fling

Implacable death's mysteriously sable
robe from her redolent shoulders,
                                    Thou from whose
feet reincarnate song suddenly leaping
flameflung,mounts,inimitably to lose
herself where the wet stars softly are keeping

their exquisite dreams—O Love! upon thy dim
shrine of intangible commemoration,
(from whose faint close as some grave languorous hymn

pledged to illimitable dissipation
unhurried clouds of incense fleetly roll)

i spill my bright incalculable soul.

VIIl

when the proficient poison of sure sleep
bereaves us of our slow tranquillities

and He without Whose favour nothing is
(being of men called Love) upward doth leap
from the mute hugeness of depriving deep,

with thunder of those hungering wings of His,

into the lucent and large signories
—i shall not smile beloved;i shall not weep:

when from the less-than-whiteness of thy face
(whose eyes inherit vacancy) will time
extract his inconsiderable doom,
when these thy lips beautifully embrace
nothing
        and when thy bashful hands assume

silence beyond the mystery of rhyme

IX

this is the garden:colours come and go,
frail azures fluttering from night's outer wing
strong silent greens serenely lingering,
absolute lights like baths of golden snow.
This is the garden:pursed lips do blow
upon cool flutes within wide glooms,and sing
(of harps celestial to the quivering string)
invisible faces hauntingly and slow.

This is the garden.   Time shall surely reap
and on Death's blade lie many a flower curled,
in other lands where other songs be sung;
yet stand They here enraptured,as among
the slow deep trees perpetual of sleep
some silver-fingered fountain steals the world.

X

it is at moments after i have dreamed
of the rare entertainment of your eyes,
when(being fool to fancy)i have deemed

with your peculiar mouth my heart made wise;
at moments when the glassy darkness holds

the genuine apparition of your smile
(it was through tears always)and silence moulds
such strangeness as was mine a little while;

moments when my once more illustrious arms
are filled with fascination,when my breast
wears the intolerant brightness of your charms:

one pierced moment whiter than the rest

—turning from the tremendous lie of sleep
i watch the roses of the day grow deep.

XI

it may not always be so;and i say
that if your lips,which i have loved,should touch
another's,and your dear strong fingers clutch
his heart,as mine in time not far away;
if on another's face your sweet hair lay
in such a silence as i know,or such
great writhing words as,uttering overmuch,
stand helplessly before the spirit at bay;

if this should be,i say if this should be—
you of my heart,send me a little word;
that i may go unto him,and take his hands,
saying,Accept all happiness from me.
Then shall i turn my face,and hear one bird
sing terribly afar in the lost lands.

XII

I have seen her a stealthily frail
flower walking with its fellows in the death
of light,against whose enormous curve of flesh
exactly cubes of tiny fragrance try;
i have watched certain petals rapidly wish
in the corners of her youth;whom,fiercely shy
and gently brutal,the prettiest wrath
of blossoms dishevelling made a pale
fracas upon the accurate moon....
Across the important gardens her body
will come toward me with its hurting sexual smell
of lilies....beyond night's silken immense swoon
the moon is like a floating silver hell
a song of adolescent ivory.

XIII

if learned darkness from our searched world

should wrest the rare unwisdom of thy eyes,
and if thy hands flowers of silence curled

upon a wish,to rapture should surprise
my soul slowly which on thy beauty dreams
(proud through the cold perfect night whisperless

to mark,how that asleep whitely she seems

whose lips the whole of life almost do guess)

if god should send the morning;and before
my doubting window leaves softly to stir,
of thoughtful trees whom night hath pondered o'er
—and frailties of dimension to occur

about us
          and birds known,scarcely to sing

(heart,could we bear the marvel of this thing?)

XIV

who's most afraid of death?thou
                              art of him
utterly afraid,i love of thee
(beloved)this

              and truly i would be
near when his scythe takes crisply the whim
of thy smoothness. and mark the fainting
murdered petals. with the caving stem.

But of all most would i be one of them

round the hurt heart which do so frailly cling....)
i who am but imperfect in my fear

Or with thy mind against my mind,to hear
nearing our hearts' irrevocable play—
through the mysterious high futile day

an enormous stride
                    (and drawing thy mouth toward

my mouth,steer our lost bodies carefully downward)

XV

come nothing to my comparable soul
which with existence has conversed in vain,
O scrupulously take thy trivial toll,
for whose cool feet this frantic heart is fain;
try me with thy perfumes which have seduced
the mightier nostrils of the fervent dead,
feed with felicities me wormperused
by whom the hungering mouth of time is fed:
and if i like not what thou givest me
to him let me complain,whose seat is where
revolving planets struggle to be free
with the astounding everlasting air—
but if i like,i'll take between thy hands
what no man feels,no woman understands.

XVI

when citied day with the sonorous homes
of light swiftly sink in the sorrowful hour,
thy counted petals O tremendous flower
on whose huge heart prospecting darkness roams

torture my spirit with the exquisite froms
and whithers of existence,
                              as by shores
soundless,the unspeaking watcher who adores

perceived sails whose mighty brightness dumbs

the utterance of his soul—so even i
wholly chained to a grave astonishment
feel in my being the delirious smart

of thrilled ecstasy,where sea and sky
marry—

          to know the white ship of thy heart

on frailer ports of costlier commerce bent

XVII

will suddenly trees leap from winter and will

the stabbing music of your white youth
wounded by my arms' bothness
(say a twilight lifting the fragile skill
of new leaves' voices,and sharp lips of spring
simply joining with the wonderless
city's sublime cheap distinct mouth)

do the exact human comely thing?

(or will the fleshless moments go and go

across this dirtied pane where softly preys
the grey and perpendicular Always—
or possibly there drift a pulseless blur
of paleness;
               the unswift mouths of snow
insignificantly whisper....

XVIII

a wind has blown the rain away and blown
the sky away and all the leaves away,
and the trees stand.   I think i too have known
autumn too long

              (and what have you to say,
wind wind wind—did you love somebody
and have you the petal of somewhere in your heart
pinched from dumb summer?
                     O crazy daddy
of death dance cruelly for us and start

the last leaf whirling in the final brain
of air!)Let us as we have seen see
doom's integration.........a wind has blown the rain

away and the leaves and the sky and the
trees stand:
            the trees stand.   The trees,
suddenly wait against the moon's face.

SONNETS—ACTUALITIES

I

when my love comes to see me it's
just a little like music,a
little more like curving colour(say
orange)
        against silence,or darkness....

the coming of my love emits
a wonderful smell in my mind,

you should see when i turn to find
her how my least heart-beat becomes less.
And then all her beauty is a vise

whose stilling lips murder suddenly me,

but of my corpse the tool her smile makes something
suddenly luminous and precise

—and then we are I and She....

what is that the hurdy-gurdy's playing

II

it is funny,you will be dead some day.
By you the mouth hair eyes,and i mean
the unique and nervously obscene

need;it's funny.   They will all be dead

knead of lustfulhunched deeplytoplay
lips and stare the gross fuzzy-pash
—dead—and the dark gold delicately smash....
grass,and the stars,of my shoulder in stead.

It is a funny,thing.   And you will be

and i and all the days and nights that matter
knocked by sun moon jabbed jerked with ecstasy
....tremble(not knowing how much better

than me will you like the rain's face and

the rich improbable hands of the Wind)

III

i have loved,let us see if that's all.
Bit into you as teeth,in the stone
of a musical fruit.   My lips pleasantly groan
on your taste.   Jumped the quick wall

of your smile into stupid gardens
if this were not enough(not really enough
pulled one before one the vague tough

exquisite

       flowers,whom hardens
richly,darkness.   On the whole
possibly have i loved....?you)
                      sheath before sheath

stripped to the Odour.   (and here's what WhoEver will know
Had you as bite teeth;
i stood with you as a foal

stands but as the trees,lay,which grow

IV

the mind is its own beautiful prisoner.
Mine looked long at the sticky moon
opening in dusk her new wings

then decently hanged himself,one afternoon.

The last thing he saw was you
naked amid unnaked things,

your flesh,a succinct wandlike animal,
a little strolling with the futile purr
of blood;your sex squeaked like a billiard-cue
chalking itself,as not to make an error,
with twists spontaneously methodical.
He suddenly tasted worms windows and roses

he laughed,and closed his eyes as a girl closes
her left hand upon a mirror.

V

even a pencil has fear to
do the posed body luckily made
a pen is dreadfully afraid
of her of this of the smile's two
eyes....too,since the world's but
a piece of eminent fragility.
Well and when—Does susceptibility
imply perspicuity,or?
                shut

up.
    Seeing
           seeing her is not
to something or to nothing as much as
being by her seen,which has got
nothing on something as i think

,did you ever hear a jazz
Band?

    or unnoise men don't make soup who drink.

VI

let's live suddenly without thinking

under honest trees,
                    a stream
does.the brain of cleverly-crinkling
-water pursues the angry dream
of the shore.   By midnight,
                              a moon
scratches the skin of the organised hills

an edged nothing begins to prune

let's live like the light that kills
and let's as silence,
                      because Whirl's after all:
(after me)love,and after you.
I occasionally feel vague how
vague i don't know tenuous Now-
spears and The Then-arrows making do
our mouths something red,something tall

VII

yours is the music for no instrument
yours the preposterous colour unbeheld

—mine the unbought contemptuous intent
till this our flesh merely shall be excelled
by speaking flower
                    (if i have made songs

it does not greatly matter to the sun,
nor will rain care
                    cautiously who prolongs
unserious twilight)Shadows have begun

the hair's worm huge,ecstatic,rathe....

yours are the poems i do not write.

In this at least we have got a bulge on death,
silence,and the keenly musical light

of sudden nothing....la bocca mia "he
kissed wholly trembling"

                              or so thought the lady.

VIII

fabulous against   ,a,fathoming jelly
of vital futile huge light as she
does not stand–ing.unsits

                        her(wrist
performs a thundering trivial)it.y

protuberant through the room's skilful of thing
silent spits discrete lumps of noise....
furniture

            unsolemnly :bur   sting
the skinfull of Ludicrous,solidity which a.   ,kissed
with is nearness.(peers:body of

                              aching toys
in unsmooth sexual luminosity spree.

—dear)the   uncouthly Her.thuglike stare the
pollenizing vacancy
when,Thy patters?hands....is swig

it does who eye   sO neatly big

IX

by little accurate saints thickly which tread
the serene nervous light of paradise—
by angelfaces clustered like bright lice

about god's capable dull important head—
by on whom glories whisperingly impinge
(god's pretty mother)but may not confuse

the clever hair nor rout the young mouth whose
lips begin a smile exactly strange—
this painter should have loved my lady.
And by this throat a little suddenly lifted

in singing—hands fragile whom almost tire
the sleepshaped lilies—

                should my lady's body
with these frail ladies dangerously respire:

impeccable girls in raiment laughter-gifted.

X

a thing most new complete fragile intense,
which wholly trembling memory undertakes
—your kiss,the little pushings of flesh,makes
my body sorry when the minute moon
is a remarkable splinter in the quick
of twilight
　　　　　....or if sunset utters one
unhurried muscled huge chromatic
fist skilfully modeling silence
—to feel how through the stopped entire day
horribly and seriously thrills
the moment of enthusiastic space
is a little wonderful,and say
Perhaps her body touched me;and to face

suddenly the lighted living hills

XI

autumn is:that between there and here
gladness flays hideously hills.
It was in the spring of this very year

(a spring of wines women and window-sills)
i met that hideous gladness,per the face
—pinxit,who knows?   Who knows?   Some "allemand"....?
of Goethe,since exempt from heaven's grace,

in an engraving belonging to my friend.
Whom i salute,by what is dear to us;
and by a gestured city stilled in the framing
twilight of Spring....and the dream of dreaming
—and i fall back,quietly amorous
of,through the autumn indisputably roaming

death's big rotten particular kiss.

XII

my love is building a building
around you,a frail slippery
house,a strong fragile house
(beginning at the singular beginning

of your smile)a skilful uncouth
prison,a precise clumsy
prison(building thatandthis into Thus,
Around the reckless magic of your mouth)

my love is building a magic,a discrete
tower of magic and(as i guess)

when Farmer Death(whom fairies hate)shall

crumble the mouth-flower fleet
He'll not my tower,
                laborious,casual

where the surrounded smile
                    hangs

                          breathless

XIII

perhaps it is to feel strike
the silver fish of her nakedness
with fins sharply pleasant,my

youth has travelled toward her these years

or to snare the timid like
of her mind to my mind that i

am come by little countries to the yes

of her youth.
                              And if somebody hears
what i say—let him be pitiful:
because i've travelled all alone
through the forest of wonderful,
and that my feet have surely known
the furious ways and the peaceful,

and because she is beautiful

XIV

the ivory performing rose

of you,worn upon my mind
all night,quitting only in the unkind

dawn its muscle amorous

pricks with minute odour these gross
days
      when i think of you and do not live:
and the empty twilight cannot grieve
nor the autumn,as i grieve,faint for your face

O stay with me slightly.   or until

with neat obscure obvious hands

Time stuff the sincere stomach of each mill

of the ingenious gods.(i am punished.
They have stolen into recent lands
the flower
         with their enormous fingers unwished

XV

my naked lady framed
in twilight is an accident

whose niceness betters easily the intent
of genius—
            painting wholly feels ashamed
before this music,and poetry cannot
go near because perfectly fearful.

meanwhile these speak her wonderful
But i(having in my arms caught

the picture)hurry it slowly

to my mouth,taste the accurate demure
ferocious
            rhythm of
                        precise
laziness.   Eat the price

of an imaginable gesture

exact warm unholy

XVI

i have found what you are like
the rain,

       (Who feathers frightened fields
with the superior dust-of-sleep. wields

easily the pale club of the wind
and swirled justly souls of flower strike

the air in utterable coolness

deeds of green thrilling light
                  with thinned
newfragile yellows

           lurch and.press
—in the woods
        which
            stutter
               and

                   sing
And the coolness of your smile is
stirringofbirds between my arms;but
i should rather than anything
have(almost when hugeness will shut
quietly)almost,
        your kiss

XVII

—GON splashes-sink
which is east eighth,a star of three annoys

me,but the stink of perfumed noise
fiercely mounts from the fireman's ball,i think

and also i think of you,getting mandolin-clink
mixed with your hair;feeling your knees
among the supercilious chimneys,

my nerves sumptuously wink
....and little-dusk has his toys to play with
windows-and-whispers,
     (will BigMorning get away with
them?j'm'en doute,)
      chérie,j'm'en doute.

the accurate key to a palace

—You,—in this window sits a Face
(it is twilight)a Face playing on a flute

XVIII

my sonnet is A light goes on in
the toiletwindow,that's straightacross from
my window,night air bothered with a rustling din

sort of sublimated tom-tom
which quite outdoes the mandolin-

man's tiny racket.   The horses sleep upstairs.
And you can see their ears.   Ears win-

k,funny stable.   In the morning they go out in pairs:
amazingly,one pair is white
(but you know that)they look at each other.   Nudge.

(if they love each other,who cares?)
They pull the morning out of the night.

I am living with a mouse who shares

my meals with him,which is fair as i judge.

XIX

(the phonograph's voice like a keen spider skipping

quickly over patriotic swill.
The,negress,in the,rocker by the,curb,tipping

and tipping,the flocks of pigeons.　And the skil-

ful loneliness,and the rather fat
man in bluishsuspenders half-reading the
Evening Something
　　　　　　　　in the normal window.　and a cat.

A cat waiting for god knows makes me

wonder if i'm alive(eye pries,

not open.　Tail stirs.)　And the. fire-escapes—
the night. makes me wonder if,if i am
the face of a baby smeared with beautiful jam

or

　my invincible Nearness rapes

laughter from your preferable,eyes

XX

you asked me to come:it was raining a little,
and the spring;a clumsy brightness of air
wonderfully stumbled above the square,
little amorous-tadpole people wiggled

battered by stuttering pearl,
                              leaves jiggled
to the jigging fragrance of newness
—and then.   My crazy fingers liked your dress
....your kiss,your kiss was a distinct brittle

flower,and the flesh crisp set
my love-tooth on edge.   So until light
each having each we promised to forget—

wherefore is there nothing left to guess:
the cheap intelligent thighs,the electric trite
thighs;the hair stupidly priceless.

XXI

(let us tremble)a personal radiance sits
hideously upon the trafficking hum
of dusk
        each street takes of shadowy
light the droll snowing delirium

(we do not speak)
                tumbled hushingly bits
of downward flower flowing without or cease

or time;a naming stealth of ecstasy
means,like a girl lasciviously frail,
                           peace
(dreaming is better)

                murdering coolness slowly
in peopling places seeks play:withs of star
link clauses of warmth
                  (after dream who knows?)
a blackish cat and a bluish cat are

eyeing,as with almost melancholy
delicacy night gargles windows.

XXII

utterly and amusingly i am pash
possibly because
                        .dusk and if it
perhaps drea-mingly Is(not-
quite trees hugging with the rash,
coherent light
)only to trace with
stiffening slow shrill eyes beyond a fit-
and-cling of stuffs the alert willing myth
of body,which will make oddly to strut
my indolent priceless smile,
                                    until
this very frail enormous star(do you see
it?)and this shall dance upon the nude
and final silence and shall the
(i do but touch you)timid lewd
moon plunge skilfully into the hill.

XXIII

notice the convulsed orange inch of moon
perching on this silver minute of evening.

We'll choose the way to the forest—no offense
to you,white town whose spires softly dare.
Will take the houseless wisping rune
of road lazily carved on sharpening air.

Fields lying miraculous in violent silence

fill with microscopic whithering
...(that's the Black People,chérie,
who live under stones.) Don't be afraid

and we will pass the simple ugliness
of exact tombs,where a large road crosses
and all the people are minutely dead.

Then you will slowly kiss me

XXIV

and this day it was Spring....us
drew lewdly the murmurous minute clumsy
smelloftheworld.   We intricately
alive,cleaving the luminous stammer of bodies
(eagerly just not each other touch)seeking,some
street which easily tickles a brittle fuss
of fragile huge humanity....
                              Numb
thoughts,kicking in the rivers of our blood,miss
by how terrible inches speech—it
made you a little dizzy did the world's smell
(but i was thinking why the girl-and-bird
of you move....moves....and also,i'll admit—)

till,at the corner of Nothing and Something,we heard
a handorgan in twilight playing like hell

&

[AND]

To
E. O.

A

POST IMPRESSIONS

I

the wind is a Lady with
bright slender eyes(who

moves)at sunset
and who—touches—the
hills without any reason

(i have spoken with this
indubitable and green person "Are
You the wind?" "Yes" "why do you touch flowers
as if they were unalive,as

if They were ideas?" "because,sir
things which in my mind blossom will
stumble beneath a clumsiest disguise,appear
capable of fragility and indecision

—do not suppose these
without any reason and otherwise
roses and mountains
different from the i am who wanders

imminently across the renewed world"
to me said the)wind being A lady in a green
dress,who;touches:the fields
(at sunset)

II

Take for example this:

if to the colour of midnight
to a more than darkness(which
is myself and Paris and all
things)the bright
rain
occurs deeply,beautifully

and i(being at a window
in this midnight)
                    for no reason feel
deeply completely conscious of the rain or rather
Somebody who uses roofs and streets skilfully to make a
possible and beautiful sound:

if a(perhaps)clock strikes,in the alive
coolness,very faintly and
finally through altogether delicate gestures of rain

a colour comes,which is morning,O do not wonder that

(just at the edge of day)i surely
make a millionth poem which will not wholly
miss you;or if i certainly create,lady,
one of the thousand selves who are your smile.

III

Paris;this April sunset completely utters;
utters serenely silently a cathedral

before whose upward lean magnificent face
the streets turn young with rain,

spiral acres of bloated rose
coiled within cobalt miles of sky
yield to and heed
the mauve
          of twilight(who slenderly descends,
daintily carrying in her eyes the dangerous first stars)
people move love hurry in a gently

arriving gloom and
see!(the new moon
fills abruptly with sudden silver
these torn pockets of lame and begging colour)while
there and here the lithe indolent prostitute
Night,argues

with certain houses

IV

I remark this beach has been used too.   much Too.   originally
spontaneous twurls-of-excrement inanely codified with superb
sunlight,   jolts of delapidation bath-houses whose opened
withins ejaculate. obscenity   the tide Did dl es a,fad ed
explosion of, pink!stocking

w h e e saysthesea-brE aking-b Re   akin g(brea)K   ing

my Nose puts on sharp robes of uncouth odour,for an onion!for
one—onion for.   putrescence is Cubical   sliced-nicelybits
Of,   shivers ofcrin Ging stink.dull, globular glows and
flatchatte ringarom a .s

—w hee e;

seasays Break snice-Ly in-twin K les Of,CleaN

a booming smell waddles toward,me,dressed like a Plum grinning
softly,New   focus-of disintegrat i o n ?   my

mind laughsin- to Slivers of (unthinking.c'est

l'heure

         exquise)i remind Me of HerThe delicate-swill tints of

hair Whose(the lit–tle m-oo-n' s o u t)   flesh   stalks
the Momentinmyarms

your expression
               my love
                    when most passionate.,

                                        my,love
is thatofa fly.pre cisel Yhalf

(squashe)d

          with,its,little,solemn,   entrails

V

my smallheaded pearshaped

lady in gluey twilight
moving,suddenly

is three animals.   The
minute waist continually

with an African gesture

utters a frivolous intense half of
Girl which(like some

floating snake upon itself always and
slowly which upward certainly is pouring)emits
a pose
        :to twitter wickedly

whereas the big and firm legs moving solemnly
like careful and furious and beautiful elephants

(mingled in whispering thickly smooth thighs
thinkingly)
remind me of Woman and

how between
her hips India is.

VI

of this sunset(which is so
filled with fear people bells)i
say your eyes can take
day away more softly horribly suddenly;

(of these two most
early stars wincing upon a single
colour,i know only that your hands
move more simply upon the evening

and à propos such light and shape as means
the moon,i somehow feel
your smile slightly is a more
minute adventure)

lady.   The clumsy dark threatens(and i do
not speak nor think nor am aware
of anything
              save that these houses bulge
like memories in one crooked street

of a mind peacefully and skilfully which is **disappearing**

VII

my eyes are fond of the east side
as i lie asleep my eyes go into Allen street the dark long cool tunnel
of raving colour,on either side the windows are packed with hardslippery
greens and helplessbaby blues and stic-ky chromes and prettylemons and
virginal pinks and wealthy vermilion and breathless-scarlet,dark colours
like 'cellos keen fiddling colours colours cOOler than harps colours
p r i c k i n glike piccolos thumPing colours like a bangofpiano colours
which,are,the,flowery pluckings of a harpsichord colours of Pure percus-
sion colours-like-trumpets they(writhe they,struggleinweird chords of
humorous,fury heapingandsqueezing tum-bling-scratchingcrowd ingworming
each by screeching Each)on either side the street's DarkcOOllonGBody
windows,are. clenched. fistsoftint.
      TUMTITUMTIDDLE
if sometimes my eyes stay at home
then my mouth will go out into the East side,my mouth goes to the peddlers,
to the peddlers of smooth,fruits of eager colours of the little,huddling
nuts and the bad candies my,mouth loves melons slitted with bright knives,
it stains itself,with currants and cherries it (swallow s bun chesofnew
grapes likeGree n A r e b u b b l e s asc end-ing inthecarts my,mouth
is,fond of tiny plums of tangerines and apples it will,Gorge indistinct
palishflesh of laZilytas tingg OO seberries,it,loves these better than,
cubesandovalsof sweetness but it swallow) s greedily sugaredellipses it
does not disdain picKles,once,it,ate a scarlet pepper and my eyes were
buttoned with pain
      THE BLACK CAT WITH
is there anything my ears love it's
to go into the east Side in a. dark street a hurDygurdY with thequeer
hopping ghosts of children.   my,ears know the fuZZy tune that's played
by the Funny hand of the paralyticwhose dod d e rin g partner whEEl
shi min chb yi nch along the whirlingPeaceful furious street people
drop,coppers into,the littletin-cup His wrappedupbody Queerly Has,my,
ears,go into Hassan's place the kanoonchir p ing the bigtwittering
zither-and the mealy,ladies dancing thicklyfoolish,with,the,tam,bou,
rine,s And the violin spitting squeakysongs into the cuspidor-col our-
edRoom and,my ears bend to the little silent handorgan propping the
curve of the tiny motheaten old manwhose Beard rests.onthetopwhose
silly,Hand revolves,perfectly,slowlywith,the handle ofa crankin It
The L's roar tortures-pleasantly myears it is,like the,Jab:of a dark
tool.   With a cleverjeRk in itlike the motionofa Sharp Knife-sN ap-
pingof fadeadf ish' shead Or,the whipping of a blackSnake cu tSudden ly
in 2 that,writhes...A..lit.tleora basket of RipeBlackbeRRies emptied
suddenl (y down the squirming sPine of the)unsuspecting street;
      THE YELLOW EYES AND

—;i Like to
Lie On My Couch at Christopher Street For my stomach goes out into The
east side my sex sitting upright on the stomach like A billiken with
hisknees huggedtogether it,goes out into the rapid hard women and
intotheslow hot women   my Stomach ruBSiTSEIf kew-re-ous-ly a mong
Them(among their stomachs andtheir sexes   )stomachsofold pe o pleLike
hideous vegetaBles weazEned with-being-put-too-long in windows and
never sold and couldn't-be-given-away because Who?wanted them,stom-
achslikEDead fishe s s olemnandputrid vast,stomachs bLurting and
cHuckling like uninteresting-landscapes made interesting by earTHQuake
empty stomachsClenche Dtothe beautiful-curveofhunger, cHuBbY stomachs
which have not,known other stomachs and their Sexis a Lone ly,flower
whose secretloveliness hur.ts itse;l.f to no-thing   signifi-cant
stomachs:Who carry-tadpole!s,,stomachs of little,girls smoothanduseless
i,like,best,the,stomachs,of the young (girls silky and lewd)like corn
s l e n derl y tottering in sun-light
       THE
nobody(knows and WhoEver would)?dance lewd dollies pretty and putrid
dollies of-love-and-of-death dollies of perfect life,

dollies of anyway
       VIOLIN

VIII

suppose
Life is an old man carrying flowers on his head.

young death sits in a café
smiling,a piece of money held between
his thumb and first finger

(i say "will he buy flowers" to you
and "Death is young
life wears velour trousers
life totters,life has a beard" i

say to you who are silent.—"Do you see
Life?he is there and here,
or that,or this
or nothing or an old man 3 thirds
asleep,on his head
flowers,always crying
to nobody something about les
roses les bluets
           yes,
              will He buy?
Les belles bottes—oh hear
,pas chères")

and my love slowly answered I think so.   But
I think I see someone else

there is a lady,whose name is Afterwards
she is sitting beside young death,is slender;
likes flowers.

PORTRAITS

I

when the spent day begins to frail
(whose grave already three or two
young stars with spades of silver dig)

by beauty i declare to you

if what i am at one o'clock
to little lips(which have not sinned
in whose displeasure lives a kiss)
kneeling,your frequent mercy begs,

sharply believe me,wholly,well
—did(wisely suddenly into
a dangerous womb of cringing air)
the largest hour push deep his din

of wallowing male(shock beyond shock
blurted)strokes,vibrant with the purr
of echo pouring in a mesh
of following tone:did this and this

spire strike midnight(and did occur
bell beyond fiercely spurting bell
a jetted music splashing fresh
upon silence)i without fail

entered became and was these twin
imminent lisping bags of flesh;
became eyes moist lithe shuddering big,
the luminous laughter,and the legs

whereas,at twenty minutes to

one,i am this blueeyed Finn
emerging from a lovehouse who
buttons his coat against the wind

II

impossibly

motivated by midnight
the flyspecked abdominous female
indubitably tellurian
strolls
          emitting minute grins

each an intaglio.
Nothing
has also carved upon her much

too white forehead a pair of
eyes which mutter thickly(as one merely
terricolous American an instant doubts
the authenticity

of these antiquities—relaxing
                                   hurries
  elsewhere;to blow

incredible wampum

III

here is little Effie's head
whose brains are made of gingerbread
when the judgment day comes
God will find six crumbs

stooping by the coffinlid
waiting for something to rise
as the other somethings did—
you imagine His surprise

bellowing through the general noise
Where is Effie who was dead?
—to God in a tiny voice,
i am may the first crumb said

whereupon its fellow five
crumbs chuckled as if they were alive
and number two took up the song,
might i'm called and did no wrong

cried the third crumb,i am should
and this is my little sister could
with our big brother who is would
don't punish us for we were good;

and the last crumb with some shame
whispered unto God,my name
is must and with the others i've
been Effie who isn't alive

just imagine it I say
God amid a monstrous din
watch your step and follow me
stooping by Effie's little,in

(want a match or can you see?)
which the six subjunctive crumbs
twitch like mutilated thumbs:
picture His peering biggest whey

coloured face on which a frown
puzzles,but I know the way—
(nervously Whose eyes approve
the blessed while His ears are crammed

with the strenuous music of
the innumerable capering damned)
—staring wildly up and down
and here we are now judgment day

cross the threshold have no dread
lift the sheet back in this way.
here is little Effie's head
whose brains are made of gingerbread

N

&:SEVEN POEMS

I

                              i will be
M o ving in the Street of her

bodyfee l inga ro undMe the traffic of
lovely;muscles-sinke x p i r i n   g S
          uddenl
Y   totouch
                    the curvedship of
                                   Her-
....kIss   her:hands
                       will play on,mE as
dea d tunes OR s-crap p-y lea Ves flut te rin g
from Hideous trees or

       Maybe Mandolins
                      l oo k-
          pigeons fly ingand

whee(:are,SpRiN,k,LiNg an in-stant with sunLight
then)l-
ing all go BlacK wh-eel-ing

oh
   ver
        mYveRylitT'le

street
where
you will come,

              at twi li ght
s(oon & there's
a   m oo
)n.

II

i'll tell you a dream i had once i was away up in the sky Blue,everything:
a bar the bar was made of brass hangIng from strings (or)someThing i was
lying on the bar it was cOOl i didn't have anything on and I was hot all
Hot and the bar was

    COOl
O My lover,

        there's just room for me in You
my stomach goes into your Little Stomach My legs are in your legs Your
arms
       under me around; my head fits(my head)in your Brain—my,head's
big
she(said laughing
)with your head.all big

III

Spring is like a perhaps hand
(which comes carefully
out of Nowhere)arranging
a window,into which people look(while
people stare
arranging and changing placing
carefully there a strange
thing and a known thing here)and

changing everything carefully

spring is like a perhaps
Hand in a window
(carefully to
and fro moving New and
Old things,while
people stare carefully
moving a perhaps
fraction of flower here placing
an inch of air there)and

without breaking anything.

IV

Who
      threw the silver dollar up into the tree?

                  I didn't said the little
lady who sews and grows every day paler-paler she sits sewing and grow-
ing and that's the truth,
who threw

      the ripe melon into the tree?you
                got me said the smoke who
runs the elevator but I bet two bits come seven come eleven mm make
the world safe for democracy it never fails and that's a fact;

who threw the

bunch of violets
        into the tree?I dunno said the silver dog,   with ripe
eyes and wagged his tail that's the god's own

and the moon kissed the little lady on her paler-paler face and said
never mind,you'll find
        But the moon creeped into the pink hand of the
smoke that shook the ivories
        and she said said She Win and you won't be

sorry   And The Moon came!along-along to the waggy silver dog
and the moon came
and the Moon said into his Ripe Eyes
        and the moon
          Smiled

      ,so

V

gee i like to think of dead it means nearer because deeper firmer
since darker than little round water at one end of the well   it's
too cool to be crooked and it's too firm to be hard but it's sharp
and thick and it loves,   every old thing falls in rosebugs and
jackknives and kittens and pennies they all sit there looking at
each other having the fastest time because they've never met before

dead's more even than how many ways of sitting on your head your
unnatural hair has in the morning

dead's clever too like POF goes the alarm off and the little striker
having the best time tickling away everybody's brain so everybody
just puts out their finger and they stuff the poor thing all full
of fingers

dead has a smile like the nicest man you've never met who maybe winks
at you in a streetcar and you pretend you don't but really you do
see and you are My how glad he winked and hope he'll do it again

or if it talks about you somewhere behind your back it makes your neck
feel pleasant and stoopid   and if dead says may i have this one and
was never introduced you say Yes because you know you want it to dance
with you and it wants to and it can dance and Whocares

dead's fine like hands do you see that water flowerpots in windows but
they live higher in their house than you so that's all you see but you
don't want to

dead's happy like the way underclothes All so differently solemn and
inti and sitting on one string

dead never says my dear, Time for your musiclesson and you like music and
to have somebody play who can but you know you never can and why have to?

dead's nice like a dance where you danced simple hours and you take all
your prickly-clothes off and squeeze-into-largeness without one word   and
you lie still as anything   in largeness and this largeness begins to give
you,the dance all over again and you,feel all again all over the way men
you liked made you feel when they touched you(but that's not all)because
largeness tells you so you can feel what you made,men feel when,you touched,
them

dead's sorry like a thistlefluff-thing which goes landing away all by
himself on somebody's roof or something where who–ever–heard–of–growing
and nobody expects you to anyway

dead says come with me he says(andwhyevernot)into the round well and
see the kitten and the penny and the jackknife and the rosebug

and you

say Sure you say   (like that)   sure i'll come with you you say for i
like kittens i do and jackknives i do and pennies i do and rosebugs i do

VI

(one!)
the wisti–twisti barber
-pole is climbing

people high,up–in

tenements talk.in sawdust Voices
                              a:whispering drunkard passes

VII

who knows if the moon's
a balloon,coming out of a keen city
in the sky—filled with pretty people?
(and if you and i should

get into it,if they
should take me and take you into their balloon,
why then
we'd go up higher with all the pretty people

than houses and steeples and clouds:
go sailing
away and away sailing into a keen
city which nobody's ever visited,where

always
        it's
            Spring)and everyone's
in love and flowers pick themselves

D

SONNETS—REALITIES

I

O It's Nice To Get Up In,the slipshod mucous kiss
of her riant belly's fooling bore
—When The Sun Begins To(with a phrasing crease
of hot subliminal lips,as if a score
of youngest angels suddenly should stretch neat necks
just to see how always squirms
the skilful mystery of Hell)me suddenly

grips in chuckles of supreme sex.

In The Good Old Summer Time.
My gorgeous bullet in tickling intuitive flight
aches,just,simply,into,her.   Thirsty
stirring. (Must be summer.   Hush.   Worms.)
But It's Nicer To Lie In Bed
                              —eh?   I'm

not.   Again.   Hush.   God.   Please hold.   Tight

II

my strength becoming wistful in a glib

girl i consider her as a leaf
                              thinks
of the sky,my mind takes to nib
-bling,of her posture.   (As an eye winks).

and almost i refrain from jumbling her
flesh whose casual mouth's coy rooting
dies also.   (my loveFist in her knuckling

thighs,
          with a sharp indecent stir
unclenches

              into fingers....she too is tired.
Not of me.   The eyes which biggish loll

the hands' will tumbling into shall

—and Love 's a coach with gilt hopeless wheels mired
where sits rigidly her body's doll
gay exactly perishing sexual,

III

the dirty colours of her kiss have just
throttled
       my seeing blood,her heart's chatter

riveted a weeping skyscraper

in me

     i bite on the eyes' brittle crust
(only feeling the belly's merry thrust
Boost my huge passion like a business

and the Y her legs panting as they press

proffers its omelet of fluffy lust)
at six exactly
       the alarm tore

two slits in her cheeks.   A brain peered at the dawn.
she got up

      with a gashing yellow yawn
and tottered to a glass bumping things.
she picked wearily something from the floor

Her hair was mussed,and she coughed while tying strings

IV

light cursed falling in a singular block
her,rain-warm-naked
                           exquisitely hashed

(little careful hunks-of-lilac laughter splashed
from the world prettily upward,mock
us....)
           and there was a clock.   tac-tic.   tac-toc.

Time and lilacs....minutes and love....do you?and
always
          (i simply understand
the gnashing petals of sex which lock
me seriously.

                 Dumb for a while.my

god—a patter of kisses,the chewed stump

of a mouth,huge dropping of a flesh from
hinging thighs
                  ....merci....i want to die
nous sommes heureux

                     My soul a limp lump

of lymph
        she kissed
              and i

                   ....chéri....nous sommes

V

the bed is not very big

a sufficient pillow shoveling
her small manure-shaped head

one sheet on which distinctly wags

at times the weary twig
of a neckless nudity
(very occasionally budding

a flabby algebraic odour

jigs
    et tout en face
always wiggles the perfectly dead
finger of thitherhithering gas.

clothed with a luminous fur

poilu

    a Jesus sags
in frolicsome wooden agony).

VI

the poem her belly marched through me as
one army.   From her nostrils to her feet

she smelled of silence.   The inspired cleat

of her glad leg pulled into a sole mass
my separate lusts
                           her hair was like a gas
evil to feel.   Unwieldy....

                          the bloodbeat
in her fierce laziness tried to repeat
a trick of syncopation Europe has

—. One day i felt a mountain touch me where
i stood (maybe nine miles off).   It was spring

sun-stirring.   sweetly to the mangling air
muchness of buds mattered.   a valley spilled
its tickling river in my eyes,
                        the killed

world wriggled like a twitched string.

VII

an amiable putrescence carpenters

the village of her mind bodily which

ravelling,to a proud continual stitch
of the unmitigated sistole
                              purrs
against my mind,the eyes' shuddering burrs
of light stick on my brain harder than can twitch
its terrors;
            the,mouth's,swallowed,muscle(itch
of groping mucous)in my mouth occurs

homelessly.   While grip Hips simply.   well
fussed flesh does surely to mesh.   New
and eager.   wittily peels the.   ploop.—OOc h get:breath
once,all over,kid how,funny Do tell
....sweat,succeeds breathings stopped
                                      to

hear,in darkness,water the lips of death

VIII

her careful distinct sex whose sharp lips comb

my mumbling gropeofstrength(staggered by the lug
of love)
       sincerely greets,with an occult shrug
asking Through her Muteness will slowly roam
my dumbNess?

         her other,wet,warm

lips limp,across my bruising smile;
as rapidly upon the jiggled norm

of agony my grunting eyes pin tailored flames
Her being at this instant commits

an impenetrable transparency.
the harsh erecting breasts and uttering tits
punish my hug
          presto!

             the bright rile
of jovial hair extremely frames

the face in a hoop of grim ecstasy

IX

in making Marjorie god hurried
a boy's body on unsuspicious
legs of girl. his left hand quarried
the quartzlike face. his right slapped
the amusing big vital vicious
vegetable of her mouth.
Upon the whole he suddenly clapped
a tiny sunset of vermouth
-colour.   Hair. he put between
her lips a moist mistake,whose fragrance hurls
me into tears,as the dusty new-
ness of her obsolete gaze begins to.   lean....
a little against me,when for two
dollars i fill her hips with boys and girls

SONNETS—ACTUALITIES

I

before the fragile gradual throne of night
slowly when several stars are opening
one beyond one immaculate curving
cool treasures of silence
                              (slenderly wholly
rising,herself uprearing wholly slowly,
lean in the hips and her sails filled with dream—
when on a green brief gesture of twilight
trembles the imagined galleon of Spring)

somewhere unspeaking sits my life;the grim
clenched mind of me somewhere begins again,
shares the year's perfect agony.   Waiting

(always)upon a fragile instant when

herself me(slowly,wholly me)will press
in the young lips unearthly slenderness

I I

when i have thought of you somewhat too
much and am become perfectly and
simply Lustful....sense a gradual stir
of beginning muscle,and what it will do
to me before shutting....understand
i love you....feel your suddenly body reach
for me with a speed of white speech

(the simple instant of perfect hunger
Yes)
        how beautifully swims
the fooling world in my huge blood,
cracking brains A swiftlyenormous light
—and furiously puzzling through,prismatic,whims,
the chattering self perceives with hysterical fright

a comic tadpole wriggling in delicious mud

III

if i should sleep with a lady called death
get another man with firmer lips
to take your new mouth in his teeth
(hips pumping pleasure into hips).

Seeing how the limp huddling string
of your smile over his body squirms
kissingly,i will bring you every spring
handfuls of little normal worms.

Dress deftly your flesh in stupid stuffs,
phrase the immense weapon of your hair.
Understanding why his eye laughs,
i will bring you every year

something which is worth the whole,
an inch of nothing for your soul.

IV

upon the room's
                silence,i will sew

a nagging button of candlelight
(halfstooping to exactly kiss the trite

worm of her nakedness
                until it go

rapidly to bed:i will get in with
it,wisely,pester skilfully,teasing
its lips,absurd eyes,the hair).   Creasing
its smoothness—and leave the bed agrin with

memories
           (this white worm and i who

love to feel what it will do
in my bullying fingers)
as for the candle,it'll

turn into a little curse

of wax.   Something,distinct and.   Amusing,brittle

V

        a blue woman with sticking out breasts hanging
clothes.   On the line. not so old
for the mother of twelve undershirts(we are told
by is it Bishop Taylor who needs hanging

that marriage is a sure cure for masturbation).

           A dirty wind,twitches the,clothes which are clean
—this is twilight,
         a little puppy hopping between
skipping
       children
         (It is the consummation
of day,the hour)she says to me you big fool
she says i says to her i says Sally
i says
     the

       mmmoon,begins to,drool

softly,in the hot alley,

a nigger's voice feels curiously cool
(suddenly-Lights golon,by schedule

VI

when you went away it was morning
(that is,big horses;light feeling up
streets;heels taking derbies (where?) a pup
hurriedly hunched over swill;one butting

trolley imposingly empty;snickering
shop doors unlocked by white-grub
faces) clothes in delicate hubbub

as you stood thinking of anything,

maybe the world....But i have wondered since
isn't it odd of you really to lie
a sharp agreeable flower between my

amused legs
                    kissing with little dints

of april,making the obscene shy
breasts tickle,laughing when i wilt and wince

VII

i like my body when it is with your
body.   It is so quite new a thing.
Muscles better and nerves more.
i like your body.   i like what it does,
i like its hows.   i like to feel the spine
of your body and its bones,and the trembling
-firm-smooth ness and which i will
again and again and again
kiss,   i like kissing this and that of you,
i like,slowly stroking the,shocking fuzz
of your electric fur,and what-is-it comes
over parting flesh....And eyes big love-crumbs,

and possibly i like the thrill

of under me you so quite new

is 5

FOREWORD

On the assumption that my technique is either complicated or original or both,the publishers have politely requested me to write an introduction to this book.

At least my theory of technique,if I have one,is very far from original;nor is it complicated.   I can express it in fifteen words,by quoting The Eternal Question And Immortal Answer of burlesk,viz. "Would you hit a woman with a child?—No,I'd hit her with a brick."   Like the burlesk comedian,I am abnormally fond of that precision which creates movement.

If a poet is anybody,he is somebody to whom things made matter very little—somebody who is obsessed by Making.   Like all obsessions,the Making obsession has disadvantages;for instance,my only interest in making money would be to make it. Fortunately,however,I should prefer to make almost anything else,including locomotives and roses.   It is with roses and locomotives(not to mention acrobats Spring electricity Coney Island the 4th of July the eyes of mice and Niagara Falls)that my "poems" are competing.

They are also competing with each other,with elephants,and with El Greco.

Ineluctable preoccupation with The Verb gives a poet one priceless advantage: whereas nonmakers must content themselves with the merely undeniable fact that two times two is four,he rejoices in a purely irresistible truth(to be found,in abbreviated costume,upon the title page of the present volume).

E. E. CUMMINGS

One

FIVE AMERICANS

I. LIZ

with breathing as(faithfully)her lownecked
dress a little topples and slightly expands

one square foot mired in silk wrinkling loth
stocking begins queerly to do a few
gestures to death,
                    the silent shoulders are both
slowly with pinkish ponderous arms bedecked
whose white thick wrists deliver promptly to
a deep lap enormous mindless hands.
and no one knows what(i am sure of this)
her blunt unslender,what her big unkeen

"Business is rotten"the face yawning said

what her mouth thinks of
                          (if it were a kiss
distinct entirely melting sinuous lean...
whereof this lady in some book had read

II. MAME

she puts down the handmirror.   "Look at"arranging
before me a mellifluous idiot grin
(with what was nose upwrinkled into nothing
earthly,while the slippery eyes drown
in surging flesh).   A thumblike index down-
dragging yanks back skin"see"(i,seeing,ceased
to breathe).   The plump left fist opening
"wisdom."   Flicker of gold.   "Yep.   No gas.   Flynn"

the words drizzle untidily from released
cheeks"I'll tell duh woild;some noive all right.
Aint much on looks but how dat baby ached."

and when i timidly hinted"novocaine?"
the eyes outstart,curl,bloat,are newly baked

and swaggering cookies of indignant light

III. GERT

joggle i think will do it although the glad
monosyllable jounce possibly can tell
better how the balloons move(as
her ghost lurks,a Beau Brummell sticking in its three-

cornered always moist mouth)—jazz,
for whose twitching lips,between you and me
almost succeeds while toddle rings the bell.
But if her tall corpsecoloured body seat
itself(with the uncouth habitual dull
jerk at garters)there's no sharpest neat
word for the thing.
                         Her voice?
                                   gruesome:a trull
leaps from the lungs"gimme uh swell fite

like up ter yknow,Rektuz,Toysday nite;
where uh guy gets gayn troze uh lobstersalad

IV. MARJ

"life?
      Listen"the feline she with radishred
legs said(crossing them slowly)"I'm
asleep.   Yep.   Youse is asleep kid
and everybody is."   And i hazarded
"god"(blushing slightly)—"O damn
ginks like dis Gawd"opening slowlyslowly
them—then carefully the rolypoly
voice squatting on a mountain of gum did
something like a whisper,"even her."
"The Madam?"I emitted;vaguely watching
that mountainous worthy in the fragile act
of doing her eyebrows.—Marj's laughter smacked
me:pummeling the curtains,drooped to a purr...

i left her permanently smiling

V. FRAN

should i entirely ask of god why
on the alert neck of this brittle whore
delicately wobbles an improbably distinct face,
and how these wooden big two feet conclude
happeningly the unfirm drooping bloated
calves
            i would receive the answer more
or less deserved,Young fellow go in peace.
which i do,being as Dick Mid once noted
lifting a Green River(here's to youse)
"a bloke wot's well behaved"...and always try
to not wonder how let's say elation
causes the bent eyes thickly to protrude—

or why her tiniest whispered invitation
is like a clock striking in a dark house

II

POEM,OR BEAUTY HURTS MR.VINAL

take it from me kiddo
believe me
my country,'tis of

you,land of the Cluett
Shirt Boston Garter and Spearmint
Girl With The Wrigley Eyes(of you
land of the Arrow Ide
and Earl &
Wilson
Collars)of you i
sing:land of Abraham Lincoln and Lydia E. Pinkham,
land above all of Just Add Hot Water And Serve—
from every B.V.D.

let freedom ring

amen.   i do however protest,anent the un
-spontaneous and otherwise scented merde which
greets one(Everywhere Why)as divine poesy per
that and this radically defunct periodical.   i would

suggest that certain ideas gestures
rhymes,like Gillette Razor Blades
having been used and reused
to the mystical moment of dullness emphatically are
Not To Be Resharpened.   (Case in point

if we are to believe these gently O sweetly
melancholy trillers amid the thrillers
these crepuscular violinists among my and your
skyscrapers—Helen & Cleopatra were Just Too Lovely,
The Snail's On The Thorn enter Morn and God's
In His andsoforth

do you get me?)according
to such supposedly indigenous
throstles Art is O World O Life
a formula:example,Turn Your Shirttails Into
Drawers and If It Isn't An Eastman It Isn't A
Kodak therefore my friends let
us now sing each and all fortissimo A-
mer
i

ca,I
love,
You.　　And there're a
hun-dred-mil-lion-oth-ers,like
all of you successfully if
delicately gelded(or spaded)
gentlemen(and ladies)—pretty

littleliverpill-
hearted-Nujolneeding-There's-A-Reason
americans(who tensetendoned and with
upward vacant eyes,painfully
perpetually crouched,quivering,upon the
sternly allotted sandpile
—how silently
emit a tiny violetflavoured nuisance:Odor?

ono.
comes out like a ribbon lies flat on the brush

III

curtains part)
the peacockappareled
prodigy of Flo's midnight
Frolic dolores

small in the head keen chassised like a Rolls
Royce
swoops smoothly
                    outward(amid
tinkling-cheering-hammering

tables)

while softly along Kirkland Street
the infantile ghost of Professor
Royce rolls

remembering that it

has for
-gotten some-
thing ah

(my

necktie

IV

workingman with hand so hairy-sturdy
you may turn O turn that airy hurdysturdygurdy
but when will turn backward O backward Time in your no thy flight
and make me a child,a pretty dribbling child,a little child.

In thy your ear:
en amérique on ne boit que de Jingyale.
things are going rather kaka
over there,over there.
yet we scarcely fare much better—

what's become of(if you please)
all the glory that or which was Greece
all the grandja
that was dada?

make me a child,stout hurdysturdygurdyman
waiter,make me a child.   So this is Paris.
i will sit in the corner and drink thinks and think drinks,
in memory of the Grand and Old days:
of Amy Sandburg
of Algernon Carl Swinburned.

Waiter a drink waiter two or three drinks
what's become of Maeterlinck
now that April's here?
(ask the man who owns one
ask Dad,He knows).

V

yonder deadfromtheneckup graduate of a
somewhat obscure to be sure university spends
her time looking picturesque under

the as it happens quite
erroneous impression that he

nascitur

VI

Jimmie's got a goil
                    goil
                            goil,
                                    Jimmie
's got a goil and
she coitnly can shimmie

when you see her shake
                          shake
                                  shake,
                                          when
you see her shake a
shimmie how you wish that you was Jimmie.

Oh for such a gurl
                    gurl
                            gurl,
                                  oh
for such a gurl to
be a fellow's twistandtwirl

talk about your Sal-
                    Sal-
                            Sal-,
                                    talk
about your Salo
-mes but gimmie Jimmie's gal.

VII

listen my children and you
shall hear the true

story of Mr Do
-nothing the wellknown parvenu
who

(having dreamed of a corkscrew)
studied with Freud a year or two
and when Freud got through
with Do-

nothing Do
-nothing could do
nothing which you
and i are accustomed to
accomplish two

or three times,and even a few
more depending on the remu-
nerativeness of the stimulus(eheu
fu
-gaces Postu-
me boo

who)

VIII

even if all desires things moments be
murdered known photographed,ourselves yawning will ask ourselves
où sont les neiges....some

guys talks big

about Lundun Burlin an gay Paree an
some guys claims der never was
nutn like Nooer Leans Shikahgo Sain
Looey Noo York an San Fran dictaphones
wireless subways vacuum
cleaners pianolas funnygraphs skyscrapers an safetyrazors

sall right in its way kiddo
but as fer i gimme de good ole daze....

in dem daze kid Christmas
meant sumpn youse knows wot
i refers ter Satter Nailyuh(comes but once er
year)i'll tell de woild one swell bangup
time wen nobody wore no cloze
an went runnin aroun wid eachudder Hell
Bent fer election makin believe dey was chust born

IX

death is more than
certain a hundred these
sounds crowds odours it
is in a hurry
beyond that any this
taxi smile or angle we do

not sell and buy
things so necessary as
is death and unlike shirts
neckties trousers
we cannot wear it out

no sir which is why
granted who discovered
America ether the movies
may claim general importance

to me to you nothing is
what particularly
matters hence in a

little sunlight and less
moonlight ourselves against the worms

hate laugh shimmy

X

nobody loses all the time

i had an uncle named
Sol who was a born failure and
nearly everybody said he should have gone
into vaudeville perhaps because my Uncle Sol could
sing McCann He Was A Diver on Xmas Eve like Hell Itself which
may or may not account for the fact that my Uncle

Sol indulged in that possibly most inexcusable
of all to use a highfalootin phrase
luxuries that is or to
wit farming and be
it needlessly
added

my Uncle Sol's farm
failed because the chickens
ate the vegetables so
my Uncle Sol had a
chicken farm till the
skunks ate the chickens when

my Uncle Sol
had a skunk farm but
the skunks caught cold and
died and so
my Uncle Sol imitated the
skunks in a subtle manner

or by drowning himself in the watertank
but somebody who'd given my Uncle Sol a Victor
Victrola and records while he lived presented to
him upon the auspicious occasion of his decease a
scrumptious not to mention splendiferous funeral with
tall boys in black gloves and flowers and everything and

i remember we all cried like the Missouri
when my Uncle Sol's coffin lurched because
somebody pressed a button
(and down went
my Uncle
Sol

and started a worm farm)

XI

now dis "daughter" uv eve(who aint precisely slim)sim

ply don't know duh meanin uv duh woid sin in
not disagreeable contras tuh dat not exacly fat

"father"(adjustin his robe)who now puts on his flat hat

XII

(and i imagine
never mind Joe agreeably cheerfully remarked when
surrounded by fat stupid animals
the jewess shrieked
the messiah tumbled successfully into the world
the animals continued eating.   And i imagine she,and
heard them slobber and
in the darkness)

stood sharp angels with faces like Jim Europe

XIII

it really must
be Nice,never to

have no imagination)or never
never to wonder about guys you used to(and them
slim hot queens with dam next to nothing

on)tangoing
(while a feller tries
to hold down the fifty bucks per
job with one foot and rock a

cradle with the other)it Must be
nice never to have no doubts about why you
put the ring
on(and watching her
face grow old and tired to which

you're married and hands get red washing
things and dishes)and to never,never really wonder i
mean about the smell
of babies and how you

know the dam rent's going to and everything and never,never
Never to stand at no window
because i can't sleep(smoking sawdust

cigarettes in the
middle of the night

XIV

ITEM

this man is o so
Waiter
this;woman is

please shut that
the pout And affectionate leer
interminable pyramidal,napkins
(this man is oh so tired of this
a door opens by itself
woman.)they so to speak were in

Love once?
now
    her mouth opens too far
and:she attacks her Lobster without
feet mingle under the
mercy.
      (exit the hors d'oeuvres)

XV

IKEY(GOLDBERG)'S WORTH I'M
TOLD $ SEVERAL MILLION
FINKLESTEIN(FRITZ)LIVES
AT THE RITZ WEAR
earl & wilson COLLARS

XVI

?

why are these pipples taking their hets off?
the king & queen
alighting from their limousine
inhabit the Hôtel Meurice(whereas
i live in a garret and eat aspirine)

but who is this pale softish almost round
young man to whom headwaiters bow so?
hush—the author of Women By Night whose latest Seeds
Of Evil sold 69 carloads before
publication the girl who goes wrong you

know(whereas when i lie down i cough too
much).   How did the traffic get so jammed?
bedad it is the famous doctor who inserts
monkeyglands in millionaires a cute idea n'est-ce pas?
(whereas,upon the other hand,myself)but let us next demand

wherefore yon mob
an accident?somebody got concus-
sion of the brain?—Not
a bit of it,my dears merely the prime
minister of Siam in native

costume,who
emerging from a pissoir
enters abruptly Notre Dame(whereas
de gustibus non disputandum est
my lady is tired of That sort of thing

XVII

this young question mark man

question mark
who suffers from
indigestion question
mark is a remarkably
charming person

personally they tell

me as for me
i only knows that
as far as
his picture goes

he's a wet dream

by Cézanne

XVIII

mr youse needn't be so spry
concernin questions arty

each has his tastes but as for i
i likes a certain party

gimme the he-man's solid bliss
for youse ideas i'll match youse

a pretty girl who naked is
is worth a million statues

XIX

she being Brand

-new;and you
know consequently a
little stiff i was
careful of her and(having

thoroughly oiled the universal
joint tested my gas felt of
her radiator made sure her springs were O.

K.)i went right to it flooded-the-carburetor cranked her

up,slipped the
clutch(and then somehow got into reverse she
kicked what
the hell)next
minute i was back in neutral tried and

again slo-wly;bare,ly nudg.   ing(my

lev-er Right-
oh and her gears being in
A 1 shape passed
from low through
second-in-to-high like
greasedlightning)just as we turned the corner of Divinity

avenue i touched the accelerator and give

her the juice,good

                    (it

was the first ride and believe i we was
happy to see how nice she acted right up to
the last minute coming back down by the Public
Gardens i slammed on

the
internalexpanding
&
externalcontracting
brakes Bothatonce and

brought allofher tremB
-ling
to a:dead.

stand-
;Still)

XX

slightly before the middle of Congressman Pudd
's 4th of July oration,with a curse and a frown
Amy Lowell got up
and all the little schoolchildren sat down

XXI

oDE

o

the sweet & aged people
who rule this world(and me and
you if we're not very
careful)

O,

the darling benevolent mindless
He—and She—
shaped waxworks filled
with dead ideas(the oh

quintillions of incredible
dodderingly godly toothless
always-so-much-interested-
in-everybody-else's-business

bipeds)OH
the bothering
dear unnecessary hairless
o

ld

XXII

on the Madam's best april the
twenty nellie

anyway and
it's flutters everything
queer;does smells he smiles is
like Out of doors he's a with
eyes and making twice the a week
you kind of,know(kind well of
A sort of the way he smile)but
and her a I mean me a
Irish,cook but well oh don't
you makes burst want to dear somehow
quickyes when(now,dark dear oh)
the iceman
how,luminously
oh how listens and,expands
my somewherealloverme heart my
the halfgloom coolish
of The what are
parks for wiggle yes has
are leap,which,anyway

give rapid lapfulls of
idiotic big hands

XXIII

(as that named Fred
-someBody:hippopotamus,scratch-
ing,one,knee with,its,
friend observes I

pass Mr Tom Larsen twirls among

pale lips the extinct
cigar)at

which

this(once flinger
of lariats lean exroper of
horned suddenly crashing things)man spits

quickly into the very bright spittoon

XXIV

my uncle
Daniel fought in the civil
war band and can play the triangle
like the devil)my

uncle Frank has done nothing for many
years but fly kites and
when the
string breaks(or something)my uncle Frank breaks into
tears.   my uncle Tom

knits and is a kewpie above the ears(but

my uncle Ed
that's
dead from the neck

up is lead all over
Brattle Street by a castrated pup

XXV ·

than(by yon sunset's wintry glow
revealed)this tall strong stalwart youth,
what sight shall human optics know
more quite ennobling forsooth?

One wondrous fine sonofabitch
(to all purposes and intents)
in which distinct and rich
portrait should be included,gents

these(by the fire's ruddy glow
united)not less than sixteen
children and of course you know
their mother,of his heart the queen

—incalculable bliss!
Picture it gents:our hero,Dan
who as you've guessed already is
the poorbuthonest workingman

(by that bright flame whose myriad tints
enrich a visage simple,terse,
seated like any king or prince
upon his uncorrupted arse

with all his hearty soul aglow)
his nightly supper sups
it isn't snowing snow you know
it's snowing buttercups

XXVI

weazened Irrefutable unastonished
two,countenances seated in arranging;sunlight
with-ered unspea-king:tWeNtY,f i n g e r s,large
four gnarled lips totter

Therefore,approaching my twentysix selves
bulging in immortal Spring express a cry of
How do you find the sun,ladies?

(graduallyverygradually"there is not enough
of it"their,hands
minutely

answered

XXVII

MEMORABILIA

stop look &

listen Venezia:incline thine
ear you glassworks
of Murano;
pause
elevator nel
mezzo del cammin' that means half-
way up the Campanile,believe

thou me cocodrillo—

mine eyes have seen
the glory of

the coming of
the Americans particularly the
brand of marriageable nymph which is
armed with large legs rancid
voices Baedekers Mothers and kodaks
—by night upon the Riva Schiavoni or in
the felicitous vicinity of the de l'Europe

Grand and Royal
Danielli their numbers

are like unto the stars of Heaven....

i do signore
affirm that all gondola signore
day below me gondola signore gondola
and above me pass loudly and gondola
rapidly denizens of Omaha Altoona or what
not enthusiastic cohorts from Duluth God only,
gondola knows Cincingondolanati i gondola don't

—the substantial dollarbringing virgins

"from the Loggia where
are we angels by O yes
beautiful we now pass through the look
girls in the style of that's the
foliage what is it didn't Ruskin
says about you got the haven't Marjorie
isn't this wellcurb simply darling"
                    —O Education:O

thos cook & son

(O to be a metope
now that triglyph's here)

XXVIII

a man who had fallen among thieves
lay by the roadside on his back
dressed in fifteenthrate ideas
wearing a round jeer for a hat

fate per a somewhat more than less
emancipated evening
had in return for consciousness
endowed him with a changeless grin

whereon a dozen staunch and leal
citizens did graze at pause
then fired by hypercivic zeal
sought newer pastures or because

swaddled with a frozen brook
of pinkest vomit out of eyes
which noticed nobody he looked
as if he did not care to rise

one hand did nothing on the vest
its wideflung friend clenched weakly dirt
while the mute trouserfly confessed
a button solemnly inert.

Brushing from whom the stiffened puke
i put him all into my arms
and staggered banged with terror through
a million billion trillion stars

XXIX

this evangelist
buttons with his big gollywog voice
the kingdomofheaven up behind and crazily
skating thither and hither in filthy sawdust
chucks and rolls
against the tent his thick joggling fists

he is persuasive

the editor cigarstinking hobgoblin swims
upward in his swivelchair one fist dangling scandal while
five other fingers snitch
rapidly through mist a defunct king as

linotypes gobblehobble

our lightheavy twic twoc ingly attacks
landing a onetwo
which doubles up suddenly his bunged hinging
victim against the
giving ropes amid
screams of deeply bulging thousands

i too omit one kelly

in response to howjedooze the candidate's new silk
lid bounds gently from his baldness
a smile masturbates softly in the vacant
lot of his physiognomy
his scientifically pressed trousers ejaculate spats

a strikingly succulent getup

but
we knew a muffhunter and he said to us Kid.
daze nutn like it.

XXX

(ponder,darling,these busted statues
of yon motheaten forum be aware
notice what hath remained
—the stone cringes
clinging to the stone,how obsolete

lips utter their extant smile....
remark

a few deleted of texture
or meaning monuments and dolls

resist Them Greediest Paws of careful
time all of which is extremely
unimportant)whereas Life

matters if or

when the your- and my-
idle vertical worthless
self unite in a peculiarly
momentary

partnership(to instigate
constructive
                Horizontal
business....even so,let us make haste
—consider well this ruined aqueduct

lady,
which used to lead something into somewhere)

XXXI

poets yeggs and thirsties

since we are spanked and put to sleep by dolls let
us not be continually astonished should
from their actions and speeches
sawdust perpetually leak

rather is it between such beddings and
bumpings of ourselves to be observed
how in this fundamental respect the well
recognised regime of childhood is reversed

meantime in dreams let us investigate
thoroughly each one his optima rerum first
having taken care to lie upon our
abdomens for greater privacy and lest

punished bottoms interrupt philosophy

XXXII

Will i ever forget that precarious moment?

As i was standing on the third rail waiting for the next train to grind me
into lifeless atoms various absurd thoughts slyly crept into my highly sexed
mind.

It seemed to me that i had first of all really made quite a mistake in being
at all born,seeing that i was wifeless and only half awake,cursed with pimples,
correctly dressed,cleanshaven above the nombril,and much to my astonishment much
impressed by having once noticed(as an infantile phenomenon)George Washington al-
most incompletely surrounded by well-drawn icecakes beheld being too strong,in
brief:an American,is you understand that i mean what i say i believe my most
intimate friends would never have gathered.

A collarbutton which had always not nothurt me not much and in the same place.

Why according to tomorrow's paper the proletariat will not rise yesterday.

Inexpressible itchings to be photographed with Lord Rothermere playing with
Lord Rothermere billiards very well by moonlight with Lord Rothermere.

A crocodile eats a native,who in revenge beats it insensible with a banana,
establishing meanwhile a religious cult based on consubstantial intangibility.

Personne ne m'aime et j'ai les mains froides.

His Royal Highness said "peek-a-boo" and thirty tame fleas left the prettily
embroidered howdah immediately.

Thumbprints of an angel named Frederick found on a lightning-rod,Boston,Mass.

such were the not unhurried reflections to which my organ of imperception gave
birth to which i should ordinarily have objected to which,considering the back-
ground,it is hardly surprising if anyone hardly should call exactly extraordin-
ary. We refer,of course,to my position. A bachelor incapable of occupation,he
had long suppressed the desire to suppress the suppressed desire of shall we
say:Idleness,while meaning its opposite?   Nothing could be clearer to all con-
cerned than that i am not a policeman.

Meanwhile the tea regressed.

Kipling again H. G. Wells,and Anatole France shook hands again and yet again
shook again hands again,the former coachman with a pipewrench of the again latter

then opening a box of newly without exaggeration shot with some difficulty sar-
dines. Mr. Wiggin took Wrs. Miggin's harm in is,extinguishing the spittoon by a
candle furnished by courtesy of the management on Thursdays,opposite which a
church stood perfectly upright but not piano item:a watermelon causes indigestion
to William Cullen Longfellow's small negro son,Henry Wadsworth Bryant.

By this time,however,the flight of crows had ceased.   I withdrew my hands from
the tennisracket.   All was over.   One brief convulsive octopus,and then our hero
folded his umbrella.

It seemed too beautiful.

Let us perhaps excuse me if i repeat himself:these,or nearly these,were the not
unpainful thoughts which occupied the subject of our attention;to speak even less
objectively,i was horribly scared i would actually fall off the rail before the
really train after all arrived.   If i should have made this perfectly clear,it
entirely would have been not my fault.

XXXIII

voices to voices,lip to lip
i swear(to noone everyone)constitutes
undying;or whatever this and that petal confutes...
to exist being a peculiar form of sleep

what's beyond logic happens beneath will;
nor can these moments be translated:i say
that even after April
by God there is no excuse for May

—bring forth your flowers and machinery:sculpture and prose
flowers guess and miss
machinery is the more accurate,yes
it delivers the goods,Heaven knows

(yet are we mindful,though not as yet awake,
of ourselves which shout and cling,being
for a little while and which easily break
in spite of the best overseeing)

i mean that the blond absence of any program
except last and always and first to live
makes unimportant what i and you believe;
not for philosophy does this rose give a damn...

bring on your fireworks,which are a mixed
splendor of piston and of pistil;very well
provided an instant may be fixed
so that it will not rub,like any other pastel.

(While you and i have lips and voices which
are for kissing and to sing with
who cares if some oneeyed son of a bitch
invents an instrument to measure Spring with?

each dream nascitur,is not made...)
why then to Hell with that:the other;this,
since the thing perhaps is
to eat flowers and not to be afraid.

XXXIV

life hurl my
yes,crumbles hand(ful released conarefetti)ev eryflitter,inga. where
mil(lions of aflickf)litter ing brightmillion of S hurl;edindodg:ing
whom areEyes shy-dodge is bright cruMbshandful,quick-hurl edinwho
Is flittercrumbs,fluttercrimbs are floatfallin,g;allwhere:
a:crimbflitteringish is arefloatsis ingfallall!mil,shy milbrightlions
my(hurl flicker handful
in)dodging are shybrigHteyes is crum bs(alll)if,ey Es

Two

I

the season 'tis,my lovely lambs,

of Sumner Volstead Christ and Co.
the epoch of Mann's righteousness
the age of dollars and no sense.
Which being quite beyond dispute

as prove from Troy(N.Y.)to Cairo
(Egypt)the luminous dithyrambs
of large immaculate unmute
antibolshevistic gents
(each manufacturing word by word
his own unrivalled brand of pyro
-technic blurb anent the(hic)
hero dead that gladly(sic)
in far lands perished of unheard
of maladies including flu)

my little darlings,let us now
passionately remember how—
braving the worst,of peril heedless,
each braver than the other,each
(a typewriter within his reach)
upon his fearless derrière
sturdily seated—Colonel Needless
To Name and General You know who
a string of pretty medals drew

(while messrs jack james john and jim
in token of their country's love
received my dears the order of
The Artificial Arm and Limb)

—or,since bloodshed and kindred questions
inhibit unprepared digestions,
come:let us mildly contemplate
beginning with his wellfilled pants
earth's biggest grafter,nothing less;
the Honorable Mr.(guess)
who,breathing on the ear of fate,
landed a seat in the legislat-
ure whereas tommy so and so
(an erring child of circumstance
whom the bulls nabbed at 33rd)

pulled six months for selling snow

I I

opening of the chambers close

quotes the microscopic pithecoid President
in a new frock
coat(scrambling all
up over the tribune dances crazily
& &)&
chatters about Peacepeacepeace(to
droppingly
descend amid thunderous anthropoid applause)pronounced

by the way Pay the

extremely artistic nevertobeextinguished fla
-me of the(very prettily indeed)arra-
nged souvenir of the in spite of himself fa
-mous soldier minus his na-
me(so as not to hurt the perspective of the(hei
-nous thought)otherwise immaculately tabulated vicinity)invei-
gles a few mildly curious rai
-ned on people(both male and female
created He

then,   And every beast of the field

III

"next to of course god america i
love you land of the pilgrims' and so forth oh
say can you see by the dawn's early my
country 'tis of centuries come and go
and are no more what of it we should worry
in every language even deafanddumb
thy sons acclaim your glorious name by gorry
by jingo by gee by gosh by gum
why talk of beauty what could be more beaut-
iful than these heroic happy dead
who rushed like lions to the roaring slaughter
they did not stop to think they died instead
then shall the voice of liberty be mute?"

He spoke.   And drank rapidly a glass of water

IV

it's jolly
odd what pops into
your jolly tête when the
jolly shells begin dropping jolly fast you
hear the rrmp and
then nearerandnearerandNEARER
and before
you can

!

& we're

NOT
(oh—
—i say

that's jolly odd
old thing,jolly
odd,jolly
jolly odd isn't
it jolly odd.

V

look at this)
a 75 done
this nobody would
have believed
would they no
kidding this was my particular

pal
funny aint
it we was
buddies
i used to

know
him lift the
poor cuss
tenderly this side up handle

with care
fragile
and send him home

to his old mother in
a new nice pine box

(collect

VI

first Jock he
was kilt a handsome
man and James and
next let me
see yes Will that was
cleverest
he was kilt and my youngest
boy was kilt last with
the big eyes i loved like you can't
imagine Harry was o
god kilt he was kilt everybody was kilt

they called them the kilties

VII

lis
-ten

you know what i mean when
the first guy drops you know
everybody feels sick or
when they throw in a few gas
and the oh baby shrapnel
or my feet getting dim freezing or
up to your you know what in water or
with the bugs crawling right all up
all everywhere over you all me everyone
that's been there knows what
i mean a god damned lot of
people don't and never
never
will know,
they don't want

to
no

VIII

come,gaze with me upon this dome
of many coloured glass,and see
his mother's pride,his father's joy,
unto whom duty whispers low

"thou must!" and who replies "I can!"
—yon clean upstanding well dressed boy
that with his peers full oft hath quaffed
the wine of life and found it sweet—

a tear within his stern blue eye,
upon his firm white lips a smile,
one thought alone:to do or die
for God for country and for Yale

above his blond determined head
the sacred flag of truth unfurled,
in the bright heyday of his youth
the upper class American

unsullied stands,before the world:
with manly heart and conscience free,
upon the front steps of her home
by the high minded pure young girl

much kissed,by loving relatives
well fed,and fully photographed
the son of man goes forth to war
with trumpets clap and syphilis

IX

16 heures
l'Etoile

the communists have fine Eyes

some are young some old none
look alike the flics rush
batter the crowd sprawls collapses
singing knocked down trampled the kicked by
flics rush(the

Flics,tidiyum,are
very tidiyum reassuringly similar,
they all have very tidiyum
mustaches,and very
tidiyum chins,and just above
their very tidiyum ears their
very tidiyum necks begin)
                         let us add

that there are 50(fifty)flics for every
one(1)communist and
all the flics are very organically
arranged
and their nucleus(composed
of captains in freshly-creased
-uniforms with only-just-
shined buttons
tidiyum
before and behind)has a nucleolus:

the Prefect of Police

(a dapper derbied
creature,swaggers daintily
twiddling
his tiny cane
and,mazurkas about tweak-
ing his wing collar pecking at his im

-peccable cravat directing being
shooting his cuffs
saluted everywhere saluting
reviewing processions of minions
tappingpeopleontheback

"allezcirculez")

—my   he's brave....
the
communists pick
up themselves friends
& their hats legs &

arms brush dirt coats
smile looking hands
spit blood teeth

the Communists have(very)fine eyes
(which stroll hither and thither through the
evening in bruised narrow questioning faces)

X

my sweet old etcetera
aunt lucy during the recent

war could and what
is more did tell you just
what everybody was fighting

for,
my sister

isabel created hundreds
(and
hundreds)of socks not to
mention shirts fleaproof earwarmers

etcetera wristers etcetera,my

mother hoped that

i would die etcetera
bravely of course my father used
to become hoarse talking about how it was
a privilege and if only he
could meanwhile my

self etcetera lay quietly
in the deep mud et

cetera
(dreaming,
et
   cetera,of
Your smile
eyes knees and of your Etcetera)

Three

I

now that fierce few
flowers(stealthily)
in the alive west
begin

requiescat this six
feet of Breton big good
body,which terminated
in fists hair wood

erect cursing hatless who
(bent by wind)slammed hard-
over the tiller;clattered
forward skidding in outrageous

sabots language trickling
pried his black
mouth with fat jibing
lips,

once upon a
(that is
over:and the sea heaving
indolent colourless forgets)time

Requiescat.
carry
carefully the blessed large silent him
into nibbling final worms

II

Among

      these
          red pieces of
day(against which and
quite silently hills
made of blueandgreen paper

scorchbend ingthem
-selves-U
pcurv E,into:
            anguish(clim
b)ing
s-p-i-r-a-
l
 and,disappear)
            Satanic and blasé

a black goat lookingly wanders

There is nothing left of the world but
into this noth
ing il treno per
Roma si-gnori?
jerk.
ilyr,ushes

III

it is winter a moon in the afternoon
and warm air turning into January darkness up
through which sprouting gently,the cathedral
leans its dreamy spine against thick sunset

i perceive in front of our lady a ring of people
a brittle swoon of centrifugally expecting
faces clumsily which devours a man,three cats,
five white mice,and a baboon.

O a monkey with a sharp face waddling carefully
the length of this padded pole;a monkey attached
by a chain securely to this always talking
individual,mysterious witty hatless.

Cats which move smoothly from neck to neck of bottles,cats
smoothly willowing out and in between bottles,who step smoothly
and rapidly along this pole over five squirming
mice;or leap through hoops of fire,creating smoothness.

People stare,the drunker applaud
while twilight takes the sting out of the vermilion
jacket of nodding hairy Jacqueline who is given a mouse
to hold lovingly,

our lady what do you think of this?   Do your proud fingers and
your arms tremble remembering something squirming fragile
and which had been presented unto you by a mystery?
...the cathedral recedes into weather without answering

IV

candles and

Here Comes a glass box
which the exhumed
hand of Saint Ignatz miraculously
inhabits.   (people tumble
down.   people crumble to their
knees.   people
begin crossing people)and

hErE cOmEs a glass box:
surrounded by priests
moving in fifty colours
,sensuously

(the crowd
howls faintly
blubbering pointing

see
yes)
It
here
comes

A Glass
Box and incense with

and oh sunlight—
the crash of the
colours(of the oh
silently
striding)priests-and-
slowly,al,ways;procession:and

Enters

this
       church.

toward which The
Expectant stutter(upon artificial limbs,
with faces like defunct geraniums)

V

will out of the kindness of their hearts a few philosophers tell me
what am i doing on top of this hill at Calchidas,in the sunlight?
down ever so far on the beach below me a little girl in white spins,
    tumbles;rolling in sand.
across this water,crowding tints:browns and whites shoving, the dot-
    ting millions of windows of thousands of houses—Lisboa.   Like
    the crackle of a typewriter,in the afternoon sky.
goats and sheep are driven by somebody along a curve of road which
    eats into a pink cliff back and up leaning out of yellowgreen
    water.

they are building a house down there by the sea,in the afternoon.

rapidly a reddish ant travels my fifth finger.
a bird chirps in a tree,somewhere nowhere
and a little girl in white is tumbling
in sand
        Clouds over
me are like bridegrooms

Naked and luminous

             (here the absurd I;life,to peer and wear clothes.
                i am altogether foolish,i suddenly make a fist
                out of ten fingers
voices rise from down ever so far—
hush.
      Sunlight,
           there are old men behind me I tell you;several, in-
           credible,sleepy

VI

but observe;although
once is never the beginning of
enough,is it(i do not pretend
to know the reason any more than.)　But look:up-

raising,hoisting,a little
perhaps that and this,deftly
propping on smallest hands
the slim hinging you
　　　　　　　　　—because
it's five o'clock

and these(i notice)trees winterbrief surly old
gurgle a nonsense of sparrows,the cathedral
shudders blackening;
the sky is washed with tone

now for a moon
to squat in first darkness
—a little moon thinner than

memory

faint
-er
　　than all the whys
which lurk
between your naked shoulderblades.—Here
comes a stout fellow in a blouse
just outside this window,touching the glass
boxes one by one with his magic
stick(in which a willing
bulb of flame bubbles)
　　　　　　　　　see

here and here they explode
silently into crocuses of brightness.　(That is enough
of life,for you.　I understand.　Once
again....)sliding

a little downward,embrace me with your body's suddenly
curving entire warm questions

VII

sunlight was over
our mouths fears hearts lungs arms hopes feet hands

under us the unspeaking Mediterranean bluer
than we had imagined
a few cries drifting through
high air
a sail a fishing boat somebody an invisible spectator,
maybe certain nobodies laughing faintly

playing moving far below us

perhaps one villa caught like pieces
of a kite in the trees,here
and here reflecting
sunlight
(everywhere sunlight keen complete
silent

and everywhere you your kisses your flesh mind breathing
beside under around myself)
                              by and by

a fat colour reared itself against the sky and the sea

...finally your eyes knew
me,we smiled to each other,releasing lay,watching
(sprawling,in
grass upon a
cliff)what had been something
else carefully slowly fatally turning into ourselves...

while in the very middle of fire all

the world becoming bright and little melted.

Four

I

the moon looked into my window
it touched me with its small hands
and with curling infantile
fingers it understood my eyes cheeks mouth
its hands(slipping)felt of my necktie wandered
against my shirt and into my body the
sharp things fingered tinily my heart life

the little hands withdrew,jerkily,themselves

quietly they began playing with a button
the moon smiled she
let go my vest and crept
through the window
she did not fall
she went creeping along the air
                                        over houses
                                                roofs

And out of the east toward
her a fragile light bent gatheringly

II

if being mortised with a dream
myself speaks

(whispering,
suggesting that our souls
inhabit whatever is between them)
knowing my lips hands the way i move
my habits laughter

i say
you will perhaps pardon,
possibly you will comprehend.   and how
this has arrived your mind may guess

if at sunset

it should,leaning against me,smile;
or(between dawn and twilight)giving

your eyes,present me also
with the terror of shrines

which noone has suspected(but
wherein silently
always
are kneeling the various deaths
which are your lover lady:together with what keen
innumerable lives he has not lived.

III

here's a little mouse)and
what does he think about,i
wonder as over this
floor(quietly with

bright eyes)drifts(nobody
can tell because
Nobody knows,or why
jerks Here &,here,
gr(oo)ving the room's Silence)this like
a littlest
poem a
(with wee ears and see?

tail frisks)
                    (gonE)
"mouse",
              We are not the same you and

i,since here's a little he
or is
it It
?   (or was something we saw in the mirror)?

therefore we'll kiss;for maybe
what was Disappeared
into ourselves
who   (look)   ,startled

IV

but if i should say
goodmorning trouble adds
up all sorts of quickly
things on the slate of that
nigger's
face(but

If i should say thankyouverymuch

mr rosenbloom picks strawberries
with beringed hands)but if

i Should say solong my
tailor
chuckles

like a woman in a dream(but if i
should say
Now the all saucers
but cups if begin to spoons dance every-

should where say over the damned table and we
hold lips Eyes everything
hands you know what
happens)but if i should,
Say,

V

in spite of everything
which breathes and moves,since Doom
(with white longest hands
neatening each crease)
will smooth entirely our minds

—before leaving my room
i turn,and(stooping
through the morning)kiss
this pillow,dear
where our heads lived and were.

VI

you are not going to,dear.   You are not going to and
i but that doesn't in the least matter.   The big
fear Who held us deeply in His fist is

no longer,can you imagine it
i can't which doesn't matter
and what does is possibly this dear,that we may resume
impact with the inutile collide

once more with the imaginable,love,and eat sunlight(do
you believe it?   i begin to and that doesn't matter)which

i suggest teach us a new terror always
which shall brighten
carefully these things we consider life.
Dear i put my eyes into you but that doesn't matter
further than of old

because you fooled the doctors,i touch you with hopes and
words and with so and so:we are together,we will
kiss or smile or move.   It's different too isn't it

different dear from moving as we,you
and i,used to move when i thought you were going to(but
that doesn't matter)
when you thought you were going to America.
                                                    Then

moving was a matter of not keeping still;we were
two alert lice in the blond hair of nothing

VII

since feeling is first
who pays any attention
to the syntax of things
will never wholly kiss you;

wholly to be a fool
while Spring is in the world

my blood approves,
and kisses are a better fate
than wisdom
lady i swear by all flowers.   Don't cry
—the best gesture of my brain is less than
your eyelids' flutter which says

we are for each other:then
laugh,leaning back in my arms
for life's not a paragraph

And death i think is no parenthesis

VIII

some ask praise of their fellows
but i being otherwise
made compose curves
and yellows,angles or silences
to a less erring end)

myself is sculptor of
your body's idiom:
the musician of your wrists;
the poet who is afraid
only to mistranslate

a rhythm in your hair,
(your fingertips
the way you move)
                    the

painter of your voice—
beyond these elements

remarkably nothing is....therefore,lady
am i content should any
by me carven thing provoke
your gesture possibly or

any painting(for its own

reason)in your lips
slenderly should create one least smile
(shyly
if a poem should lift to
me the distinct country of your
eyes,gifted with green twilight)

IX

supposing i dreamed this)
only imagine,when day has thrilled
you are a house around which
i am a wind—

your walls will not reckon how
strangely my life is curved
since the best he can do
is to peer through windows,unobserved

—listen,for(out of all
things)dream is noone's fool;
if this wind who i am prowls
carefully around this house of you

love being such,or such,
the normal corners of your heart
will never guess how much
my wonderful jealousy is dark

if light should flower:
or laughing sparkle from
the shut house(around and around
which a poor wind will roam

X

you are like the snow only
purer fleeter,like the rain
only sweeter frailer you

whom certain
flowers resemble but trembling(cowards
which fear
to miss within your least gesture the hurting
skill which lives)and since

nothing lingers
beyond a little instant,
along with rhyme and with laughter
O my lady
(and every brittle marvelous breathing thing)

since i and you are on our ways to dust

of your fragility
(but chiefly of your smile,
most suddenly which is
of love and death a marriage)you give me

courage
so that against myself
the sharp days slobber in vain:

Nor am i afraid that
this,which we call autumn,cleverly
dies and over the ripe world wanders with
a near and careful
smile in his mouth(making

everything suddenly old and with his awkward eyes
pushing
sleep under and thoroughly
into all beautiful things)

winter,whom Spring shall kill

XI

because
you go away i give roses who
will advise even yourself,lady
in the most certainly(of what we
everywhere do not touch)deep
things;
            remembering ever so
tinily these,your crisp
eyes actually shall contain new faeries

(and if your slim lips are amused,no wisest

painter of fragile
Marys will understand
how smiling may be made as
skilfully.)   But carry
also,with that indolent and with
this flower wholly whom you do
not ever fear,
                me in your heart

softly;not all
but the beginning

of mySelf

XII

you being in love
will tell who softly asks in love,

am i separated from your body smile brain hands merely
to become the jumping puppets of a dream?   oh i mean:
entirely having in my careful how
careful arms created this at length
inexcusable,this inexplicable pleasure—you go from several
persons:believe me that strangers arrive
when i have kissed you into a memory
slowly,oh seriously
—that since and if you disappear

solemnly
myselves
ask "life,the question how do i drink dream smile

and how do i prefer this face to another and
why do i weep eat sleep—what does the whole intend"
they wonder.   oh and they cry "to be,being,that i am alive
this absurd fraction in its lowest terms
with everything cancelled
but shadows
—what does it all come down to?   love?   Love
if you like and i like,for the reason that i
hate people and lean out of this window is love,love
and the reason that i laugh and breathe is oh love and the reason

that i do not fall into this street is love."

XIII

Nobody wears a yellow
flower in his buttonhole
he is altogether a queer fellow
as young as he is old

when autumn comes,
who twiddles his white thumbs
and frisks down the boulevards

without his coat and hat

—(and i wonder just why that
should please him or i wonder what he does)

and why(at the bottom of this trunk,
under some dirty collars)only a
moment
(or
was it perhaps a year)ago i found staring

me in the face a dead yellow small rose

XIV

it is so long since my heart has been with yours

shut by our mingling arms through
a darkness where new lights begin and
increase,
since your mind has walked into
my kiss as a stranger
into the streets and colours of a town—

that i have perhaps forgotten
how,always(from
these hurrying crudities
of blood and flesh)Love
coins His most gradual gesture,

and whittles life to eternity

—after which our separating selves become museums
filled with skilfully stuffed memories

XV

i am a beggar always
who begs in your mind

(slightly smiling,patient,unspeaking
with a sign on his
breast
BLIND)yes i

am this person of whom somehow
you are never wholly rid(and who

does not ask for more than
just enough dreams to
live on)
       after all,kid

you might as well
toss him a few thoughts

a little love preferably,
anything which you can't
pass off on other people:for
instance a
plugged promise—

then he will maybe(hearing something
fall into his hat)go wandering
after it with fingers;till having

found
what was thrown away
           himself
taptaptaps out of your brain,hopes,life

to(carefully turning a
corner)never bother you any more.

XVI

if within tonight's erect
everywhere of black muscles fools
a weightless slowness(deftly

muting the world's texture with drifted

gifts of featheriest slenderness and
how gradually which descending are suddenly
received)or by doomfull connivance

accurately thither and hither myself

struts unremembered(rememberingly
with in both pockets curled hands moves)
why then toward morning he is a ghost whom

assault these whispering fists of hail

(and a few windows awaken certain faces
busily horribly blunder through new light
hush we are made of the same thing as perhaps

nothing,he murmurs carefully lying down)

XVII

how this uncouth enchanted
person,arising from a
restaurant,looks breathes or moves
—climbing(past light after
light)to turn,disappears

the very swift and
invisibly living
rhythm of your Heart possibly

will understand;
or why(in

this most exquisite of cities)all
of the long night a fragile imitation of
(perhaps)myself carefully wanders
streets dark and,deep

with rain....

(he,slightly whom or
cautiously this person

and this imitation resemble,
descends into the earth with the year
a cigarette between his ghost-lips

gradually)
remembering badly,softly
your
kissed thrice suddenly smile

XVIII

i go to this window

just as day dissolves
when it is twilight(and
looking up in fear

i see the new moon
thinner than a hair)

making me feel
how myself has been coarse and dull
compared with you,silently who are
and cling
to my mind always

But now she sharpens and becomes crisper
until i smile with knowing
—and all about
herself

the sprouting largest final air

plunges
              inward with hurled
downward thousands of enormous dreams

Five

I

after all white horses are in bed

will you walking beside me,my very lady,
if scarcely the somewhat city
wiggles in considerable twilight

touch(now)with a suddenly unsaid

gesture lightly my eyes?
And send life out of me and the night
absolutely into me....a wise
and puerile moving of your arm will
do suddenly that

       will do
more than heroes beautifully in shrill
armour colliding on huge blue horses,
and the poets looked at them,and made verses,

through the sharp light cryingly as the knights flew.

II

touching you i say(it being Spring
and night)"let us go a very little beyond
the last road—there's something to be found"

and smiling you answer"everything
turns into something else,and slips away....
(these leaves are Thingish with moondrool
and i'm ever so very little afraid")
                                        i say
"along this particular road the moon if you'll
notice follows us like a big yellow dog.   You

don't believe?   look back.(Along the sand
behind us,a big yellow dog that's....now it's red
a big red dog that may be owned by who
knows)
            only turn a little your.   so.   And

there's the moon,there is something faithful and mad"

III

along the brittle treacherous bright streets
of memory comes my heart,singing like
an idiot,whispering like a drunken man

who(at a certain corner,suddenly)meets
the tall policeman of my mind.
                                    awake
being not asleep,elsewhere our dreams began
which now are folded:but the year completes
his life as a forgotten prisoner

—"Ici?"—"Ah non,mon chéri;il fait trop froid"—
they are gone:along these gardens moves a wind bringing
rain and leaves,filling the air with fear
and sweetness....pauses.   (Halfwhispering....halfsinging

stirs the always smiling chevaux de bois)

when you were in Paris we met here

IV

our touching hearts slenderly comprehend
(clinging as fingers,loving one another
gradually into hands)and bend
into the huge disaster of the year:

like this most early single star which tugs

weakly at twilight,caught in thickening fear
our slightly fingering spirits starve and smother;
until autumn abruptly wholly hugs

our dying silent minds,which hand in hand
at some window try to understand
the
    (through pale miles of perishing air,haunted
with huddling infinite wishless melancholy,
suddenly looming)accurate undaunted

moon's bright third tumbling slowly

V

if i have made,my lady,intricate
imperfect various things chiefly which wrong
your eyes(frailer than most deep dreams are frail)
songs less firm than your body's whitest song
upon my mind—if i have failed to snare
the glance too shy—if through my singing slips
the very skilful strangeness of your smile
the keen primeval silence of your hair

—let the world say "his most wise music stole
nothing from death"—
                        you only will create
(who are so perfectly alive)my shame:
lady through whose profound and fragile lips
the sweet small clumsy feet of April came

into the ragged meadow of my soul.

W
[ViVa]

I

      ,mean-
hum
a)now

(nit
y unb
uria

ble fore(hurry
into
heads are
legs think wrists

argue)short(eyes do
bang hands angle
scoot bulbs marry a become)
ened
(to is

see!so
long door
golf slam bridge train shriek
chewing whistles hugest
to
morrow from smiles sin

k
ingly ele
vator glide pinn
)pu(
acle to

rubber)tres(plants how grin
ho)cen(tel
und
ead the

not stroll
living spawn imitate)ce(re
peat

credo fais do
do neighbours re babies
            while:

II

oil tel duh woil doi sez
dooyuh unnurs tanmih eesez pullih nizmus tash,oi
dough un giv uh shid oi sez.   Tom
oidoughwuntuh doot,butoiguttuh
braikyooz,datswut eesez tuhmih.   (Nowoi askyuh
woodundat maik yurarstoin
green?   Oilsaisough.)—Hool
spairruh luckih?   Thangzkeed.   Mairsee.
Muh jax awl gawn.   Fur Croi saik
ainnoughbudih gutnutntuhplai?

HAI

yoozwidduhpoimnuntwaiv un duhyookuhsumpnruddur
givusuhtoonunduhphugnting

III

the surely

Cued
motif smites truly to Beautifully
retire through its english

the Forwardflung backwardSpinning hoop returns fasterishly
whipped the top leaps bounding upon other tops to caroming
off persist displacing Its own and their Lives who
grow slowly and first into different deaths

Concentric geometries of transparency slightly
joggled sink through algebras of proud

inwardlyness to collide spirally with iron arithmethics
and mesh witH
Which when both

march outward into the freezing fire of Thickness)points

uPDownwardishly
find everywheres noisecoloured
curvecorners gush silently perpetuating solids(More
fluid Than gas

IV

there are 6 doors.
Next door(but
four)gentlemen are trinightly entertained by a whore
who Talks in the daytime,when who

is asleep with only several
faces and a multitude of chins:next door
but three dwells;a(ghost)Who
screams Faintly always

who Is bluish;next
Door but two occupy a man
and his wife:Both very young noisily
who kiss throw silently things

Each at other(if not
quarrelling in a luxury of telescoped
languages)she smokes three
castles He looks jewish

,next door but One
a on Dirty bed Mangy from person Porous
sits years its of self fee(bly
Perpetually coughing And thickly spi)tting

But next door nobody
seems to live at present(l'on
parle de repapering;i
don't think so.maybe:somebody?)or,bedbugs

V

myself,walking in Dragon st
one fine August
night,i just
happened to meet

"how do you do" she smiling
said "thought you
were earning your living
or probably dead"

so Jones was murdered by
a man named Smith and
we sailed on the
Leviathan

VI

but mr can you maybe listen there's
me &
some people
and others please
don't
confuse.Some

people

's future is toothsome like
(they got
pockets full may take a littl
e nibble now And then
bite)candy

others
fly,their;puLLing:bright
futures
against the deep sky in

May mine's tou
ching this crump
led cap mumble some
thing to oh no
body will
(can you give
a)listen to
who may

you

be
any
how?
down
to
smoking
found
Butts

VII

Space being(don't forget to remember)Curved
(and that reminds me who said o yes Frost
Something there is which isn't fond of walls)

an electromagnetic(now I've lost
the)Einstein expanded Newton's law preserved
conTinuum(but we read that beFore)

of Course life being just a Reflex you
know since Everything is Relative or

to sum it All Up god being Dead(not to

mention inTerred)
              LONG LIVE that Upwardlooking
Serene Illustrious and Beatific
Lord of Creation,MAN:
                  at a least crooking
of Whose compassionate digit,earth's most terrific

quadruped swoons into billiardBalls!

VIII

(one fine day)

let's take the train
for because dear

whispered again
in never's ear
(i'm tho thcared

giggling lithped now
we muthn't pleathe
don't as pop weird
up her hot ow

you hurt tho nithe
steered his big was)
thither to thence
swore many a vow
but both made sense

in when's haymow
with young fore'er
(oh & by the way
asked sis breath
of brud breathe
how is aunt death

did always teethe

IX

y is a WELL KNOWN ATHLETE'S BRIDE

(lullaby)
& z

=an infrafairy of floating
ultrawrists who
lullabylullaby

(I could have been
You,You
might have been I)
                    " ?" quoth the

front;and there was yz
SHOT AND KILLED her
(in his arms)Self

          & Him
self in the hoe tell days are

teased:

      let(however)us
Walk very(therefore and)softly among one's own
memory(but)along perhaps the
By invisibilities spattered(or if

it may be socalled)memory
Of(without more ado about less
than nothing)

          2 boston
Dolls;found
with
Holes in each other

's lullaby and
other lulla wise by UnBroken
LULLAlullabyBY

                    the She-in-him with
the He-in-her(&

both all hopped
                up)prettily
then which did
lie
Down,honestly

now who go(BANG(BANG

X

   thethe
the pink

Tartskids with
thecas–tanets
in5/4; Time

    chick.chick
but:that Mat isse like

–with–the–chinese–eyebrowsMan
gave me,A,

(peach
   a soft eyes syriansang asong tohim self
all

about the desertbyIt self
       while) nextto
Mesmoked eleven camels
       !

and i got a Bad almond
chick.
   thepinkisht artskiDs...

  with thema Tiss eeyeb Rowspeach es
a soft desert smoked bad me whilepin Kishcam elscasta?netsits
Elf
 allaBout .

     (chic)
       –kchi

cK,

XI

a
  mong crum
            bling people(a
long ruined streets
hither and)softly

thither between(tumb
ling)
      houses(as
the kno

wing spirit prowls,its
nose winces
before a dissonance of

Rish and Foses)
                until
                      (finding one's self
at some distance from the
crooked town)a

harbour fools the sea(
while
        emanating the triple
starred

Hotel du Golf...that notable structure
or ideal edifice...situated or established
...far from the noise of waters
)one's

eye perceives
              (as the ego approaches)
painfully sterilized contours;
within

which
"ladies&gentlemen"
—under

glass—
are:
asking.

?each
oth?
er

rub,
!berq;
:uestions

XII

poor But TerFLY

went(flesh is grass)
from Troy,

n.y.
the way of(all
flesh is grass)with one "Paul"

a harvard boy
alas!
(who simply wor
shipped her)who

after not coming once in seven years explO
ded like a toy eloping to Ire(land must be
heav

en
FoR

my

motH)with a grass wid
OW

er who smelt rath
er like her fath
er who smelt rath

er(Er
camef
romth
AIR

XIII

remarked Robinson Jefferson

to Injustice Taughed
your story is so interested

but you make me laft
welates Wouldwoe Washington
to Lydia E. McKinley

when Buch tooked out his C.O.D.
Abe tucks it up back inley
clamored Clever Rusefelt
to Theodore Odysseus Graren't

we couldn't free the negro
because he ant
but Coolitch wiped his valley forge

with Sitting Bull's T.P.
and the duckbilled platitude lays & lays

and Lays aytash unee

XIV

what time is it i wonder never mind
consider rather heavenly things and but
the stars for instance everything is planned
next to that patch of darkness there's a what
is it oh yes chair but not Cassiopeia's

might those be stockings dribbling from the table
all which seemed sweet deep and inexplicable
not being dollars toenails or ideas
thoroughly 's stolen(somewhere between

our unlighted hearts lust lurks
slovenly and homeless and when
a kiss departs our lips are made of thing

in beginning corners dawn smirks

and there's the moon,thinner than a watchspring

XV

well)here's looking at ourselves

two solids in(all
one it)
solution(of
course you must shake well)

indolently dreaming puzzling

over that one
oh just thinking it over
(at that just supposing
we had met and just
but you know

supposing we

just had let it go at
that)that
seems important doesn't
it and
doesn't that seem
puzzling but we both might have found the solution

of that in

the importance of the
fact that(in spite of the fact
that i and that
you had carefully
ourselves decided what this cathedral ought to

look like)it doesn't look

at
all like what you
and what i(of course)
carefully had decided oh

no(but

XVI

    tell me not how electricity or
god was invented but
    why(captured by a
policeman's majestic and buried eye)

the almost large he-
    shaped object vomits cleverly
against a quai wall almost spray
    -ing threecoloured puke over

    this younger than
i am newspaper guy who refused
    to shake hands with
ludendorff and your humble moving through the

gloominess of(try to
    imagine)whispering
of a named
    Krassin

XVII

FULL SPEED ASTERN)

m

   usil(age)ini
sticks
tuh de mans

l

(hutch)hutchinson says sweet guinea
pigs do it it buy uh cupl un
wait

k

(relijinisde)o(peemuvdepipl)
marx okays jippymugun
roomur

j

 e(wut)
hova
in big cumbine wid

i

(check
undublcheck)
babbitt

(GOD SAVE THE UNCOMMONWEALTH OF HUMANUSETTS

XVIII

"Gay" is the captivating cognomen of a Young Woman of cambridge,mass.
to whom nobody seems to have mentioned ye olde freudian wish;
when i contemplate her uneyes safely ensconced in thick glass
you try if we are a gentleman not to think of(sh)

the world renowned investigator of paper sailors—argonauta argo
harmoniously being with his probably most brilliant pupil mated,
let us not deem it miraculous if their(so to speak)offspring has that largo
appearance of somebody who was hectocotyliferously propagated

when Miss G touched n.y. our skeleton stepped from his cupboard
gallantly offering to demonstrate the biggest best busiest city
and presently found himself rattling for that well known suburb
the bronx(enlivening an otherwise dead silence with harmless quips,out of Briggs
     by Kitty)

arriving in an exhausted condition,i purchased two bags of lukewarm peanuts
with the dime which her mama had generously provided(despite courteous
     protestations)
and offering Miss Gay one(which she politely refused)set out gaily for the hyenas
suppressing my frank qualms in deference to her not inobvious perturbations

unhappily,the denizens of the zoo were that day inclined to be uncouthly erotic
more particularly the primates—from which with dignity square feet turned
     abruptly Miss Gay away:
"on the whole"(if you will permit a metaphor savouring slightly of the demotic)
Miss Gay had nothing to say to the animals and the animals had nothing to say to
     Miss Gay

during our return voyage,my pensive companion dimly remarked something about
     "stuffed
fauna" being "very interesting"...we also discussed the possibility of rain...
in distant proximity to a Y.W.c.a. she suddenly luffed
—thanking me;and(stating that she hoped we might "meet again

sometime")vanished,gunwale awash.   I thereupon loosened my collar
and dove for the nearest 1;surreptitiously cogitating
the dictum of a new england sculptor(well on in life)re the helen moller
dancers,whom he considered "elevating—that is,if dancing CAN be elevating"

Miss(believe it or)Gay is a certain Young Woman unacquainted with the libido
and pursuing a course of instruction at radcliffe college,cambridge,mass.
i try if you are a gentleman not to sense something un poco putrido
when we contemplate her uneyes safely ensconced in thick glass

XIX

i will cultivate within
me scrupulously the Inimitable which
is loneliness,these unique dreams
never shall soil their raiment

with phenomena:such
being a conduct worthy of

more ponderous
wishes or
hopes less
tall than mine"(opening the windows)

"and there is a philosophy" strictly at
which instant(leaped
into the

street)this deep immediate mask and
expressing "as for myself,because i
am slender and fragile
i borrow contact from that you and from

this you sensations,imitating a few fatally

exquisite"(pulling Its shawl carefully around
it)"things i mean the
Rain is no respecter of persons
the snow doesn't give a soft white
damn Whom it touches

XX

but granted that it's nothing paradoxically enough beyond mere personal

pride which tends to compel me to decline to admit i've died)
seeing your bald intellect collywobbling on its feeble stem is

believing science $= (2b)^{-n}$ herr professor m

XXI

helves surling out of eakspeasies per(reel)hapsingly
proregress heandshe-ingly people
trickle curselaughgroping shrieks bubble
squirmwrithed staggerful unstrolls collaps ingly
flash a of-faceness stuck thumblike into pie
is traffic this recalls hat gestures bud
plumptumbling hand voices Eye Doangivuh sud-
denly immense impotently Eye Doancare Eye
And How replies the upsquirtingly careens
the to collide flatfooting with Wushyuhname
a girl-flops to the Geddup curb leans
carefully spewing into her own Shush Shame

as(out from behind Nowhere)creeps the deep thing
everybody sometimes calls morning

XXII

Lord John Unalive(having a fortune of fifteengrand
£
thanks to the socalled fact that maost faolks rally demannd canned
saounds)
gloats
upon the possession of quotes keltyer close
" "

aureally(yawning while all the dominoes)fall:down;in,rows

XXIII

buncha hardboil guys frum duh A.C. fulla
hooch kiddin eachudder bout duh clap an
talkin big how dey could kill
sixereight cops—"I sidesteps im an draws
back huly jeezus"—an—"my
specialty is takin fellers' goils away
frum dem"—"somebody hung uh gun on
Marcus"—"duh Swede rolls down tree flights an Sam
begins boxin im on duh
koib"—you
know
alotta sweet bull like dat
                              ...suddenly
i feels so lonely fer duh good ole days we
spent in '18 kickin duh guts outa dem
doity frogeaters an humpin duh
swell janes on
duh boollevares an wid tears
streamin down my face i hauls
out uh flask an offers it tuh duh whole gang accrost
duh table—"fellers
have some
on
me"—dey was petrified.

De room swung roun an crawled up into
itself,
an awful big light squoits down my spine like
i was dead er sumpn:next i

knows me(er
somebody is sittin in uh green
field watchin four crows drop into
sunset,playin uh busted harmonica

XXIV

from the cognoscenti

bingbongwhom chewchoo
laugh dingle nails personally
bung loamhome picpac
obviously scratches tomorrowlobs

wholeagainst you gringlehow
exudes thursday fasters
by button of whisper sum blinked
he belowtry eye nowbrow

sangsung née whitermuch grab
sicksilk soak sulksuck whim
poke if inch dimmer twist on
permament and slap tremendous

sorrydaze bog triperight
election who so thumb o'clock
asters miggle dim a ram
flat hombre sin bangaroom

slim guesser goose pin yessir wheel
no sendwisp ben jiffyclaus
bug fainarain wee celibate
amaranth clutch owch

so chuck slop hight evolute
my eerily oh gargle
to jip hug behemoth
truly pseudo yours podia

of radarw leschin

XXV

murderfully in midmost o.c.an

launch we a Hyperluxurious Supersieve
(which Ultima Thule Of Plumbing shall receive

the philophilic name S.S.VAN MERDE)

having first put right sleuthfully aboard
all to—mendaciously speaking—a man

wrongers who write what they are dine to live

XXVI

ohld song

you Know
a fly and
his reflection walking upon

a mirror this is
friday 1

what

3 a fly
&

her his Its image
strutting(very
jerkily)not toucH-

ing because separated by an impregnable

Because(amount of inter
-vening)anyway You
know Separated what
i Mean

      (oweld song by
      ;neither you nor i and

by the way)

   ,which is not fly

XXVII

the first president to be loved by his
bitterest enemies" is dead

the only man woman or child who wrote
a simple declarative sentence with seven grammatical
errors "is dead"
beautiful Warren Gamaliel Harding
"is" dead
he's
"dead"
if he wouldn't have eaten them Yapanese Craps

somebody might hardly never not have been unsorry,perhaps

XXVIII

serene immediate silliest and whose
vast one function being to enter a Toy and
emerging(believably enlarged)make how
many stopped millions of female hard for their
millions of stopped male to look at(now
-fed infantile eyes drooling unmind
grim yessing childflesh perpetually acruise
and her quick way of slowly staring and such hair)
the Californian handpicked thrill mechanically
packed and released for all this very diminishing
vicarious ughhuh world(the pertly papped
muchmouthed)her way of beginningly finishing
(and such hair)the expensively democratic tyrannically
dumb

Awake,chaos:we have napped.

XXIX

in a middle of a room
stands a suicide
sniffing a Paper rose
smiling to a self

"somewhere it is Spring and sometimes
people are in real:imagine
somewhere real flowers,but
I can't imagine real flowers for if I

could,they would somehow
not Be real"
(so he smiles
smiling)"but I will not

everywhere be real to
you in a moment"
The is blond
with small hands

"& everything is easier
than I had guessed everything would
be;even remembering the way who
looked at whom first,anyhow dancing"

(a moon swims out of a cloud
a clock strikes midnight
a finger pulls a trigger
a bird flies into a mirror)

XXX

i sing of Olaf glad and big
whose warmest heart recoiled at war:
a conscientious object-or

his wellbelovéd colonel(trig
westpointer most succinctly bred)
took erring Olaf soon in hand;
but—though an host of overjoyed
noncoms(first knocking on the head
him)do through icy waters roll
that helplessness which others stroke
with brushes recently employed
anent this muddy toiletbowl,
while kindred intellects evoke
allegiance per blunt instruments—
Olaf(being to all intents
a corpse and wanting any rag
upon what God unto him gave)
responds,without getting annoyed
"I will not kiss your fucking flag"

straightway the silver bird looked grave
(departing hurriedly to shave)

but—though all kinds of officers
(a yearning nation's blueeyed pride)
their passive prey did kick and curse
until for wear their clarion
voices and boots were much the worse,
and egged the firstclassprivates on
his rectum wickedly to tease
by means of skilfully applied
bayonets roasted hot with heat—
Olaf(upon what were once knees)
does almost ceaselessly repeat
"there is some shit I will not eat"

our president,being of which
assertions duly notified
threw the yellowsonofabitch
into a dungeon,where he died

Christ(of His mercy infinite)
i pray to see;and Olaf,too

preponderatingly because
unless statistics lie he was
more brave than me:more blond than you.

XXXI

memory believes
fragrance of a town(whose
dormers choke
and snore the steeples writhe with

rain)faces(at windows)do not
speak and are ghosts or
huddled in the darkness of
cafés people drink

smile if here there(like lopsided
imaginations)
filled with newly murdered
flowers whispering barns

bulge a tiniest street or
three contains these prettiest
deaths without effort while
hungering churches(topped

with effigies of crowing
gold)nuzzle against summer
thunder(together)smell only
such blue slender hands of god

XXXII

Wing Wong,uninterred at twice
fortyeight,succeeded in producing

sixtyfour maxims

whose)centripetal wisdom in
thirtytwo seconds centrifugally
is refuted by these(

particularly belonging to
a
retired
general)sixteen years

of rapid
animal whose swir
-ling(not too frequently
)skirt exhumes(which
buries again quick-

ly its
self in)while
a transparent blouse
even recklessly
juggles the jouncing
fruit of eager bosoms"
                              Wing

Wong

XXXIII

innerly

UningstrolL
(stamens&pistil
   silent
A s groupingThe
6around one
darks to 7th s
   o howpale)
bluedmufFletomben

   outerly

jeT
ting lip ssixs ting
sWervesca
rletlycaR v Ingharness
Of
curvish(

  ,males await she
patiently 1

)littlecrownGrave
whose whorlclown of spreadnessed bE
rich from–soft quits(now)ly
Comes;
:lush
ly–smootHdumb droopnew–gree

N.lyestmostsaresl e A v e S

XXXIV

don't cries to please my
mustn't broke)life Is
like that please stroke

for now stroke answers(but
now don't you're hurting o
Me please you're killing)death

is like now That please
squirtnowing for
o squirting we're replies(at

which now O fear turned o Now
handspring trans
forming it

self int
o eighteen)Don't
(for)Please(tnights,on whose for

eheads shone
eternal pleasedon't;
rising:from the Shall.

XXXV

what is strictly fiercely and wholly dies
his impeccable feathered with green facts
preening solemnity ignoring,through
its indolent lascivious caring eyes

watches;truly,curvingly while reacts
(sharp now with blood now accurately wan)
keenly,to dreamings more than truth untrue,

the best mouth i have seen on any man—
a little fluttering,at the enchanted dike
of whose lean lips,hovers how slenderly
the illustrious unknown

                              (warily as
their master's spirit stooping,Crusoelike
examines fearingly and tenderly

a recent footprint in the sand of was)

XXXVI

sunset)edges become swiftly
corners(Besides
which,i note how
fatally toward

twilight the a little
tilted streets spill lazily
multitudes out of final

towers;captured:in
the narrow light

    of

inverno)this
is the season of
crumbling & folding
hopes,hark;feet(fEEt
f-e-e-t-noWheregoingaLwaYS

XXXVII

how
ses humble.

Over thin earths chatterish

strut cuddle & shrink:
as through immediately
yeswind-faces peer

skies;whiteLy
are which stumbling eyes which
why in(thundering)by
When eaten

spaces grouse rocket know
quite,

slightly or
how at the yearhour tree-
    spires shout appalling

        deathmoney into
            spiralS
               and

Now(comes

un,

   season of in:wardly
of him(every)

who does
(where)not move
;is

   .crowned the with shrill
Nonleaf daemons and large The downlife gods of
shut
)

XXXVIII

n(o)w

     the
how
    dis(appeared cleverly)world

iS Slapped:with;liGhtninG
!

  at
which(shal)lpounceupcrackw(ill)jumps

of
  THuNdeRB
         loSSo!M iN
-visiblya mongban(gedfrag-
ment ssky?wha tm)eani ngl(essNessUn
rolli)ngl yS troll s(who leO v erd)oma insCol

Lide.!high
       n , o ; w   :
                theraIncomIng

o all the roofs roar
        drownInsound(
&
(we(are like)dead
)Whoshout(Ghost)atOne(voiceless)O
ther or im)
    pos
    sib(ly as
    leep)
      But l!ook—
        s

    U

     n:starT birDs(lEAp)Openi ng
t hing ; s(
—sing
)all are aLl(cry alL See)o(ver All)Th(e grEEn

?eartH)N,ew

XXXIX

An(fragrance)Of

(Begins)
millions

Of Tints(and)
&
(grows)Slowly(slowly)Voyaging

tones intimate tumult
(Into)bangs
minds into
dream(An)quickly

Not

un deux trois
der
    die

Stood(apparition.)
WITH(THE ROUND AIR IS FILLED)OPENING

XL

thou

firsting a hugeness of twi
-light
pale
beyond soft-
liness than dream more sing

(buoyant & who
silently shall to rea- disa)

ular,

(ppear ah!Star
whycol

our
ed
shy lurch small invin

cible nod oc
cul
t ke
ylike writhe of brea

Thing

XLI

twi-
    is -Light bird
ful
-ly dar
kness eats

a distance a
c(h)luck
(l)ing of just bells (touch)ing
?mind

(moon begins The
)
now,est hills er dream;new
.oh if

    when:
&
a
nd O impercept i bl

XLII

structure,miraculous challenge,devout am

upward deep most invincible unthing
—stern sexual timelessness,outtowering
this noisy impotence of not and same

answer,beginning,ecstasy,to dare:
prouder than all mountains,more than all
oceans various
                    and while everywhere
beneath thee and about thyself a small
hoping insect,humanity,achieves
(moult beyond difficult moult)amazing doom
who standest as thou hast stood and thou shalt stand.

Nor any dusk but kneelingly believes
thy secret and each morning stoops to blend

her star with what huge merciful forms presume

XLIII

if there are any heavens my mother will(all by herself)have
one.   It will not be a pansy heaven nor
a fragile heaven of lilies–of–the–valley but
it will be a heaven of blackred roses

my father will be(deep like a rose
tall like a rose)

standing near my

swaying over her
(silent)
with eyes which are really petals and see

nothing with the face of a poet really which
is a flower and not a face with
hands
which whisper
This is my beloved my

                              (suddenly in sunlight
he will bow,

& the whole garden will bow)

XLIV

i'd think "wonder

if" if
i were a
child "we can see a bat in this
twilight")
          there one is

look

how it goes   like   a dream

(and between houses,really a kind of
mouse)but he has little wings
and here's my
hotel this is the
door(opening it i

think things
which
were supposed to
be out of my
reach
        ,they are like
jam on the shelf everybody guessed

was too high)

look

        (it's back again   there   therehere
And)i say "won't you"(remembering)
knowing that you
are afraid "go first" of dreams and little

bats & mice(and

                    you,
you say "let's" going in
"take
hands" smiling "coming up
these dark stairs.

XLV

you
in win
ter who sit
dying thinking
huddled behind dir
ty glass mind muddled
and cuddled by dreams(or some
times vacantly gazing through un
washed panes into a crisp todo of
murdering uncouth faces which pass rap
idly with their breaths.)"people are walking deaths
in this season" think "finality lives up
on them a little more openly than usual
hither,thither who briskly busily carry the as
tonishing & spontaneous & difficult ugliness
of themselves with a more incisive simplicity a
more intensively brutal futility"And sit
huddling dumbly behind three or two partly tran
sparent panes which by some loveless trick sepa
rate one stilled unmoving mind from a hun
dred doomed hurrying brains(by twos
or threes which fiercely rapidly
pass with their breaths)in win
ter you think,die slow
ly "toc tic" as i
have seen trees(in
whose black bod
ies leaves
hide

XLVI

i met a man under the moon
on Sunday.
by way of saying
nothing he
smiled(but
just by the dirty collar of his

jacket were two glued uncarefully ears
in
that face a box of
skin lay eyes like
new tools)

whence i guessed that he also had climbed the pincian
to appreciate rome at nightfall;and because against this
wall his white sincere small
hands with their guessing fingers

did-not-move exquisitely
,like dead children
(if he had been playing a fiddle i had

been dancing:which is
why something about me reminded him of ourselves)

as Nobody came slowly over the town

XLVII

when rain whom fear
not children but men
speaks(among leaves Easily
through voices womenlike telling

of death love earth dark)

and thousand
thrusts squirms stars
Trees,swift each with its

Own motion deeply to wickedly

comprehend the innocently Doomed
brief all which somewhere is

fragrantly,

arrive
        (when
Rain comes;
predicating forever,assuming
the laughter of afterwards—
i spirally understand

What

touching means
or What does a hand
with your hair
in my imagination

XLVIII

come a little further—why be afraid—
here's the earliest star(have you a wish?)
touch me,
before we perish
(believe that not anything which has ever been
invented can spoil this or this instant)
kiss me a little:
the air
darkens and is alive—
o live with me in the fewness of
these colours;
alone who slightly
always are beyond the reach of death

and the English

XLIX

a light Out)
        & first of all foam

-like hair spatters creasing pillow
next everywhere hidinglyseek
no o god dear wait sh please o no O
3rd Findingest whispers understand
sobs bigly climb what(love being some-
thing possibly more intricate)i(breath
in breath)have nicknamed ecstasy and And

spills smile cheaply thick

—who therefore Thee(once and once only,Queen
among centuries universes between
Who out of deeplyness rose to undeath)

salute.   and having worshipped for my doom
pass ignorantly into sleep's bright land

L

when hair falls off and eyes blur And
thighs forget(when clocks whisper
and night shouts)When minds
shrivel and hearts grow brittler every
Instant(when of a morning Memory stands,
with clumsily wilted fingers
emptying youth colour and what was
into a dirtied glass)Pills for Ills
(a recipe against Laughing Virginity Death)

then dearest the
way trees are Made leaves
open Clouds take sun mountains
stand And oceans do Not sleep matters
nothing;then(then the only hands so to speak are
they always which creep budgingly over some
numbered face capable of a largest nonglance the
least unsmile
or whatever weeds feel and fish think of)

LI

a clown's smirk in the skull of a baboon
(where once good lips stalked or eyes firmly stirred)
my mirror gives me,on this afternoon;
i am a shape that can but eat and turd
ere with the dirt death shall him vastly gird,
a coward waiting clumsily to cease
whom every perfect thing meanwhile doth miss;
a hand's impression in an empty glove,
a soon forgotten tune,a house for lease.
I have never loved you dear as now i love

behold this fool who,in the month of June,
having of certain stars and planets heard,
rose very slowly in a tight balloon
until the smallening world became absurd;
him did an archer spy(whose aim had erred
never)and by that little trick or this
he shot the aeronaut down,into the abyss
—and wonderfully i fell through the green groove
of twilight,striking into many a piece.
I have never loved you dear as now i love

god's terrible face,brighter than a spoon,
collects the image of one fatal word;
so that my life(which liked the sun and the moon)
resembles something that has not occurred:
i am a birdcage without any bird,
a collar looking for a dog,a kiss
without lips;a prayer lacking any knees
but something beats within my shirt to prove
he is undead who,living,noone is.
I have never loved you dear as now i love.

Hell(by most humble me which shall increase)
open thy fire!for i have had some bliss
of one small lady upon earth above;
to whom i cry,remembering her face,
i have never loved you dear as now i love

LII

it)It will it
Will come(we
being
unwound & gone into the ground)but

though

with wormS eyes
writhe amor(Though through

our hearts hugely squirm
roots)us
          ly;though
hither nosing lymoles cru.Ising

thither:t,ouch soft-ly me and eye(you
leSs

)ly(un
          der the mi
                    croscopic world's

whens,wheels;wonders:
murders.cries:hopes;
houses,clouds.kisses,
lice;headaches:ifs.

)
 yet shall
our Not to
be

deciphered
selves

merely Continue to experience

a neverish subchemistry of
alWays
)fiercely live whom on

Large Darkness And The Middle Of
The
E

a
r
t
H

LIII

breathe with me this fear
(which beyond night shall go)
remembering only dare
(Wholly consider how

these immaculate thin
things half daemon half
tree among sunset dream
acute from root to leaf)

but should voices(whom lure
an eagerest strict flame)
demand the metaphor
of our projectile am

tell such to murder time
(forgetting what's to know
wholly imagining fire)
only consider How

LIV

if i love You
(thickness means
worlds inhabited by roamingly
stern bright faeries

if you love
me)distance is mind carefully
luminous with innumerable gnomes
Of complete dream

if we love each(shyly)
other,what clouds do or Silently
Flowers resembles beauty
less than our breathing

LV

speaking of love(of
which Who knows the
meaning;or how dreaming
becomes

if your heart's mind)i
guess a grassblade
Thinks beyond or
around(as poems are

made)Our picking it. this
caress that laugh
both quickly signify
life's only half(through

deep weather then
or none let's feel
all)mind in mind flesh
In flesh succeeding disappear

LVI

lady will you come with me into
the extremely little house of
my mind.   Clocks strike.   The

moon's round,through the window

as you see and really i have no
servants.   We could almost live

at the top of these stairs,there's a free
room.   We almost could go(you
and i)into a together whitely big
there is but if so or so

slowly i opened the window a
most tinyness,the moon(with white wig
and polished buttons)would take you away

—and all the clocks would run down the next day.

LVII

somewhere i have never travelled,gladly beyond
any experience,your eyes have their silence:
in your most frail gesture are things which enclose me,
or which i cannot touch because they are too near

your slightest look easily will unclose me
though i have closed myself as fingers,
you open always petal by petal myself as Spring opens
(touching skilfully,mysteriously)her first rose

or if your wish be to close me,i and
my life will shut very beautifully,suddenly,
as when the heart of this flower imagines
the snow carefully everywhere descending;

nothing which we are to perceive in this world equals
the power of your intense fragility:whose texture
compels me with the colour of its countries,
rendering death and forever with each breathing

(i do not know what it is about you that closes
and opens;only something in me understands
the voice of your eyes is deeper than all roses)
nobody,not even the rain,has such small hands

LVIII

is there a flower(whom
i meet anywhere)
able to be and seem
so quite softly as your hair

what bird has perfect fear
(of suddenly me)like these
first deepest rare
quite who are your eyes

(shall any dream
come a more millionth mile
shyly to its doom
than you will smile)

LIX

my darling since
you and
i are thoroughly haunted by
what neither is any
echo of dream nor
any flowering of any

echo(but the echo
of the flower of

Dreaming)somewhere behind us
always trying(or sometimes trying under
us)to is it
find somehow(but O gracefully)a
we,entirely whose least

breathing may surprise
ourselves
            —let's then
despise what is not courage my

darling(for only Nobody knows
where truth grows why
birds fly and
especially who the moon is.

LX

because i love you)last night

clothed in sealace
appeared to me
your mind drifting
with chuckling rubbish
of pearl weed coral and stones;

lifted,and(before my
eyes sinking)inward,fled;softly
your face smile breasts gargled
by death:drowned only

again carefully through deepness to rise
these your wrists
thighs feet hands

poising
          to again utterly disappear;
rushing gently swiftly creeping
through my dreams last
night,all of your
body with its spirit floated
(clothed only in

the tide's acute weaving murmur

LXI

if you and i awakening

discover that(somehow
in the dark)this world has been
Picked,like a piece
of clover,from the green meadow of

time

lessness;quietly
                    turning
toward me the
guessable mirrors which your eyes are

You will communicate a little

more than twice all that
so
gently
while we were asleep while
we were each other disappeared:but i

slightly

smiling,
gradually shall reenter the

singular kingdom

(sleep)
        .while some
thing else
kisses busily
a
memory,which how exquisitely
flutters in

the cornerless tomorrow

LXII

item:is

Clumsily with of
what manshaped whimpered how
girllike
laughtering blocks when

builds
its invisibly skil
ful toyTown
which upups to dowNdown
(and only where remembers

look,
this was of a child
's shy foot among cool ferns

)
therefore togethering our

wholly lives Givehurling
with your my most
:locking

foreverfully

blend
we a universe of gulls'
drift Of thickly
starhums wherefore

& wormSmile eternal;quite
perhaps as sternly
much not life nor stop as
a tear is darker than a mile.

LXIII

be unto love as rain is unto colour;create
me gradually(or as these emerging now
hills invent the air)
                        breathe simply my each how
my trembling where my still unvisible when.   Wait

if i am not heart,because at least i beat
—always think i am gone like a sun which must go
sometimes,to make an earth gladly seem firm for you:
remember(as those pearls more than surround this throat)

i wear your dearest fears beyond their ceaselessness

(nor has a syllable of the heart's eager dim
enormous language loss or gain from blame or praise)
but many a thought shall die which was not born of dream
while wings welcome the year and trees dance(and i guess

though wish and world go down,one poem yet shall swim

LXIV

granted the all
                 saving our young kiss only
must unexist,solemnly and per rules
apparelling its soullessness by lonely
antics of ridiculous molecules)

nakedest(aiming for hugely the
ignorant most precise essential flame
never which waked)& perfectingly We

dive

     out of tinying time
                 (into supreme

Now:
     feeling memory shrink from such brief
selves as fiercely seek findingly new
textures of actual cool stupendous is

nor may truth opening encompass true)
while your contriving fate,my sharpening life

are(behind each no)touching every yes

LXV

but being not amazing:without love
separate,smileless—merely imagine your

sorrow a certain reckoning demands...

marvelling And what may have become of
with his gradual acute lusting glance
an alert clumsily foolishwise

(tracking the beast Tomorrow by her spoor)
over the earth wandering hunter whom you
knew once?

       what if(merely suppose)

mine should overhear and answer Who
with the useless flanks and cringing feet
is this(shivering pale naked very poor)
creature of shadow,that among first light

groping washes my nightmare from his eyes?

LXVI

nothing is more exactly terrible than
to be alone in the house,with somebody and
with something)
                        You are gone.   there is laughter

and despair impersonates a street

i lean from the window,behold ghosts,
                                        a man
hugging a woman in a park.   Complete.

and slightly(why?or lest we understand)
slightly i am hearing somebody
coming up stairs,carefully
(carefully climbing carpeted flight after
carpeted flight.   in stillness,climbing
the carpeted stairs of terror)

and continually i am seeing something

inhaling gently a cigarette(in a mirror

LXVII

put off your faces,Death:for day is over
(and such a day as must remember he
who watched unhands describe what mimicry,

with angry seasalt and indignant clover
marrying to themselves Life's animals)

but not darkness shall quite outmarch forever
—and i perceive,within transparent walls
how several smoothly gesturing stars are clever
to persuade even silence:therefore wonder

opens a gate;the prisoner dawn embraces

hugely some few most rare perfectly dear
(and worlds whirl beyond worlds:immortal yonder
collidingly absorbs eternal near)

day being come,Love,put on your faces

LXVIII

but if a living dance upon dead minds
why,it is love;but at the earliest spear
of sun perfectly should disappear
moon's utmost magic,or stones speak or one
name control more incredible splendor than
our merely universe,love's also there:
and being here imprisoned,tortured here
love everywhere exploding maims and blinds
(but surely does not forget,perish,sleep
cannot be photographed,measured;disdains
the trivial labelling of punctual brains...
—Who wields a poem huger than the grave?
from only Whom shall time no refuge keep
though all the weird worlds must be opened?
)Love

LXIX

so standing,our eyes filled with wind,and the
whining rigging over us,i implore you to
notice how the keen ship lifts(skilfully
like some bird which is all birds but more fleet)
herself against the air—and whose do you
suppose possibly are certain hands,terse
and invisible,with large first new stars
knitting the structure of distinct sunset

driving white spikes of silence into joists
hewn from hugest colour
                              (and which night hoists
miraculously above the always
beyond such wheres and fears or any when
unwondering immense directionless
horizon)
              —do you perhaps know these workmen?

LXX

here is the ocean,this is moonlight:say
that both precisely beyond either were—
so in darkness ourselves go,mind in mind

which is the thrilling least of all(for love's
secret supremely clothes herself with day)

i mean,should any curious dawn discuss
our mingling spirits,you would disappear
unreally;as this planet(understand)

forgets the entire and perpetual sea

—but if yourself consider wonderful
that your(how luminous)life toward twilight will
dissolve reintegrate beckon through me,
i think it is less wonderful than this

only by you my heart always moves

No Thanks

TO

Farrar & Rinehart
Simon & Schuster
Coward-McCann
Limited Editions
Harcourt, Brace
Random House
Equinox Press
Smith & Haas
Viking Press
Knopf
Dutton
Harper's
Scribner's
Covici, Friede

I

mOOn Over tOwns mOOn
whisper
less creature huge grO
pingness

whO perfectly whO
flOat
newly alOne is
dreamest

oNLY THE MooN o
VER ToWNS
SLoWLY SPRoUTING SPIR
IT

2

moon over gai
-té.a
sharp crone dodders be-
tween taxis swirl hues crowds mov
-ing ing ing
among who dreams whom mutterings dream &

:the moon over death over edgar the
moon
          over smellings of gently smell of deads
(lovers grip sprawl twitch lovers)
& one dog?piglike big!sorrows

always;finally and always,the iflike moon over moving
me—the
moon
m
ov—in

g
over(moving)you beautifully also;at

denfert the fat strongman has put
down his carpet from which rise slim curving mighty
children while a python over the way freezes
a serpent becomes a
rod smiles
the liontamer nearby hieroglyphs
soar dip
dip
soar equalling noise solemn

dolls re
-volve whirlswans rabbitsare:
swimswim
painted-with-horses-with-painted-
with eyes and the.m

oon over juillet moon over s
-unday

O:
m
o
o
n
o
  (ver no(w ove(r all;
                  o
ver pinkthisgreen acr)o)greenthatpink)
acrobata

mong
trees climbing on
A

pi llarofch airso vertheseu pstareth oseings
over
(a hard a
hard a girl a girl)sing
-ing ing(ing
sing)ing a soft a song a softishsongly

v
  o
   i
    c
     e o
        ver
(whi!tethatr?apidly
legthelessne sssuc kedt oward
black,this

)roUnd ingrOundIngly rouNdar(round)ounDing
                                 ;ball
                                 balll
                                 ballll
                                 balllll

3

that which we who're alive in spite of mirrors
(have died beyond the clock)we,of ourselves

who more a part are(less who are aware)

than of my books could even be your shelves
(that which we die for;not when or unless
if or to prove,imperfectly or since

but through spontaneous deft strictly horrors

which stars may not observe;while roses wince)
that which we die for lives(may never cease
views with smooth vigilant perpetual eyes
each exact victim,how he does not stir)

O love,my love!soul clings and heart conceives

and mind leaps(and that which we die for lives
as wholly as that which we live for dies)

4

i
(meet)t(touch)
ems crouch(
lunge
)ing bruiseD
Suddenly by thousand

starings rinsed with
thoroughly million yells they
f-oo-l(whom,blinds;blood)pa-nt
stab are

(slopped givers of not)bang
spurting mesh(faith
-ful which -ly try are ing)al

most fe(hug)males(one-t
wo-l oop-l

eftsthrowr ightsm issingupperc

uts-lurc hhurt-re
coil charge &)swooN

Crowdloomroar:ing;diskface,es
(are two
notSoft soft one are

hard one notHard)not
boys boy-
ish(a stopped A)with!notgirl'swith?dumb
(thewith girl)ness(ish The eyesthe

Is)aRe
iS ar(ise)wi
it(wit(hprettyw)ith)mr
jeff dick
son fec

i
(m
c)
t

(m
x
x

x
ii)

I

5

a)glazed mind layed in a
                              urinal
howlessly and without why
(quite minus gal or
                  pal

slightly too sick to rightly die)
"gedup"
            the gentscoon coos
gently:tug?g(ing intently it

refuses.
        to refuse;
just,look)ing dead but not complete
-ly not(not as look men

who are turned to seem)
                              "stetti"
and
        willbeishfully bursting un-
eats wasvino isspaghett(i

6

exit a kind of unkindness exit

little
mr Big
notbusy
Busi
ness notman

(!ye
galleon
wilts
b:
  e;n,d

i
 ng
like like,like bad,like
candy:& you

are dead
you captain)

Memo 1
wife in impossibly
hell Memo
1 son
in improbably yale

7

sonnet entitled how to run the world)

A always don't there B being no such thing
for C can't casts no shadow D drink and

E eat of her voice in whose silence the music of spring
lives F feel opens but shuts understand
G gladly forget little having less

with every least each most remembering
H highest fly only the flag that's furled

(sestet entitled grass is flesh or swim
who can and bathe who must or any dream
means more than sleep as more than know means guess)

I item i immaculately owe
dying one life and will my rest to these

children building this rainman out of snow

8

the(
    Wistfully

dead seem generous)don't
All suspect each(nor

have i observed
some chucking some
legally into Oblivion wave little

flags weeping flatter
thoroughly imploring threaten)the
wistFully dead you directly perceive or minus
news alimony blackmail whathavewe

and propaganda(it is incredible But
others don't
scream murmur wink
at kid anæsthetize marry bump off
or otherwise amplify others)

the so to speak witsfulLy dead
are not relatively
speaking uncultured(who
Very distinctly confine

their omnipotent literally their
putting it more than mildly Absolute
destructivity to non–

entities e.
g. the)
    whis-per it
        (

Living

9

o pr
gress verily thou art m
mentous superc
lossal hyperpr
digious etc i kn
w & if you d

n't why g
  to yonder s
called newsreel s
called theatre & with your
wn eyes beh

ld The
          (The president The
          president of The president
          of the The)president of

          the(united The president of the
          united states The president of the united
          states of The President Of The)United States

          Of America unde negant redire quemquam supp
sedly thr
w
  i
    n
      g
        a
          b
            aseball

10

little man
(in a hurry
full of an
important worry)
halt stop forget relax

wait

(little child
who have tried
who have failed
who have cried)
lie bravely down

sleep

big rain
big snow
big sun
big moon
(enter

us)

I I

ci-gît 1 Foetus(unborn to not die

safely whose epoch fits him like a grave)
with all his toys(money men motors "my"
yachts wolfhounds women)and the will to shave

that Ghost is dead(whom noone might inter)
fleeing himself for selves more strangely made
(wears pain at joy,come summer puts on fur

answers eats moves remembers is afraid)

each hates a Man whom both would call their friend
and who may envy neither;nor bewail
(would rather make than have and give than lend
—being through failures born who cannot fail)

having no wealth but love,who shall not spend
my fortune(although endlessness should end)

12

why why

How many winds make wonderful
and is luck The skeleton of life
or did anybody Open a moment

are Not

more than(if Green invents because
where might Where live
can fisherMen swim and
who's myself's Antimere
Should words carry weapons)are

not Less than(that

by doDreaming heteronomously
metameric me are picked from
dumb sleePdeep
ness squirmcurl

ing homonomously metameric You

13

r-p–o–p–h–e–s–s–a–g–r
                    who
        a)s w(e loo)k
        upnowgath
                PPEGORHRASS
                            eringint(o-
            aThe):l
                eA
                    !p:
    S   a
                        (r
        rIvInG   .gRrEaPsPhOs)
                                        to
        rea(be)rran(com)gi(e)ngly
        ,grasshopper;

14

mouse)Won
derfully is
anyone else entirely who doesn't
move(Moved more suddenly than)whose

tiniest smile?may Be
bigger than the fear of all
hearts never which have
(Per

haps)loved(or than
everyone that will Ever love)we
've
hidden him in A leaf

and,
Opening
beautiful earth
put(only)a Leaf among dark

ness.sunlight's
thenlike?now
Disappears
some

thing(silent:
madeofimagination
;the incredible soft)ness
(his ears(eyes

15

one nonsufficiently inunderstood
re
   with some difficulty
        one father of
one(ask super-)wonderful(mother)child is a good
Husband to him(and whose what he conceives to be Love
did
     stretchandstretchandstretchandstretchand
                  did)
who begins stuttering each sentence we both
consid
    (notb- notbr- notbre- notbrea-k
               The kid)
er Santa Claus a criminal(hears Darwin;asks about Death)
concept

    O hairlesschested females,well
attend!list,every nonelastic male—
uplook,all joybegotten whelps whom soothe
psychotic myths like Jonah And The Whale

:oiwun uhsoi roitee runow dutmoi
jak roids wid yooze
        Vury Sin Silly
           :oi

16

may i feel said he
(i'll squeal said she
just once said he)
it's fun said she

(may i touch said he
how much said she
a lot said he)
why not said she

(let's go said he
not too far said she
what's too far said he
where you are said she)

may i stay said he
(which way said she
like this said he
if you kiss said she

may i move said he
is it love said she)
if you're willing said he
(but you're killing said she

but it's life said he
but your wife said she
now said he)
ow said she

(tiptop said he
don't stop said she
oh no said he)
go slow said she

(cccome?said he
ummm said she)
you're divine!said he
(you are Mine said she)

o
sure)but
nobody unders(no
but Rully yes i
know)but what it comes

to(listen you don't have to

i mean Reely)but(no listen don't
be sil why sure)i mean the(o
well ughhuh sure why not yuh course yeh well
naturally i und certain i o posi but

i know sure that's)but listen here's

(correct you said it yeah)but
listen but(it's Rilly yeh
ughhuh yuh)i know

(o sure i

know yes
of

course)but what i mean is Nobody Understands Her RERLY

this little
pair had a little scare
right in the middle of a bed bed
bed)when each other courted both
was very very thwarted)and
when which was aborted
what was dead dead dead)

whereupon mary
quite contrary didn't
die
(may be seen to inexactly pass and unprecisely
to repass where
flesh is heiry montparnasse
is goosed by raspail).

But he turned into a fair
y!a fair
y!!a
fair
y!!!
but she turned into a fair-y(and
it seems to be doing nicely

who before dying demands not rebirth

of such than hungrily more swiftness as
with(feel)pauseless immeasurably Now
cancels the childfully diminishing earth
—never whose proudly life swallowed is by

(with hope two eyes a memory this brow
five or three dreamfuls of despair that face)

large one coloured nonthings of gluttonous sky—
nor(as a blind,how timidly,throb;which
hints being;suggests identity)breathes fleet
perfectly far from tangible domains
rare with most early soul
                              him shall untouch

meaningless precision and complete fate

(he must deny mind:may believe in brains.

20

go(perpe)go

(tu)to(al
adve

nturin
g p
article

s of s
ini
sterd
exte

ri)go to(ty)the(om
nivorou salways lugbrin
g ingseekfindlosin g
motilities
are)go to

the
ant
(al
ways

alingwaysing)
go to the ant thou go
(inging)

to the
ant,thou ant-

eater

21

IN)
　　all those who got
　　athlete's mouth jumping
　　on&off bandwaggons
　　　　　　　　(MEMORIAM

22

when muckers pimps and tratesmen
delivered are of vicians
and all the world howls stadesmen
beware of politisions

beware of folks with missians
to turn us into rissions
and blokes with ammunicions
who tend to make incitions

and pity the fool who cright
god help me it aint no ews
eye like the steak all ried
but eye certainly hate the juse

he does not have to feel because he thinks
(the thoughts of others,be it understood)
he does not have to think because he knows
(that anything is bad which you think good)

because he knows,he cannot understand
(why Jones don't pay me what he knows he owes)
because he cannot understand,he drinks
(and he drinks and he drinks and he drinks and)

not bald.   (Coughs.)   Two pale slippery small eyes

balanced upon one broken babypout
(pretty teeth wander into which and out
of)Life,dost Thou contain a marvel than
this death named Smith less strange?
                                        Married and lies

afraid;aggressive and:American

24

"let's start a magazine

to hell with literature
we want something redblooded

lousy with pure
reeking with stark
and fearlessly obscene

but really clean
get what I mean
let's not spoil it
let's make it serious

something authentic and delirious
you know something genuine like a mark
in a toilet

graced with guts and gutted
with grace"

squeeze your nuts and open your face

this(that

grey)white
(man)horse

floats
on 4
3rdtoes

p
(drooli
ngly supp
ort 2 be

nt
toothpick
s)

ro
ude

stly(stuck in a spanked behind

26

what does little Ernest croon
in his death at afternoon?
(kow dow r 2 bul retoinis
wus de woids uf lil Oinis

27

little joe gould has lost his teeth and doesn't know where
to find them(and found a secondhand set which click)little
gould used to amputate his appetite with bad brittle
candy but just(nude eel)now little joe lives on air

Harvard Brevis Est for Handkerchief read Papernapkin no laundry
bills likes People preferring Negroes Indians Youse
n.b. ye twang of little joe(yankee)gould irketh sundry
who are trying to find their minds(but never had any to lose)

and a myth is as good as a smile but little joe gould's quote oral
history unquote might(publishers note)be entitled a wraith's
progress or mainly awash while chiefly submerged or an amoral
morality sort-of-aliveing by innumerable kind-of-deaths

(Amérique Je T'Aime and it may be fun to be fooled
but it's more fun to be more to be fun to be little joe gould)

28

that famous fatheads find that each
    and every thing must have an end
(the silly cause of trivial which
    thinkless unwishing doth depend

    upon the texture of their p-ss)
isn't(and that it mayn't be twirled
    around your little finger is)
what's right about the g. o. world

what's wrong with(between me and we)
    the g--d -ld w. isn't that it
can't exist(and is that the
    g. o. w. is full of)delete

29

most(people

simply

can't)
won't(most
parent people mustn't

shouldn't)most daren't

(sortof people well
youknow kindof)
aint

&

even
(not having
most ever lived

people always)don't

die(becoming most
buried unbecomingly
very

by

most)people

30

kumrads die because they're told)
kumrads die before they're old
(kumrads aren't afraid to die
kumrads don't
and kumrads won't
believe in life)and death knows whie

(all good kumrads you can tell
by their altruistic smell
moscow pipes good kumrads dance)
kumrads enjoy
s.freud knows whoy
the hope that you may mess your pance

every kumrad is a bit
of quite unmitigated hate
(travelling in a futile groove
god knows why)
and so do i
(because they are afraid to love

31

does yesterday's perfection seem not quite

so clever as the pratfall of a clown
(should stink of failure more than wars of feet

all things whose slendering sweetness touched renown)
suddenly themselves if all dreams unmake
(when in a most smashed unworld stands unslain

he which knows not if any anguish struck
how thin a ghost so deep and he might live)
yes,partly nor some edgeless star could give
that anguish room;but likes it only this

eternal mere one bursting soul
                                        why,then

comes peace unto men who are always men
while a man shall which a god sometimes is

I the lost shoulders S the empty spine

32

numb(and
that was
and that
was cling)

on
win
ter
sc

ribbled
lonely truth(from
hang
from droop

w
ar
pin
g dre

ams
whichful sarcasms
papery deathfuls)awaits
yes

this alive secretly i
frantic this serene
mightily how rooted
who of iron

33

emptied.hills.listen.
,not,alive,trees,dream(
ev:ery:wheres:ex:tend:ing:hush

)
 andDark
IshbusY
ing-roundly-dis

tinct;chuck
lings,laced
ar:e.by(

fleet&panelike&frailties
!throughwhich!brittlest!whitewhom!
f
  l o a t ?)
            r
              h y t h m s

34

snow)says!Says
over un
      graves
          der,speaking
(says.word
Less)ly(goes

folds?folds)cold
stones(o–l–d)names
aren'ts

)L
  iv
es(c
    omeS

says)s;n;o;w(says

W
I

elds)
un
  forgetting
          un.
der(theys)the

:se!crumbs things?Its
noyesiyou
he–she
(Weres

how dark and single,where he ends,the earth
(whose texture feels of pride and loneliness
alive like some dream giving more than all
life's busy little dyings may possess)

how sincere large distinct and natural
he comes to his disappearance;as a mind
full without fear might faithfully lie down
to so much sleep they only understand

enormously which fail—look:with what ease
that bright how plural tide measures her guest
(as critics will upon a poet feast)

meanwhile this ghost goes under,his drowned girth
are mountains;and beyond all hurt of praise
the unimaginable night not known

36

into a truly
curving form
enters my
soul

feels all small
facts dissolved
by the lewd guess
of fabulous immensity

the sky screamed
the sun died)
the ship lifts
on seas of iron

breathing height eating
steepness the
ship climbs
murmuring silver mountains

which
disappear(and
only
was night

and through only this night a
mightily form moves
whose passenger and whose
pilot my spirit is

conceive a man,should he have anything
would give a little more than it away

(his autumn's winter being summer's spring
who moved by standing in november's may)
from whose(if loud most howish time derange

the silent whys of such a deathlessness)
remembrance might no patient mind unstrange
learn(nor could all earth's rotting scholars guess
that life shall not for living find the rule)

and dark beginnings are his luminous ends
who far less lonely than a fire is cool
took bedfellows for moons mountains for friends

—open your thighs to fate and(if you can
withholding nothing)World,conceive a man

38

SNOW

cru
  is
    ingw Hi
sperf
    ul
lydesc

BYS FLUTTERFULLY IF

(endbegi ndesginb ecend)tang
lesp
    ang
le
  s
   ofC omeg o

CRINGE WITHS

lilt(
   -ing-
      lyful
of)!
    (s
r

BIRDS BECAUSE AGAINS

emarkable
        s)h?
          y & a
            (from n
o(into whe)re f
        ind)
nd
  ArE

GLIB SCARCELYEST AMONGS FLOWERING

39

move
deeply,rain
(dream hugely)wish
firmly.   splendidly advancing colour

strike
into form
(actually)realness
kill

(make
strangely)known(establish
new)come,what
Being!open us open

our
selves.   create
(suddenly announce:hurl)
blind full steep love

40

as if as

if a mys
teriouSly("i am alive"

)
 brave

ly and(th
e moon's al-down)most whis
per(here)ingc r O

wing;ly:cry.be,gi N s agAains

t b
ecomin
gsky?t r e e s
!

m ore&(o uto f)mor e torn(f og r

e
elingwhiRls)are pouring rush fields drea
mf(ull

     y

       are.)
&
som

ewhereishbudofshape

now,s
tI
r
ghost

?s

tirf lic;k
e rsM-o
:ke(c.

    l

i,

m
  !
b
)& it:s;elf,

mmamakmakemakesWwOwoRworLworlD

here's to opening and upward,to leaf and to sap
and to your(in my arms flowering so new)
self whose eyes smell of the sound of rain

and here's to silent certainly mountains;and to
a disappearing poet of always,snow
and to morning;and to morning's beautiful friend
twilight(and a first dream called ocean)and

let must or if be damned with whomever's afraid
down with ought with because with every brain
which thinks it thinks,nor dares to feel(but up
with joy;and up with laughing and drunkenness)

here's to one undiscoverable guess
of whose mad skill each world of blood is made
(whose fatal songs are moving in the moon

42

out of a supermetamathical subpreincestures
pooped universe(of croons canned
à la vallee and preserved goldfishian gestures)
suddenly sally rand

handsomely who did because she could what the movies try
to do because they can't i mean move
yes sir she jes was which the radio aint(proov
-ing that the quickness of the fand intrigues the fly)

for know all men(χαίρετε)
as it was in the beginning it(rejoice)
was and ever shall be nor every partialness beats one entirety
neither may shadow down flesh neither may vibration create voice

if therefore among foul pains appears an if emerges a joy let
's thank indecent
god p.s. the most successful b.o.fully speaking concession at the recent
world's fair was the paytoilet

43

theys sO alive
      (who is
          ?niggers)

     Not jes
     livin
     not Jes alive But
     So alive(they

    s
    born alive)
    some folks aint born
    somes born dead an
    somes born alive(but

   niggers
  is
  all
 born
so
Alive)

    ump-A-tum
        ;tee–die

    uM-tuM
      tidl
       -id

     umptyumpty(OO———

                !

    ting
   Bam-
 :do)
,chippity.

44

the boys i mean are not refined
they go with girls who buck and bite
they do not give a fuck for luck
they hump them thirteen times a night

one hangs a hat upon her tit
one carves a cross in her behind
they do not give a shit for wit
the boys i mean are not refined

they come with girls who bite and buck
who cannot read and cannot write
who laugh like they would fall apart
and masturbate with dynamite

the boys i mean are not refined
they cannot chat of that and this
they do not give a fart for art
they kill like you would take a piss

they speak whatever's on their mind
they do whatever's in their pants
the boys i mean are not refined
they shake the mountains when they dance

45

sometimes
      in)Spring a someone will lie(glued
among familiar things newly which are
transferred with dusk)wondering why this star
does not fall into his mind
               feeling
throughout ignorant disappearing me
hurling vastness of love(sometimes in Spring
somewhere between what is and what may be
unknown most secret i will breathe such crude
perfection as divides by timelessness
that heartbeat)
          mightily forgetting all
which will forget him(emptying our soul
of emptiness)priming at every pore
a deathless life with magic until peace
outthunders silence.
             And(night climbs the air

46

swi(
    across!gold's

rouNdly
)ftblac
kl(ness)y

a-motion-upo-nmotio-n

Less?
    thE
(against
is
)Swi

mming

(w-a)s
bIr

d,

47

ondumonde"

(first than caref
ully;pois
edN-o wt he
n
,whysprig
              sli

nkil
  -Y-
  strol(pre)ling(cise)dy(ly)na(
  mite)

    :yearnswoons;

    &Isdensekil-
    ling-whipAlert-floatScor
    ruptingly)

                ça-y-est
                droppe5
                qu'est-ce que tu veux
                Dwrith
                il est trop fort le nègre
                esn7othingish8s
                c'est fini
                pRaW,lT;O:
              allons
          9
        &
                    .

                (musically-who?

    pivoting)
    SmileS

      "ahlbrhoon

48

floatfloafloflf
lloloa
tatoatloatf loat fl oat
f loatI ngL

y

&fris
klispin
glyT
  w
   irlEric

 ,

t,
;d
; :a:
nC.eda:Nci;ddaanncciinn

(GIY)

a
 nda
   n-saint
dance!Dan
Sai ntd anc

&e&

—cupidoergosum
spun=flash
omiepsicronlonO—
megaeta?
    p
     aul D-as-in-tip-toe r

apeR

49

silent unday by silently not night

did the great world(in darkly taking rain)
drown,beyond sound
                    down(slowly
                          beneath
                                sight
fall
   ing(fall
         ing through touch
                  less stillness(seized

among what ghostly nevers of again)
silent not night by silently unday
life's bright less dwindled to a leastful most
under imagination.   When(out of sheer

nothing)came a huger than fear a

white with madness wind and broke oceans and tore
mountains from their sockets and strewed the black air
with writhing alive skies—and in death's place
new fragrantly young earth space opening was.
Were your eyes:lost,believing;hushed with when

50

much i cannot)
tear up the world:& toss
it away;or
cause one causeless cloud to purely grow

but,never
doubt my weakness
makes more than most
strength(less than these how

less than least flowers of rain)thickly
i fail slenderly i
win(like touch all stars or
to live in the moon

a while)and shall
carve time so we'll before
what's death
come(in one bed.

51

at dusk
        just when
the Light is filled with birds
seriously
i begin

to climb the best hill,
driven by black wine.
a village does not move behind
my eye

the windmills are
silent
their flattened arms
complain steadily against the west

one Clock dimly cries
nine,i stride among the vines
(my heart pursues
against the little moon

a here and there lark
                    who;rises,
and;droops
as if upon a thread invisible)

A graveyard dreams through its
cluttered and brittle emblems,or
a field(and i pause among
the smell of minute mown lives)oh

my spirit you
tumble
climb
        and mightily fatally

i remark how through deep lifted
fields Oxen distinctly move,a
yellowandbluish cat(perched why
Curvingly at this)window;yes

women sturdily meander in my
mind,woven by always upon
sunset,
crickets within me whisper

whose erect blood finally
trembles,emerging to perceive
buried in cliff
                    precisely

at the Ending of this road,
a candle in a shrine:
its puniest flame persists
shaken by the sea

52

Spring(side

walks are)is
most(windows where blaze

naLOVEme
crazily
ships

bulge hearts by
darts pierced lazily writhe
lurch faceflowers stutter
treebodies wobbly-

ing thing
-birds)sing-
u
(cities are houses
people are flies who

buzz on)-lar(windows called sidewalks
of houses called cities)spring
most singular-
ly(cities are houses are)is(are owned

by a m- by
a -n by a
-oo-

is old as
the jews are a moon is

as round as)Death

53

what a proud dreamhorse pulling(smoothloomingly)through
(stepp)this(ing)crazily seething of this
raving city screamingly street wonderful

flowers And o the Light thrown by Them opens

sharp holes in dark places paints eyes touches hands with new-
ness and these startled whats are a(piercing clothes thoughts kiss
-ing wishes bodies)squirm-of-frightened shy are whichs small
its hungry for Is for Love Spring thirsty for happens
only and beautiful
                          there is a ragged beside the who limps
man crying silence upward
                          —to have tasted Beautiful to have known
Only to have smelled Happens—skip dance kids hop point at
red blue yellow violet white orange green-
ness

    o what a proud dreamhorse moving(whose feet
almost walk air).   now who stops. Smiles.he
                                   stamps

54

Jehovah buried,Satan dead,
do fearers worship Much and Quick;
badness not being felt as bad,
itself thinks goodness what is meek;
obey says toc,submit says tic,
Eternity's a Five Year Plan:
if Joy with Pain shall hang in hock
who dares to call himself a man?

go dreamless knaves on Shadows fed,
your Harry's Tom,your Tom is Dick;
while Gadgets murder squawk and add,
the cult of Same is all the chic;
by instruments,both span and spic,
are justly measured Spic and Span:
to kiss the mike if Jew turn kike
who dares to call himself a man?

loudly for Truth have liars pled,
their heels for Freedom slaves will click;
where Boobs are holy,poets mad,
illustrious punks of Progress shriek;
when Souls are outlawed,Hearts are sick,
Hearts being sick,Minds nothing can:
if Hate's a game and Love's a fuck
who dares to call himself a man?

King Christ,this world is all aleak;
and lifepreservers there are none:
and waves which only He may walk
Who dares to call Himself a man.

55

worshipping Same
they squirm and they spawn
and a world is for them,them;whose
death's to be born)

his birth is their fear is their blind fear
—haunts all unsleep
this cry of one fiend,
a thousand dreams thick

(cringing they brood
breeding they wince)
his laugh is a million griefs wide(it
shall bury much stench)

and a hundred joys high are such shoulders
as cowards will scheme
to harness:let all
unfools of unbeing

set traps for his heart,
lay snares for his feet
(who wanders through only white darkness
who moves in black light

dancing isn'ts on why,digging bridges with mirrors
from whispers to stars;
climbing silence for ifs
diving under because)

only who'll say
"and this be my fame,
the harder the wind blows the
taller i am"

56

this mind made war
being generous
this heart could dare)
unhearts can less

unminds must fear
because and why
what filth is here
unlives do cry

on him they shat
they shat encore
he laughed and spat
(this life could dare

freely to give
as gives a friend
not those who slave
unselves to lend

for hope of hope
must coo or boo
may strut or creep
ungenerous who

ape deftly aims
they dare not share)
such make their names
(this poet made war

whose naught and all
sun are and moon
come fair come foul
he goes alone

daring to dare
for joy of joy)
what stink is here
unpoets do cry

unfools unfree
undeaths who live
nor shall they be
and must they have

at him they fart
they fart full oft
(with mind with heart
he spat and laughed

with self with life
this poet arose
nor hate nor grief
can go where goes

this whyless soul
a loneliest road
who dares to stroll
almost this god

this surely dream
perhaps this ghost)
humbly and whom
for worst or best

(and proudly things
only which grow
and the rain's wings
the birds of snow

things without name
beyond because
things over blame
things under praise

glad things or free
truly which live
always shall be
may never have)

do i salute
(by moon by sun
i deeply greet
this fool and man

57

when
        from a sidewalk
                    out of(blown never quite to
-gether by large sorry)creatures out
of(clumsily shining out of)instru-
ments,waltzing;undigestibly:groans.bounce

!o-ras-ourh an-dorg-an ble-at-ssw-ee-t-noth ings orarancidhurd
ygurdygur glingth umpssomet hings(whi,le sp,arrow,s wince
among those skeletons of these trees)
                                    when
                                        sunbeams loot
furnished rooms through whose foul windows absurd
clouds cruise nobly ridiculous skies

(the;mselve;s a;nd scr;a;tch-ing lousy full.of.rain
beggars yaw :nstretchy :awn)
                        then,
                            o my love
                                    ,then
it's Spring
        immortal Always & lewd shy New

and upon the beyond imagining spasm rise
we
    you-with-me
                around(me)you
                    IYou

58

love is a place
& through this place of
love move
(with brightness of peace)
all places

yes is a world
& in this world of
yes live
(skilfully curled)
all worlds

59

sh estiffl
ystrut sal
lif san
dbut sth

epouting(gWh.ono:w
s li psh ergo
wnd ow n,
                    r
Eve

aling 2 a
-sprout eyelands)sin
uously&them&twi
tching,begins

unununun?
butbutbut??
  tonton??
ing????

—Out-&
       steps;which
flipchucking
.grins
gRiNdS

d is app ea r in gly
eyes grip live loop croon mime
nakedly hurl asquirm the
dip&giveswoop&swoon&ingly

seethe firm swirl hips whirling climb to
GIVE
(yoursmine mineyours yoursmine
!
i()t)

60

(b
  eLl
     s?
       bE

-ginningly(come-swarm:faces
ar;rive go.faces a(live)
sob bel
ls

(pour wo
         (things)
                 men
                      selves-them

inghurl)bangbells(yawnchurches
suck people)reel(dark-
ly(whirling
in

(b
  ellSB
        el
          Ls)

-to sun(crash).Streets
glit
ter
a,strut:do;colours;are:m,ove

o im
     -pos-
          sibl
               y

(ShoutflowereD
flowerish boom
b el Lsb El l
s!cry)

(be
   llsbe
        lls)
            b
             (be
                llsbell)
                       ells
                            (sbells)

61

love's function is to fabricate unknownness

(known being wishless;but love,all of wishing)
though life's lived wrongsideout,sameness chokes oneness
truth is confused with fact,fish boast of fishing

and men are caught by worms(love may not care
if time totters,light droops,all measures bend
nor marvel if a thought should weigh a star
—dreads dying least;and less,that death should end)

how lucky lovers are(whose selves abide
under whatever shall discovered be)
whose ignorant each breathing dares to hide
more than most fabulous wisdom fears to see

(who laugh and cry)who dream,create and kill
while the whole moves;and every part stands still:

62

we)under)over,the thing of floating Of
;elate
shyly a-live keen parallel specks float-ing create
height,
        liv-

ing
   ly who:seemSwoop
                        (whir
-ling be,yond!thought
are.more(Than girl

's
tears boy Dream's)forge

tful:e
        ver than,is e
                    ven:th
                            e(s
                              e
                                a's;m
                                    e,
                                      m(or.y

63

birds(
        here,inven
ting air
U
)sing

tw
iligH(
t's
    v
       va
          vas
vast

ness.Be)look
now
     (come
soul;
&:and

who
    s)e
        voi
c
es
(
 are
    ar
      a

64

Do.
omful
relaxing

-ly)i
downrise outwrithein-
ing upfall and

Am the glad deep the living from nowh
-ere(!firm!)exp-
anding,am a fe

-rvently(susta-
inin
-gness Am

root air rock day)
:you;
smile,hands

(an-
onymo
-Us

65

if night's mostness(and whom did merely day
close)
      opens
          if more than silence silent are more
flowering than stars whitely births of mind

if air is throbbing prayers whom kneeling eyes
(until perfectly their imperfect gaze
climbs this steep fragrance of eternity)
world by than worlds immenser world will pray

so(unlove disappearing)only your
less than guessed more than beauty begins the
most not imagined life adventuring
who would feel if spring's least breathing should cause
a colour
        and i do not know him
                    (and

while behind death's death whenless voices sing
everywhere your selves himself recognize)

66

death(having lost)put on his universe
and yawned:it looks like rain
(they've played for timelessness
with chips of when)
that's yours;i guess
you'll have to loan me pain
to take the hearse,
see you again.

Love(having found)wound up such pretty toys
as themselves could not know:
the earth tinily whirls;
while daisies grow
(and boys and girls
have whispered thus and so)
and girls with boys
to bed will go,

67

    come(all you mischief-
   hatchers hatch
mischief)all you

  guilty
   scamper(you bastards throw dynamite)
    let knowings magic
   with bright credos each divisible fool

  (life imitate gossip fear unlife
mean
 -ness,and
  to succeed in not
   dying)

  Is will still occur;birds disappear
  becomingly:a thunderbolt compose poems
not because harm symmetry
  earthquakes starfish(but
   because nobody
    can sell the Moon to The)moon

68

be of love(a little)
More careful
Than of everything
guard her perhaps only

A trifle less
(merely beyond how very)
closely than
Nothing,remember love by frequent

anguish(imagine
Her least never with most
memory)give entirely each
Forever its freedom

(Dare until a flower,
understanding sizelessly sunlight
Open what thousandth why and
discover laughing)

69

reason let others give and realness bring—
ask the always impossible of me
and shall who wave among your deepening
thighs a greedier wand than even death's

what beneath breathing selves transported are
into how suddenly so huge a home
(only more than immeasurable dream
wherelessly spiralling)beyond time's sky

and through this opening universe will wraiths
of doom rush(which all ghosts of life became)
and does our fatally unshadowing fate
put on one not imaginable star

:then a small million of dark voices sing
against the awful mystery of light

70

brIght

bRight s??? big
(soft)

soft near calm
(Bright)
calm st?? holy

(soft briGht deep)
yeS near sta? calm star big yEs
alone
(wHo

Yes
near deep whO big alone soft near
deep calm deep
????Ht ?????T)
Who(holy alone)holy(alone holy)alone

morsel miraculous and meaningless

secret on luminous whose selves and lives
imperishably feast all timeless souls

(the not whose spiral hunger may appease
what merely riches of our pretty world
sweetly who flourishes,swiftly which fails

but out of serene perfectly Nothing hurled
into young Now entirely arrives
gesture past fragrance fragrant;a than pure

more signalling of singular most flame
and surely poets only understands)
honour this loneliness of even him

who fears and eyes lifts lifting hopes and hands
—nourish my failure with thy freedom:star

isful beckoningly fabulous crumb

AND
THANKS
TO
R.H.C.

New Poems

[from COLLECTED POEMS]

INTRODUCTION

The poems to come are for you and for me and are not for mostpeople
—it's no use trying to pretend that mostpeople and ourselves are alike.
Mostpeople have less in common with ourselves than the squarerootof-
minusone. You and I are human beings;mostpeople are snobs.

Take the matter of being born. What does being born mean to most-
people? Catastrophe unmitigated. Socialrevolution. The cultured
aristocrat yanked out of his hyperexclusively ultravoluptuous super-
palazzo,and dumped into an incredibly vulgar detentioncamp swarming
with every conceivable species of undesirable organism. Mostpeople
fancy a guaranteed birthproof safetysuit of nondestructible selflessness.
If mostpeople were to be born twice they'd improbably call it dying—

you and I are not snobs. We can never be born enough. We are human
beings;for whom birth is a supremely welcome mystery,the mystery of
growing:the mystery which happens only and whenever we are faithful
to ourselves. You and I wear the dangerous looseness of doom and find it
becoming. Life,for eternal us,is now;and now is much too busy being a
little more than everything to seem anything,catastrophic included.

Life,for mostpeople,simply isn't. Take the socalled standardofliving.
What do mostpeople mean by "living"? They don't mean living. They
mean the latest and closest plural approximation to singular prenatal
passivity which science,in its finite but unbounded wisdom,has suc-
ceeded in selling their wives. If science could fail,a mountain's a mammal.
Mostpeople's wives can spot a genuine delusion of embryonic omni-
potence immediately and will accept no substitutes

—luckily for us,a mountain is a mammal. The plusorminus movie to
end moving,the strictly scientific parlourgame of real unreality,the
tyranny conceived in misconception and dedicated to the proposition
that every man is a woman and any woman a king,hasn't a wheel to stand
on. What their most synthetic not to mention transparent majesty,
mrsandmr collective foetus,would improbably call a ghost is walking.
He isn't an undream of anaesthetized impersons,or a cosmic comfort-
station,or a transcendentally sterilized lookiesoundiefeelietastiesmellie.
He is a healthily complex,a naturally homogeneous,citizen of immor-
tality. The now of his each pitying free imperfect gesture,his any birth or
breathing,insults perfected inframortally millenniums of slavishness.
He is a little more than everything,he is democracy;he is alive:he is
ourselves.

Miracles are to come. With you I leave a remembrance of miracles:
they are by somebody who can love and who shall be continually reborn,

a human being;somebody who said to those near him,when his fingers would not hold a brush "tie it into my hand"—

nothing proving or sick or partial. Nothing false,nothing difficult or easy or small or colossal. Nothing ordinary or extraordinary,nothing emptied or filled,real or unreal;nothing feeble and known or clumsy and guessed. Everywhere tints childrening,innocent spontaneous,true. Nowhere possibly what flesh and impossibly such a garden,but actually flowers which breasts are among the very mouths of light. Nothing believed or doubted;brain over heart, surface:nowhere hating or to fear; shadow,mind without soul. Only how measureless cool flames of making; only each other building always distinct selves of mutual entirely opening;only alive. Never the murdered finalities of wherewhen and yesno, impotent nongames of wrongright and rightwrong;never to gain or pause,never the soft adventure of undoom,greedy anguishes and cringing ecstasies of inexistence;never to rest and never to have:only to grow.

Always the beautiful answer who asks a more beautiful question

E. E. CUMMINGS

I

un
der fog
's
touch

slo

ings
fin
gering
s

wli

whichs
turn
in
to whos

est

people
be
come
un

kind)
YM&WC
(of sort of)
A soursweet bedtime

-less un-
(wonderful)
story atrickling a
-rithmetic o-

ver me you & all those & that
"I may say professor"
asleep
wop "shapley

has compared the universe
to a
uh" pause
"Cookie

but" nonvisibly smi-
ling through man
-ufactured harmlessly accurate
gloom "I

think he might now be inclined to describe
it rather as
a" pause "uh"
cough

"Biscuit"
(& so on & so unto canned
swoonsong
came "I wish you good" the mechanical

dawn
"morning")& that those you
i St
ep

into the not
merely immeasurable into
the mightily alive the
dear beautiful eternal night

3

a football with white eyebrows the
3
rd chief something or must be off

duty wanderfuling aft spits)
int
o immensity(upon once whom

fiercely by pink mr seized green
mrs
opening is it horribly smith spouts

cornucopiously not unrecognizable whats of
t
oo vertiginously absorbed which à la

4

(of Ever-Ever Land i speak
sweet morons gather roun'
who does not dare to stand or sit
may take it lying down)

down with the human soul
and anything else uncanned
for everyone carries canopeners
in Ever-Ever Land

(for Ever-Ever Land is a place
that's as simple as simple can be
and was built that way on purpose
by simple people like we)

down with hell and heaven
and all the religious fuss
infinity pleased our parents
one inch looks good to us

(and Ever-Ever Land is a place
that's measured and safe and known
where it's lucky to be unlucky
and the hitler lies down with the cohn)

down above all with love
and everything perverse
or which makes some feel more better
when all ought to feel less worse

(but only sameness is normal
in Ever-Ever Land
for a bad cigar is a woman
but a gland is only a gland)

5

lucky means finding
Holes where
pockets aren't lucky
's to spend

laughter
not money lucky are
Breathe
grow dream

die love not
Fear eat sleep kill
and have you am luck
-y is we lucky luck-

ier
luck
-I-
est

6

Q:dwo
we know of anything which can
be as dull as one englishman
A:to

7

&-moon-He-be-hind-a-mills

tosses like thin bums dream
ing i'm thick in a hot young queen with

a twot with a twitch like kingdom
come(moon
The

sq
uirmwri
th-ing out of wonderful
thunder!of?ocean.a

ndn
ooneandfor
e-ver)moon She over this new eng
land fragrance of pasture and now ti

p toe ingt o
a child who alone st
and

s(not a
fraid of moon You)

not-mere-ly-won-der-ing-&

8

this little bride & groom are
standing)in a kind
of crown he dressed
in black candy she

veiled with candy white
carrying a bouquet of
pretend flowers this
candy crown with this candy

little bride & little
groom in it kind of stands on
a thin ring which stands on a much
less thin very much more

big & kinder of ring & which
kinder of stands on a
much more than very much
biggest & thickest & kindest

of ring & all one two three rings
are cake & everything is protected by
cellophane against anything(because
nothing really exists

9

so little he is
so.
      Little
ness be

(ing)
comes ex
-pert-
Ly expand:grO

w
 i
?n
  g

Is poet iS
(childlost
so;ul
)foundclown a

-live a
,bird
     !O
& j &

ji
&
jim,jimm
;jimmy

s:
 A
V
o(
  .
   :
   ;

10

nor woman
       (just as it be

           gan to snow he dis
           a

               ppeare
               d leavi
                 ng on its

                   elf pro
                     pped uprigh
                       t that in this o
                   ther w

                   ise how e
                   mpty park bundl
                   e of what man can

               't hurt any more h
           u
           sh
   nor child)

II

my specialty is living said
a man(who could not earn his bread
because he would not sell his head)

squads right impatiently replied
two billion pubic lice inside
one pair of trousers(which had died)

12

The Mind's(

i never you never
he she or it

never we you and they never
saw so
much heard so much smelled so much

tasted
plus touched quite so And
How much nonexistence
eye sed bea

yew tea mis
eyesucks unyewkuntel finglestein idstings
yewrety oride lesgo eckshun

kemeruh daretoi
nig

)Ah,Soul

13

if i

or anybody don't
know where it her his

my next meal's coming from
i say to hell with that
that doesn't matter(and if

he she it or everybody gets a
bellyful without
lifting my finger i say to hell
with that i

say that doesn't matter)but
if somebody
or you are beautiful or
deep or generous what
i say is

whistle that
sing that yell that spell
that out big(bigger than cosmic
rays war earthquakes famine or the ex

prince of whoses diving into
a whatses to rescue miss nobody's
probably handbag)because i say that's not

swell(get me)babe not(understand me)lousy
kid that's something else my sweet(i feel that's

true)

14

hanged

if n
y in a real hot spell
with o

man

what bubbies going
places on such
babies aint plenty
good enough for

i

eu
can have
you

rope

15

economic secu
rity" is a cu
rious excu

se
(in

use among pu
rposive pu
nks)for pu

tting the arse
before the torse

16

beware beware beware
because because because
equals(transparent or

science must
bait laws with
stars to catch telescopes

)why.
Being is
patience is patient is(patiently

all the eyes of these with listening
hands only fishermen are
prevented by cathedrals

17

only as what(out of a flophouse)floats
on murdered feet into immense no

Where
          which to map while these not eyes quite try
almost their mind immeasurably roots
among much soundless rubbish of guitars
and watches
              only as this(which might have been
a man and kept a date and played a tune)
death's dollhead wandering under weakening stars

Feels;if
          & god said & there was
                              is born:
one face who.
              and hands hold his whose unlife
bursts

          only so;only if you should turn
the infinite corner of love,all that i am
easily disappears(leaving no proof

not the least shadow of a.   Not one smallest dream)

18

must being shall

one only thing must:the opening of a
(not some not every but any)
heart—wholly,idiotically—before
such nonsense which
is the overlove & underwish of
beauty;before keen if
dim quiveringly
spangle & thingless
& before flashing soft neverwheres &
sweet nothingly gushing tinsel;silently
yes before angel curvings upon a mostless
more of star

o-

pening of(writhing your exploding my)heart
before how worlds delicate
of bombast—papery what
& vast solidities,unwinding
dizzily &
mirrors;sprung dimensionless
new alls of joy:quietly & before illimitably
spiralling candy of tiniest
forever—crazily from totally sprouted by alive
green each very lifting
& seriously voice
-like finger of

the tree

19

may my heart always be open to little
birds who are the secrets of living
whatever they sing is better than to know
and if men should not hear them men are old

may my mind stroll about hungry
and fearless and thirsty and supple
and even if it's sunday may i be wrong
for whenever men are right they are not young

and may myself do nothing usefully
and love yourself so more than truly
there's never been quite such a fool who could fail
pulling all the sky over him with one smile

20

the people who
rain(are move as)proces
-sion Its of like immens-
ely(a feet which is prayer

among)float withins he
upclimbest And(sky she
)open new(
dark we all findingly Spring the

Fragrance unvisible)ges
-tured together-
ly singing ams
trample(they flyingly silence

21

porky & porkie
sit into a moon)

blacker than dreams
are round like a spoon are
both making silence

two-made-of-one

& nothing tells anywhere
"snow will come soon" &
pretending they're birds sit

creatures of quills
(asleep who must go

things-without-wings

22

you shall above all things be glad and young.
For if you're young,whatever life you wear

it will become you;and if you are glad
whatever's living will yourself become.
Girlboys may nothing more than boygirls need:
i can entirely her only love

whose any mystery makes every man's
flesh put space on;and his mind take off time

that you should ever think,may god forbid
and(in his mercy)your true lover spare:
for that way knowledge lies,the foetal grave
called progress,and negation's dead undoom.

I'd rather learn from one bird how to sing
than teach ten thousand stars how not to dance

50 Poems

to m. m.

I

!blac
k
agains
t

(whi)

te sky
?t
rees whic
h fr

om droppe

d

,
le
af

a:;go

e
s wh
IrlI
n

.g

2

fl

a
tt
ene

d d

reaml
essn
esse

s wa

it
sp
i

t)(t

he
s
e

f

ooli
sh sh
apes

ccocoucougcoughcoughi

ng with me
n more o
n than in the

m

3

If you can't eat you got to

smoke and we aint got
nothing to smoke:come on kid

let's go to sleep
if you can't smoke you got to

Sing and we aint got

nothing to sing;come on kid
let's go to sleep

if you can't sing you got to
die and we aint got

Nothing to die,come on kid

let's go to sleep
if you can't die you got to

dream and we aint got
nothing to dream(come on kid

Let's go to sleep)

4

nobody loved this
he)with its
of eye stuck
into a rock of

forehead.No
body

loved
big that quick
sharp
thick snake of a

voice these

root
like legs
or
feethands;

nobody
ever could ever

had love loved whose his
climbing shoulders queerly twilight
:never,no
(body.

Nothing

5

am was. are leaves few this. is these a or
scratchily over which of earth dragged once
-ful leaf. & were who skies clutch an of poor
how colding hereless. air theres what immense
live without every dancing. singless on-
ly a child's eyes float silently down
more than two those that and that noing our
gone snow gone
                    yours mine
                              We're
alive and shall be:cities may overflow(am
was)assassinating whole grassblades,five
ideas can swallow a man;three words im
-prison a woman for all her now:but we've
such freedom such intense digestion so
much greenness only dying makes us grow

6

flotsam and jetsam
are gentlemen poeds
urseappeal netsam
our spinsters and coeds)

thoroughly bretish
they scout the inhuman
itarian fetish
that man isn't wuman

vive the millenni
um three cheers for labor
give all things to enni
one bugger thy nabor

(neck and senecktie
are gentlemen ppoyds
even whose recktie
are covered by lloyd's

7

moan
(is)
ing

the she of the
sea
un

der a who
a he a moon a
magic out

of the black this which of
one street leaps quick
squirmthicklying lu

minous night
mare som
e w

hereanynoevery
ing(danc)ing
wills&weres

8

the Noster was a ship of swank
(as gallant as they come)
until she hit a mine and sank
just off the coast of Sum

precisely where a craft of cost
the Ergo perished later
all hands(you may recall)being lost
including captain Pater

9

warped this perhapsy
stumbl
i
 NgflounderpirouettiN
                          g

:seized(

tatterdemalion
dow
     nupfloatsw
                    oon
InG

s ly)tuck.s its(ghostsoul sheshape)

elf into leasting forever most
magical maybes of certainly
never the iswas

teetertiptotterish

sp-
    inwhirlpin
                 -wh
EEling
;a!who,

(

whic hbubble ssomethin
gabou tlov
e)

1 0

spoke joe to jack

leave her alone
she's not your gal

jack spoke to joe
's left crashed
pal dropped

o god alice
yells but who shot
up grabbing had
by my throat me

give it him good
a bottle she
quick who stop damned
fall all we go spill

and chairs tables the and
bitch whispers jill
mopping too bad

dear sh not yet
jesus what blood

darling i said

11

red-rag and pink-flag
blackshirt and brown
strut-mince and stink-brag
have all come to town

some like it shot
and some like it hung
and some like it in the twot
nine months young

12

(will you teach a
wretch to live
straighter than a needle)

ask
    her
        ask
            when
                (ask and
                ask
                and ask
again and)ask a
brittle little
person fiddling
in
the
rain

(did you kiss
a girl with nipples
like pink thimbles)

ask
    him
        ask
            who
                (ask and
                ask
                and ask
ago and)ask a
simple
crazy
thing
singing
in the snow

13

proud of his scientific attitude

and liked the prince of wales wife wants to die
but the doctors won't let her comma considers frood
whom he pronounces young mistaken and
cradles in rubbery one somewhat hand
the paper destinies of nations sic
item a bounceless period unshy
the empty house is full O Yes of guk
rooms daughter item son a woopsing queer
colon hobby photography never has plumbed
the heights of prowst but respects artists if
they are sincere proud of his scientif
ic attitude and liked the king of)hear

ye!the godless are the dull and the dull are the damned

14

the way to hump a cow is not
to get yourself a stool
but draw a line around the spot
and call it beautifool

to multiply because and why
dividing thens by nows
and adding and(i understand)
is hows to hump a cows

the way to hump a cow is not
to elevate your tool
but drop a penny in the slot
and bellow like a bool

to lay a wreath from ancient greath
on insulated brows
(while tossing boms at uncle toms)
is hows to hump a cows

the way to hump a cow is not
to push and then to pull
but practicing the art of swot
to preach the golden rull

to vote for me(all decent mem
and wonens will allows
which if they don't to hell with them)
is hows to hump a cows

mrs

& mr across the way are kind of
afraid)afraid

of what(of

a crazy man)don't
ask me how i know(a he of head
comes to some dirty window every)twilight i

feel(his lousy eyes roaming)wonderful all

sky(a little mouth)stumbling(can't
keep up with how big very
them)now(it tears
off rag its

of

mind chucks away flimsy
which but)always(they're
more much further off)further these
those three disappear finally what's left

behind is(just a head of he

is)merely(a pair of ears with some
lips plus a couple of)holes probably that's what
(mr & mrs are

sort of really

really kind
of afraid of)these(down pull & who'll

shades

16

)when what hugs stopping earth than silent is
more silent than more than much more is or
total sun oceaning than any this
tear jumping from each most least eye of star

and without was if minus and shall be
immeasurable happenless unnow
shuts more than open could that every tree
or than all life more death begins to grow

end's ending then these dolls of joy and grief
these recent memories of future dream
these perhaps who have lost their shadows if
which did not do the losing spectres mime

until out of merely not nothing comes
only one snowflake(and we speak our names

17

youful

larger
of smallish)

Humble a
rosily
,nimblest;

c–urlin–g
noworld
Silent is

blue
(sleep!new

girlgold

ecco a letter starting "dearest we"
unsigned:remarkably brief but covering
one complete miracle of nearest far

"i cordially invite me to become
noone except yourselves r s v p"

she cannot read or write,la moon.   Employs
a very crazily how clownlike that
this quickly ghost scribbling from there to where

—name unless i'm mistaken chauvesouris—
whose grammar is atrocious;but so what

princess selene doesn't know a thing
who's much too busy being her beautiful yes.
The place is now
                    let us accept
                              (the time

forever,and you'll wear your silver shoes

there is a here and

that here was a
town(and the town is

so aged the ocean
wanders the streets are so
ancient the houses enter the

people are so feeble the feeble go to
sleep if the people sit down)
and this light is so dark the mountains
grow up from

the sky is so near the earth does not
open her
eyes(but the
feeble are people the feeble
are so wise the people

remember being born)
when and
if nothing disappears they
will disappear always who are filled

with never are more than
more is are mostly
almost are feebler than feeble are

fable who are less than these are least is who
are am(beyond when behind where under

un)

20

harder perhaps than a newengland bed

these ends of arms which pinch that purple book
between what hands had been before they died

squirming:now withered and unself her gnarled
vomits a rock of mindscream into life;
possibly darker than a spinster's heart

my voice feels who inquires is your cough
better today?nn-nn went head face goes

(if how begins a pillow's green means face

or why a quilt's pink stops might equal head).
Then with the splendor of an angel's fart

came one trembling out of huge each eye look
"thank you" nicely the lady's small grin said
(with more simplicity than makes a world)

21

six

are in a room's dark around)
five

(are all dancesing singdance all are

three
with faces made of cloud dancing and
three
singing with voices made of earth and

six are in a room's dark around)

five
(six are in a room's)
one

is red

and(six are in)
four are

white

(three singdance six dancesing three
all around around all
clouds singing three and
and three dancing earths

three menandwomen three

and all around all and
all around five all
around five around)

five flowers five

(six are in a room's dark)
all five are one

flowers five flowers and all one is fire

22

nouns to nouns

wan
wan

too nons too

and
and

nuns two nuns

w an d
ering

in sin

g
ular untheknowndulous s

pring

23

a pretty a day
(and every fades)
is here and away
(but born are maids
to flower an hour
in all,all)

o yes to flower
until so blithe
a doer a wooer
some limber and lithe
some very fine mower
a tall;tall

some jerry so very
(and nellie and fan)
some handsomest harry
(and sally and nan
they tremble and cower
so pale:pale)

for betty was born
to never say nay
but lucy could learn
and lily could pray
and fewer were shyer
than doll.   doll

24

these people socalled were not given hearts
how should they be?their socalled hearts would think
these socalled people have no minds but if
they had their minds socalled would not exist

but if these not existing minds took life
such life could not begin to live id est
breathe but if such life could its breath would stink

and as for souls why souls are wholes not parts
but all these hundreds upon thousands of
people socalled if multiplied by twice
infinity could never equal one)

which may your million selves and my suffice
to through the only mystery of love
become while every sun goes round its moon

25

as freedom is a breakfastfood
or truth can live with right and wrong
or molehills are from mountains made
—long enough and just so long
will being pay the rent of seem
and genius please the talentgang
and water most encourage flame

as hatracks into peachtrees grow
or hopes dance best on bald men's hair
and every finger is a toe
and any courage is a fear
—long enough and just so long
will the impure think all things pure
and hornets wail by children stung

or as the seeing are the blind
and robins never welcome spring
nor flatfolk prove their world is round
nor dingsters die at break of dong
and common's rare and millstones float
—long enough and just so long
tomorrow will not be too late

worms are the words but joy's the voice
down shall go which and up come who
breasts will be breasts thighs will be thighs
deeds cannot dream what dreams can do
—time is a tree(this life one leaf)
but love is the sky and i am for you
just so long and long enough

wherelings whenlings
(daughters of ifbut offspring of hopefear
sons of unless and children of almost)
never shall guess the dimension of

him whose
each
foot likes the
here of this earth

whose both
eyes
love
this now of the sky

—endlings of isn't
shall never
begin
to begin to

imagine how(only are shall be were
dawn dark rain snow rain
-bow &
a

moon
's whis-
per
in sunset

or thrushes toward dusk among whippoorwills or
tree field rock hollyhock forest brook chickadee
mountain.   Mountain)
whycoloured worlds of because do

not stand against yes which is built by
forever & sunsmell
(sometimes a wonder
of wild roses

sometimes)
with north
over
the barn

buy me an ounce and i'll sell you a pound.
Turn
gert
     (spin!
helen)the
slimmer the finger the thicker the thumb(it's
whirl,
girls)
round and round

early to better is wiser for worse.
Give
liz
    (take!
tommy)we
order a steak and they send us a pie(it's
try,
boys)
mine is yours

ask me the name of the moon in the man.
Up
sam
     (down!
alice)a
hole in the ocean will never be missed(it's
in,
girls)
yours is mine

either was deafer than neither was dumb.
Skip
fred
     (jump!
neddy)but
under the wonder is over the why(it's
now,
boys)
here we come

28

there are possibly 2½ or impossibly 3
individuals every several fat
thousand years.   Expecting more would be
neither fantastic nor pathological but

dumb.   The number of times a wheel turns
doesn't determine its roundness:if swallows tryst
in your barn be glad;nobody ever earns
anything, everything little looks big in a mist

and if(by Him Whose blood was for us spilled)
than all mankind something more small occurs
or something more distorting than socalled
civilization i'll kiss a stalinist arse

in hitler's window on wednesday next at 1
E.S.T. bring the kiddies let's all have fun

29

anyone lived in a pretty how town
(with up so floating many bells down)
spring summer autumn winter
he sang his didn't he danced his did.

Women and men(both little and small)
cared for anyone not at all
they sowed their isn't they reaped their same
sun moon stars rain

children guessed(but only a few
and down they forgot as up they grew
autumn winter spring summer)
that noone loved him more by more

when by now and tree by leaf
she laughed his joy she cried his grief
bird by snow and stir by still
anyone's any was all to her

someones married their everyones
laughed their cryings and did their dance
(sleep wake hope and then)they
said their nevers they slept their dream

stars rain sun moon
(and only the snow can begin to explain
how children are apt to forget to remember
with up so floating many bells down)

one day anyone died i guess
(and noone stooped to kiss his face)
busy folk buried them side by side
little by little and was by was

all by all and deep by deep
and more by more they dream their sleep
noone and anyone earth by april
wish by spirit and if by yes.

Women and men(both dong and ding)
summer autumn winter spring
reaped their sowing and went their came
sun moon stars rain

30

the silently little blue elephant shyly(he was terri
bly
warped by his voyage from every to no)who
still stands still as found some lost thing(like a
curtain on which tiny the was painted in round
blue but quite now it's swirly and foldish so only through)the
little blue elephant at the zoo(jumbled
to queer this what that a here and
there a peers at you)has(elephant the blue)put some just
a now and now little the(on his quiet
head his magical shoulders him doll
self)hay completely thus or that wispily
is to say according to his perfect
satisfaction vanishing from a this world into bigger
much some out of(not visible to us)whom only his dream
ing own soul looks
and
the is all floatful and remembering

31

not time's how(anchored in what mountaining roots
of mere eternity)stupendous if
discoverably disappearing floats
at trillionworlded the ecstatic ease

with which vast my complexly wisdoming friend's
—a fingery treesoul onlying from serene
whom queries not suspected selves of space—
life stands gradually upon four minds

(out of some undering joy and overing grief
nothing arrives a so prodigious am
a so immediate is escorts us home
through never's always until absolute un

gulps the first knowledge of death's wandering guess)
while children climb their eyes to touch his dream

32

newlys of silence
(both an only

moon the with star

one moving are twilight
they beyond near)

girlest she slender

is cradling in joy her
flower than now

(softlying wisdoms

enter guess)
childmoon smile to

your breathing doll

33

one slipslouch twi
tterstamp
coon wid a plon
kykerplung
guit
ar
  (pleez make me glad)dis

dumdam slamslum slopp
idy wurl
sho am
wick
id id
ar
  (now heer we kum dearie)bud

hooz
gwine ter
hate
dad hurt
fool wurl no gal no
boy
   (day simbully loves id)fer

ids dare
pain dares un
no
budy elses un ids
dare dare
joy
   (eye kinely thank yoo)

34

my father moved through dooms of love
through sames of am through haves of give,
singing each morning out of each night
my father moved through depths of height

this motionless forgetful where
turned at his glance to shining here;
that if(so timid air is firm)
under his eyes would stir and squirm

newly as from unburied which
floats the first who,his april touch
drove sleeping selves to swarm their fates
woke dreamers to their ghostly roots

and should some why completely weep
my father's fingers brought her sleep:
vainly no smallest voice might cry
for he could feel the mountains grow.

Lifting the valleys of the sea
my father moved through griefs of joy;
praising a forehead called the moon
singing desire into begin

joy was his song and joy so pure
a heart of star by him could steer
and pure so now and now so yes
the wrists of twilight would rejoice

keen as midsummer's keen beyond
conceiving mind of sun will stand,
so strictly(over utmost him
so hugely)stood my father's dream

his flesh was flesh his blood was blood:
no hungry man but wished him food;
no cripple wouldn't creep one mile
uphill to only see him smile.

Scorning the pomp of must and shall
my father moved through dooms of feel;
his anger was as right as rain
his pity was as green as grain

septembering arms of year extend
less humbly wealth to foe and friend
than he to foolish and to wise
offered immeasurable is

proudly and(by octobering flame
beckoned)as earth will downward climb,
so naked for immortal work
his shoulders marched against the dark

his sorrow was as true as bread:
no liar looked him in the head;
if every friend became his foe
he'd laugh and build a world with snow.

My father moved through theys of we,
singing each new leaf out of each tree
(and every child was sure that spring
danced when she heard my father sing)

then let men kill which cannot share,
let blood and flesh be mud and mire,
scheming imagine,passion willed,
freedom a drug that's bought and sold

giving to steal and cruel kind,
a heart to fear,to doubt a mind,
to differ a disease of same,
conform the pinnacle of am

though dull were all we taste as bright,
bitter all utterly things sweet,
maggoty minus and dumb death
all we inherit,all bequeath

and nothing quite so least as truth
—i say though hate were why men breathe—
because my father lived his soul
love is the whole and more than all

35

you which could grin three smiles into a dead
house clutch between eyes emptiness toss one

at nobody shoulder and thick stickingly un

stride after glide massacre monday did
more)ask a lifelump buried by the star
nicked ends next among broken odds of yes
terday's tomorrow(than today can guess

or fears to dare whatever dares to fear)

i very humbly thank you which could grin
may stern particular Love surround your trite
how terrible self hood with its hands and feet

(lift and may pitying Who from sharp soft worms

of spiralling why and out of black because
your absolute courage with its legs and arms

36

i say no world

can hold a you
shall see the not
because
and why but
(who
stood within his steam be-
ginning and
began to sing all
here is hands machine no

good too quick i know this
suit you pay
a store too
much yes what
too much o much cheap
me i work i know i say i have
not any
never
no vacation here

is hands is work since i am
born is good
but there this cheap this suit too
quick no suit there every
-thing
nothing i
say the
world not fit
you)he is

not(i say the world
yes any world is much
too not quite big enough to
hold one tiny this with
time's
more than
most how
immeasurable
anguish

pregnant one fearless
one good yes
completely kind
mindheart one true one generous child-
man
-god one eager
souldoll one
unsellable not buyable alive
one i say human being)one

goldberger

37

these children singing in stone a
silence of stone these
little children wound with stone
flowers opening for

ever these silently lit
tle children are petals
their song is a flower of
always their flowers

of stone are
silently singing
a song more silent
than silence these always

children forever
singing wreathed with singing
blossoms children of
stone with blossoming

eyes
know if a
lit tle
tree listens

forever to always children singing forever
a song made
of silent as stone silence of
song

38

love is the every only god

who spoke this earth so glad and big
even a thing all small and sad
man,may his mighty briefness dig

for love beginning means return
seas who could sing so deep and strong

one querying wave will whitely yearn
from each last shore and home come young

so truly perfectly the skies
by merciful love whispered were,
completes its brightness with your eyes

any illimitable star

39

denied night's face
have shadowless they?
i bring you peace
the moon of day

predicted end
who never began
of god and fiend?
i give you man

extracted hate
from whispering grass?
joy in time shut
and starved on space?

love's murdered eye
dissected to mere
because and why?
take this whole tear.

By handless hints
do conjurers rule?
do mannikins
forbid the soul?

is death a whore
with life's disease
which quacks will cure
when pimps may please?

must through unstrange
synthetic now
true histories plunge?
rains a grey snow

of mothery same
rotting keen dream?
i rise which am
the sun of whom

40

a peopleshaped toomany-ness far too

and will it tell us who we are and will
it tell us why we dream and will it tell
us how we drink crawl eat walk die fly do?

a notalive undead too-nearishness

and shall we cry and shall we laugh and shall
entirely our doom steer his great small
wish into upward deepness of less fear
much than more climbing hope meets most despair?

all knowing's having and have is(you guess)
perhaps the very unkindest way to kill
each of those creatures called one's self so we'll

not have(but i imagine that yes is
the only living thing)and we'll make yes

41

up into the silence the green
silence with a white earth in it

you will(kiss me)go

out into the morning the young
morning with a warm world in it

(kiss me)you will go

on into the sunlight the fine
sunlight with a firm day in it

you will go(kiss me

down into your memory and
a memory and memory

i)kiss me(will go)

42

love is more thicker than forget
more thinner than recall
more seldom than a wave is wet
more frequent than to fail

it is most mad and moonly
and less it shall unbe
than all the sea which only
is deeper than the sea

love is less always than to win
less never than alive
less bigger than the least begin
less littler than forgive

it is most sane and sunly
and more it cannot die
than all the sky which only
is higher than the sky

43

hate blows a bubble of despair into
hugeness world system universe and bang
—fear buries a tomorrow under woe
and up comes yesterday most green and young

pleasure and pain are merely surfaces
(one itself showing,itself hiding one)
life's only and true value neither is
love makes the little thickness of the coin

comes here a man would have from madame death
neverless now and without winter spring?
she'll spin that spirit her own fingers with
and give him nothing(if he should not sing)

how much more than enough for both of us
darling.   And if i sing you are my voice,

44

air,

be
comes
or

(a)

new
(live)
now

;&

th
(is no littler
th

an a:

fear no bigger
th
an a

hope)is

st
anding
st

a.r

45

enters give
whose lost is his found
leading love
whose heart is her mind)

supremely whole
uplifting the,
of each where all
was is to be

welcomes welcomes
her dreams his face
(her face his dreams
rejoice rejoice)

—opens the sun:
who music wear
burst icy known
swim ignorant fire

(adventuring
and time's dead which;
falling falling
both locked in each

down a thief by
a whore dragged goes
to meet her why
she his because

46

grEEn's d

an
cing on hollow was

young Up
floatingly clothes tumbledish
olD(with

sprouts o
ver and)a-
live
wanders remembe

r
ing per
F
ectl
y

crumb
ling eye
-holes oUt of whe
reful whom(leas

tly)
smiles the
infinite nothing

of
M

an

47

(sitting in a tree-)
o small you
sitting in a tree-

sitting in a treetop

riding on a greenest

riding on a greener
(o little i)
riding on a leaf

o least who
sing small thing
dance little joy

(shine most prayer)

48

mortals)

climbi
     ng i
     nto eachness begi
     n
dizzily
       swingthings
of speeds of
trapeze gush somersaults
open ing
       hes shes
&meet&
     swoop
         fully is are ex
               quisite theys of re
turn
     a
     n
     d
fall which now drop who all dreamlike

(im

49

i am so glad and very
merely my fourth will cure
the laziest self of weary
the hugest sea of shore

so far your nearness reaches
a lucky fifth of you
turns people into eachs
and cowards into grow

our can'ts were born to happen
our mosts have died in more
our twentieth will open
wide a wide open door

we are so both and oneful
night cannot be so sky
sky cannot be so sunful
i am through you so i

50

what freedom's not some under's mere above
but breathing yes which fear will never no?
measureless our pure living complete love
whose doom is beauty and its fate to grow

shall hate confound the wise?doubt blind the brave?
does mask wear face?have singings gone to say?
here youngest selves yet younger selves conceive
here's music's music and the day of day

are worlds collapsing?any was a glove
but i'm and you are actual either hand
is when for sale?forever is to give
and on forever's very now we stand

nor a first rose explodes but shall increase
whole truthful infinite immediate us

1 x 1
[One Times One]

1

I

nonsun blob a
cold to
skylessness
sticking fire

my are your
are birds our all
and one gone
away the they

leaf of ghosts some
few creep there
here or on
unearth

II

neither could say
(it comes so slow
not since not why)
both didn't know

exeunt they
(not false not true
not you not i)
it comes so who

III

it's over a(see just
over this)wall
the apples are(yes
they're gravensteins)all
as red as to lose
and as round as to find.

Each why of a leaf says
(floating each how)
you're which as to die
(each green of a new)
you're who as to grow
but you're he as to do

what must(whispers)be must
be(the wise fool)
if living's to give
so breathing's to steal—
five wishes are five
and one hand is a mind

then over our thief goes
(you go and i)
has pulled(for he's we)
such fruit from what bough
that someone called they
made him pay with his now.

But over a(see just
over this)wall
the red and the round
(they're gravensteins)fall
with kind of a blind
big sound on the ground

I V

of all the blessings which to man
kind progress doth impart
one stands supreme i mean the an
imal without a heart.

Huge this collective pseudobeast
(sans either pain or joy)
does nothing except preexist
its hoi in its polloi

and if sometimes he's prodded forth
to exercise her vote
(or made by threats of something worth
than death to change their coat

—which something as you'll never guess
in fifty thousand years
equals the quote and unquote loss
of liberty my dears—

or even is compelled to fight
itself from tame to teem)
still doth our hero contemplate
in raptures of undream

that strictly(and how)scienti
fic land of supernod
where freedom is compulsory
and only man is god.

Without a heart the animal
is very very kind
so kind it wouldn't like a soul
and couldn't use a mind

V

squints a blond
job at her
diamond
solitaire

while guesswho nibbles his ton of torse

squirms a pool
of pink fat
screams a hole
in it

that birth was wicked and life is worse

squats a big
dove on g
w's wig
so what he

is much too busy sitting the horse

VI

my(his from daughter's mother's zero mind
fahrenheit)old infrequently more and
more much(as aprils elsewhere stroll)exhumed

most innocently undecaying friend
hangs at yon gilty ceiling per both pale
orbs thus excluding a leanderless

drowning in sub(at the next)nakedness
(table but three)hero's carnivorous(smile
by lipstick smell by matchabelli)tits

as(while thumb a plus fingers all with blind
him of who)i discreetly(masturbates
one honest breadcrumb)say "i understand

quite what you mean by"
                          sold!to the dollarfull shea
with a weakness for living literature
                                  "loyaltea"

VII

ygUDuh

    ydoan
    yunnuhstan

    ydoan o
    yunnuhstan dem
    yguduh ged

    yunnuhstan dem doidee
    yguduh ged riduh
    ydoan o nudn
LISN bud LISN

        dem
        gud
        am

        lidl yelluh bas
        tuds weer goin

duhSIVILEYEzum

VIII

applaws)

"fell
ow
sit
isn'ts"

(a paw s

IX

a salesman is an it that stinks Excuse

Me whether it's president of the you were say
or a jennelman name misder finger isn't
important whether it's millions of other punks
or just a handful absolutely doesn't
matter and whether it's in lonjewray

or shrouds is immaterial it stinks

a salesman is an it that stinks to please

but whether to please itself or someone else
makes no more difference than if it sells
hate condoms education snakeoil vac
uumcleaners terror strawberries democ
ra(caveat emptor)cy superfluous hair

or Think We've Met subhuman rights Before

X

a politician is an arse upon
which everyone has sat except a man

XI

mr u will not be missed
who as an anthologist
sold the many on the few
not excluding mr u

XII

it was a goodly co
which paid to make man free
(for man is enslaved by a dread dizziz
and the sooner it's over the sooner to biz
don't ask me what it's pliz)

then up rose bishop budge from kew
a anglican was who
(with a rag and a bone and a hank of hair)'d
he picked up a thousand pounds or two
and he smote the monster merde

then up rose pride and up rose pelf
and ghibelline and guelph
and ladios and laddios
(on radios and raddios)
did save man from himself

ye duskiest despot's goldenest gal
did wring that dragon's tail
(for men must loaf and women must lay)
and she gave him a desdemonial
that took his breath away

all history oped her teeming womb
said demon for to doom
yea(fresh complexions being oke
with him)one william shakespeare broke
the silence of the tomb

then up rose mr lipshits pres
(who always nothing says)
and he kisséd the general menedjerr
and they smokéd a robert burns cigerr
to the god of things like they err

XIII

plato told

him:he couldn't
believe it(jesus

told him;he
wouldn't believe
it)lao

tsze
certainly told
him,and general
(yes

mam)
sherman;
and even
(believe it
or

not)you
told him:i told
him;we told him
(he didn't believe it,no

sir)it took
a nipponized bit of
the old sixth

avenue
el;in the top of his head:to tell

him

XIV

pity this busy monster,manunkind,

not.   Progress is a comfortable disease:
your victim(death and life safely beyond)

plays with the bigness of his littleness
—electrons deify one razorblade
into a mountainrange;lenses extend

unwish through curving wherewhen till unwish
returns on its unself.
                    A world of made
is not a world of born—pity poor flesh

and trees,poor stars and stones,but never this
fine specimen of hypermagical

ultraomnipotence.   We doctors know

a hopeless case if—listen:there's a hell
of a good universe next door;let's go

XV

("fire stop thief help murder save the world"

what world?
          is it themselves these insects mean?
when microscopic shriekings shall have snarled
threads of celestial silence huger than
eternity,men will be saviours
                —flop
grasshopper,exactly nothing's soon;
scream,all ye screamers,till your if is up
and vanish under prodigies of un)

"have you" the mountain,while his maples wept
air to blood,asked "something a little child
who's just as small as me can do or be?"
god whispered him a snowflake "yes:you may
sleep now,my mountain" and this mountain slept

while his pines lifted their green lives and smiled

XVI

one's not half two.   It's two are halves of one:
which halves reintegrating,shall occur
no death and any quantity;but than
all numerable mosts the actual more

minds ignorant of stern miraculous
this every truth—beware of heartless them
(given the scalpel,they dissect a kiss;
or,sold the reason,they undream a dream)

one is the song which fiends and angels sing:
all murdering lies by mortals told make two.
Let liars wilt,repaying life they're loaned;
we(by a gift called dying born)must grow

deep in dark least ourselves remembering
love only rides his year.
                              All lose,whole find

X

XVII

one(Floatingly)arrive

(silent)one by(alive)
from(into disappear

and perfectly)nowhere
vivid anonymous
mythical guests of Is

unslowly more who(and
here who there who)descend
-ing(mercifully)touch
deathful earth's any which

Weavingly now one by
wonder(on twilight)they
come until(over dull

all nouns)begins a whole
verbal adventure to

illimitably Grow

XVIII

as any(men's hells having wrestled with)
man drops into his own paradise
thankfully
             whole and the green whereless truth
of an eternal now welcomes each was
of whom among not numerable ams

(leaving a perfectly distinct unhe;
a ticking phantom by prodigious time's
mere brain contrived:a spook of stop and go)
may i achieve another steepest thing—

how more than sleep illimitably my
—being so very born no bird can sing
as easily creation up all sky

(really unreal world,will you perhaps do
the breathing for me while i am away?)

XIX

when you are silent,shining host by guest
a snowingly enfolding glory is

all angry common things to disappear
causing through mystery miracle peace:

or(if begin the colours of your voice)
from some complete existence of to dream
into complete some dream of to exist
a stranger who is i awakening am.

Living no single thing dares partly seem
one atomy once,and every cannot stir
imagining;while you are motionless—

whose moving is more april than the year
(if all her most first little flowers rise

out of tremendous darkness into air)

XX

what if a much of a which of a wind
gives the truth to summer's lie;
bloodies with dizzying leaves the sun
and yanks immortal stars awry?
Blow king to beggar and queen to seem
(blow friend to fiend:blow space to time)
—when skies are hanged and oceans drowned,
the single secret will still be man

what if a keen of a lean wind flays
screaming hills with sleet and snow:
strangles valleys by ropes of thing
and stifles forests in white ago?
Blow hope to terror;blow seeing to blind
(blow pity to envy and soul to mind)
—whose hearts are mountains,roots are trees,
it's they shall cry hello to the spring

what if a dawn of a doom of a dream
bites this universe in two,
peels forever out of his grave
and sprinkles nowhere with me and you?
Blow soon to never and never to twice
(blow life to isn't:blow death to was)
—all nothing's only our hugest home;
the most who die,the more we live

XXI

dead every enormous piece
of nonsense which itself must call
a state submicroscopic is—
compared with pitying terrible
some alive individual

ten centuries of original soon
or make it ten times ten are more
than not entitled to complain
—plunged in eternal now if who're
by the five nevers of a lear

XXII

no man,if men are gods;but if gods must
be men,the sometimes only man is this
(most common,for each anguish is his grief;
and,for his joy is more than joy,most rare)

a fiend,if fiends speak truth;if angels burn

by their own generous completely light,
an angel;or(as various worlds he'll spurn
rather than fail immeasurable fate)
coward,clown,traitor,idiot,dreamer,beast—

such was a poet and shall be and is

—who'll solve the depths of horror to defend
a sunbeam's architecture with his life:
and carve immortal jungles of despair
to hold a mountain's heartbeat in his hand

XXIII

love is a spring at which
crazy they drink who've climbed
steeper than hopes are fears
only not ever named
mountains more if than each
known allness disappears

lovers are mindless they
higher than fears are hopes
lovers are those who kneel
lovers are these whose lips
smash unimagined sky
deeper than heaven is hell

XXIV

(once like a spark)

if strangers meet
life begins—
not poor not rich
(only aware)
kind neither
nor cruel
(only complete)
i not not you
not possible;
only truthful
—truthfully,once
if strangers(who
deep our most are
selves)touch:
forever

(and so to dark)

XXV

what over and which under
burst lurch things phantoms curl
(mouth seekingly lips wander
a finding whom of girl)

dolls clutching their dolls wallow
toys playing writhe with toys
(than are all unworlds hollow
silence has deeper eyes

purest than fear's obscener
brightest than hate's more black
keenest than dying's keener
each will kissed breast awake)

slow tottering visions bigly
come crashing into go
(all than were nevers ugly
beautiful most is now)

XXVI

when god decided to invent
everything he took one
breath bigger than a circustent
and everything began

when man determined to destroy
himself he picked the was
of shall and finding only why
smashed it into because

XXVII

old mr ly
fresh from a fu
ruddy as a sun
with blue true two

man
neral
rise
eyes

"this world's made 'bout
right it's the people that
abuses it you can git
anything you like out

of it if
you gut a mind
to there's something
for everybody it's a"

old mr lyman
ruddy as a sunrise
fresh with blue come
true from

a funeral
eyes
"big
thing"

XXVIII

rain or hail
sam done
the best he kin
till they digged his hole

:sam was a man

stout as a bridge
rugged as a bear
slickern a weazel
how be you

(sun or snow)

gone into what
like all them kings
you read about
and on him sings

a whippoorwill;

heart was big
as the world aint square
with room for the devil
and his angels too

yes,sir

what may be better
or what may be worse
and what may be clover
clover clover

(nobody'll know)

sam was a man
grinned his grin
done his chores
laid him down.

Sleep well

XXIX

let it go—the
smashed word broken
open vow or
the oath cracked length
wise—let it go it
was sworn to
            go

let them go—the
truthful liars and
the false fair friends
and the boths and
neithers—you must let them go they
were born
            to go

let all go—the
big small middling
tall bigger really
the biggest and all
things—let all go
dear
        so comes love

XXX

Hello is what a mirror says
it is a maid says Who
and(hearing not a which)replies
in haste I must be you

no sunbeam ever lies

Bang is the meaning of a gun
it is a man means No
and(seeing something yes)will grin
with pain You so&so

true wars are never won

XXXI

a-

float on some
?
i call twilight you

'll see

an in
-ch
of an if

&

who
is
the

)

more
dream than become
more

am than imagine

XXXII

i've come to ask you if there isn't a
new moon outside your window saying if

that's all,just if"
                    "that's all there is to say"

(and she looked)"especially in winter"(like a leaf
opening)
            as we stood,one(truthed
by wisping tinily the silverest

alive silentness god ever breathed

upon beginning)
                    "beautiful o most
beautiful" her,my life worships and
(night)
            then "everything beautiful can grow"

my,her life marvels "here'll be a canoe

and a whole world and then a single hair
again" marvels "and liars kill their kind

but" her,my "love creates love only" our

XXXIII

open green those
(dear)
worlds of than great
more eyes,and what
were summer's beside their
glories

downward if they'll
or
goldenly float
so(dreaming out
of dreams among)no year
will fall

this than,a least
dare
of snow less quite
is nothing but
herself,and than this(mere
most)breast

spring's million(who
are
and do not wait)
buds imitate
upward each first flower
of two

XXXIV

nothing false and possible is love
(who's imagined,therefore limitless)
love's to giving as to keeping's give;
as yes is to if,love is to yes

must's a schoolroom in the month of may:
life's the deathboard where all now turns when
(love's a universe beyond obey
or command,reality or un-)

proudly depths above why's first because
(faith's last doubt and humbly heights below)
kneeling,we—true lovers—pray that us
will ourselves continue to outgrow

all whose mosts if you have known and i've
only we our least begin to guess

XXXV

except in your
honour,
my loveliest,
nothing
may move may rest
—you bring

(out of dark the
earth)a
procession of
wonders
huger than prove
our fears

were hopes:the moon
open
for you and close
will shy
wings of because;
each why

of star(afloat
on not
quite less than all
of time)
gives you skilful
his flame

so is your heart
alert,
of languages
there's none
but well she knows;
and can

perfectly speak
(snowflake
and rainbow mind
and soul
november and
april)

who younger than
begin
are,the worlds move
in your
(and rest,my love)
honour

XXXVI

true lovers in each happening of their hearts
live longer than all which and every who;
despite what fear denies,what hope asserts,
what falsest both disprove by proving true

(all doubts,all certainties,as villains strive
and heroes through the mere mind's poor pretend
—grim comics of duration:only love
immortally occurs beyond the mind)

such a forever is love's any now
and her each here is such an everywhere,
even more true would truest lovers grow
if out of midnight dropped more suns than are

(yes;and if time should ask into his was
all shall,their eyes would never miss a yes)

XXXVII

we love each other very dearly
                 ,more
than raindrops need synbeams or snowflakes make
possible mayflowers:

           quite eyes of air
not with twilight's first thrushes may awake
more secretly than our(if disappear
should some world)selves

              .No doing shall undo
(nor madness nor mere death nor both who is
la guerre)your me or simplify my you
,darling

      sweet this creative never known
complexity was born before the moon
before God wished Himself into a rose

and even(
          we'll adventure the into
most immemorial of whens
)before

each heartbeat which i am alive to kiss

XXXVIII

yes is a pleasant country:
if's wintry
(my lovely)
let's open the year

both is the very weather
(not either)
my treasure,
when violets appear

love is a deeper season
than reason;
my sweet one
(and april's where we're)

XXXIX

all ignorance toboggans into know
and trudges up to ignorance again:
but winter's not forever,even snow
melts;and if spring should spoil the game,what then?

all history's a winter sport or three:
but were it five,i'd still insist that all
history is too small for even me;
for me and you,exceedingly too small.

Swoop(shrill collective myth)into thy grave
merely to toil the scale to shrillerness
per every madge and mabel dick and dave
—tomorrow is our permanent address

and there they'll scarcely find us(if they do,
we'll move away still further:into now

XL

darling!because my blood can sing
and dance(and does with each your least
your any most very amazing now
or here)let pitiless fear play host
to every isn't that's under the spring
—but if a look should april me,
down isn't's own isn't go ghostly they

doubting can turn men's see to stare
their faith to how their joy to why
their stride and breathing to limp and prove
—but if a look should april me,
some thousand million hundred more
bright worlds than merely by doubting have
darkly themselves unmade makes love

armies(than hate itself and no
meanness unsmaller)armies can
immensely meet for centuries
and(except nothing)nothing's won
—but if a look should april me
for half a when,whatever is less
alive than never begins to yes

but if a look should april me
(though such as perfect hope can feel
only despair completely strikes
forests of mind,mountains of soul)
quite at the hugest which of his who
death is killed dead.   Hills jump with brooks:
trees tumble out of twigs and sticks;

1

XLI

how

tinily
of

squir(two be
tween sto
nes)ming a gr

eenes
t you b
ecome

s whi
(mysterious
ly)te

one
t

hou

XLII

might these be thrushes climbing through almost(do they

beautifully wandering in merciful
miracles wonderingly celebrate day
and welcome earth's arrival with a soul)

sunlight?yes
           (always we have heard them sing
the dark alive but)
              look:begins to grow
more than all real,all imagining;

and we who are we?surely not i not you
behold nor any breathing creature this?
nothing except the impossible shall occur

—see!now himself uplifts of stars the star
(sing!every joy)—wholly now disappear
night's not eternal terrors like a guess.

Life's life and strikes my your our blossoming sphere

XLIII

if(among
silent skies
bluer than believing)a
little gay
earth opening
is all the flowers of his eyes
:april's they

this if now
or this(young
trembling any)into flame
twig or limb
explodes and o
each living ablaze greenly thing
;may has come

love(by yes
every new
bird no bigger than to sing)
leaf is wing
and tree is voice
more leastfully than i am you
,we are spring

XLIV

these(whom;pretends

blue nothing)
are
built of soon carved
of to born of
be

One

:petals
him starrily her
and around
ing swim
snowing

ly upward with Joy,

no
where(no)when
may
breathe
so sky so

.wish

XLV

i think you like"

a strawberry
bang this
blueeyed world(on
which are wintry

handlebars

glued)updives pursued
by its wigglesome whisperful
body and
almost

isn't(grabbed into skies of

grin)"my
flowers"(the humble
man than sunlight
older with ships than

dreams more hands are

offering jonquils)down again
who but zooms
through
one perfectly beautiful bow

"my home ionian isles

XLVI

open your heart:
i'll give you a treasure
of tiniest world
a piece of forever with

summitless younger than
angels are mountains
rivery forests
towerful towns(queen

poet king float
sprout heroes of moonstar
flutter to and
swim blossoms of person)through

musical shadows while hunted
by daemons
seethe luminous
leopards(on wingfeet of thingfear)

come ships go
snowily sailing
perfect silence.
Absolute ocean

XLVII

until and i heard
a certain a bird
i dreamed i could sing
but like nothing
                    are the joys
of his voice

until and who came
with a song like a dream
of a bird with a song
like not anything
                    under skies
over grass

until and until
into flame i can feel
how the earth must fly
if a truth is a cry
                    of a whole
of a soul

until i awoke
for the beautiful sake
of a grave gay brave
bright cry of alive
                    with a trill
like until

XLVIII

so isn't small one littlest why,
it into if shall climb all the
blue heaven green earth neither sea
here's more than room for three of me

and only while your sweet eyes close
have disappeared a million whys;
but opening if are those eyes
every because is murdered twice

XLIX

trees
    were in(give
give)bud when to me
you
made for by love
love said did
o no yes

earth was in
            (live
live)spring
with all beautiful
things when to
me
you gave gave darling

birds are
       in(trees are in)
song
when to me you
leap and i'm born we
're sunlight of
oneness

L

which is the very
(in sad this havingest
world)most merry
most fair most rare
—the livingest givingest
girl on this whirlingest
earth?
      why you're
by far the darlingest

who(on this busily
nowhere rollingest
it)'s the dizzily
he most him
—the climbingly fallingest
fool in this trickiest
if?
   why i'm
by much the luckiest

what of the wonder
(beingest growingest)
over all under
all hate all fear
—all perfectly dyingest
my and foreverless
thy?
      why our
is love and neverless

L I

"sweet spring is your
time is my time is our
time for springtime is lovetime
and viva sweet love"

(all the merry little birds are
flying in the floating in the
very spirits singing in
are winging in the blossoming)

lovers go and lovers come
awandering awondering
but any two are perfectly
alone there's nobody else alive

(such a sky and such a sun
i never knew and neither did you
and everybody never breathed
quite so many kinds of yes)

not a tree can count his leaves
each herself by opening
but shining who by thousands mean
only one amazing thing

(secretly adoring shyly
tiny winging darting floating
merry in the blossoming
always joyful selves are singing)

"sweet spring is your
time is my time is our
time for springtime is lovetime
and viva sweet love"

LII

life is more true than reason will deceive
(more secret or than madness did reveal)
deeper is life than lose:higher than have
—but beauty is more each than living's all

multiplied with infinity sans if
the mightiest meditations of mankind
cancelled are by one merely opening leaf
(beyond whose nearness there is no beyond)

or does some littler bird than eyes can learn
look up to silence and completely sing?
futures are obsolete;pasts are unborn
(here less than nothing's more than everything)

death,as men call him,ends what they call men
—but beauty is more now than dying's when

LIII

o by the by
has anybody seen
little you-i
who stood on a green
hill and threw
his wish at blue

with a swoop and a dart
out flew his wish
(it dived like a fish
but it climbed like a dream)
throbbing like a heart
singing like a flame

blue took it my
far beyond far
and high beyond high
bluer took it your
but bluest took it our
away beyond where

what a wonderful thing
is the end of a string
(murmurs little you-i
as the hill becomes nil)
and will somebody tell
me why people let go

LIV

if everything happens that can't be done
(and anything's righter
than books
could plan)
the stupidest teacher will almost guess
(with a run
skip
around we go yes)
there's nothing as something as one

one hasn't a why or because or although
(and buds know better
than books
don't grow)
one's anything old being everything new
(with a what
which
around we come who)
one's everyanything so

so world is a leaf so tree is a bough
(and birds sing sweeter
than books
tell how)
so here is away and so your is a my
(with a down
up
around again fly)
forever was never till now

now i love you and you love me
(and books are shuter
than books
can be)
and deep in the high that does nothing but fall
(with a shout
each
around we go all)
there's somebody calling who's we

we're anything brighter than even the sun
(we're everything greater
than books
might mean)
we're everyanything more than believe
(with a spin
leap
alive we're alive)
we're wonderful one times one

marion's book

XAIPE

to
hildegarde
watson

I

this(let's remember)day died again and
again;whose golden,crimson dooms conceive

an oceaning abyss of orange dream

larger than sky times earth:a flame beyond
soul immemorially forevering am—
and as collapsing that grey mind by wave
doom disappeared,out of perhaps(who knows?)

eternity floated a blossoming

(while anyone might slowly count to soon)
rose—did you see her?darling,did you(kiss
me)quickly count to never?you were wrong

—then all the way from perfect nowhere came

(as easily as we forget something)
livingest the imaginable moon

hush)
noones
are coming
out in the gloam
ing together are
standing together un
der a particular tree
are all breathing bright darkness to
gether are slowly all together

very magically smiling and if

we are not perfectly careful be
lieve me you and i'll go strolling
right through these each illimit
able to speak very
softly altogeth
er miracu
lous citi
zens of
(hush

3

purer than purest pure
whisper of a whisper

so(big with innocence)
forgivingly a once
of eager glory,no
more miracle may grow

—childfully serious
flower of holiness

a pilgrim from beyond
the future's future;and
immediate like some
newly remembered dream—

flaming a coolly bell
touches most mere until

(eternally)with(now)
luminous the shadow
of love himself:who's we
—nor can you die or i

and every world,before
silence begins a star

4

this out of within itself moo
ving lump of twilight squirts a two
ne like nothing verdi slightly knu

as and some six cents hit the whigh
shaped hathole thangew yelps one shi
ly glad old unman who is eye

5

swim so now million many worlds in each

least less than particle of perfect dark—
how should a loudness called mankind unteach
whole infinite the who of life's life(hark

what silence)?"   "Worlds? o no:i'm certain they're
(look again)flowers."   "Don't worlds open and
worlds close?"   "Worlds do,but differently;or

as if worlds wanted us to understand
they'd never close(and open)if that fool
called everyone(or you or i)were wise."

"You mean worlds may have better luck,some day?"
"Or worse!poor worlds;i mean they're possible
—but" lifting "flowers" more all stars than eyes

"only are quite what worlds merely might be

6

dying is fine)but Death

?o
baby
i

wouldn't like

Death if Death
were
good:for

when(instead of stopping to think)you

begin to feel of it,dying
's miraculous
why?be

cause dying is

perfectly natural;perfectly
putting
it mildly lively(but

Death

is strictly
scientific
& artificial &

evil & legal)

we thank thee
god
almighty for dying

(forgive us,o life!the sin of Death

7

we miss you,jack—tactfully you(with one cocked
eyebrow)subtracting clichés un by un
till the god's truth stands art-naked:you and the fact

that rotgut never was brewed which could knock you down

(while scotch was your breakfast every night all day)
a 3ringbrain you had and a circusheart
and we miss them more than any bright word may cry
—even the crackling spark of(hung in a)"fert

ig"
   (tent-sky wholly wallendas)
                      ready were all

erect your yous to cross the chasm of time
lessness;but two dim disks of stare are still
wondering if the stunt was really a dream—

here's,wherever you aren't or are,good luck!
aberdeen plato–rabelais peter jack

8

o

the round
little man we
loved so isn't

no!w

a gay of a
brave and
a true of a

who have

r
olle
d i

nt

o
n
o

w(he)re

9

possibly thrice we glimpsed—
                              more likely twice
that(once crammed into someone's kitchenette)

wheezing bulgily world of genial plac
-idity(plus,out of much its misbutt-
oned trouserfly tumbling,faded five
or so lightyears of pyjamastring)

a(vastly and particularly)live
that undeluded notselfpitying

lover of all things excellently rare;
obsolete almost that phenomenon
(too gay for malice and too wise for fear)
of shadowy virtue and of sunful sin

namely(ford madox ford)and eke to wit
a human being
                —let's remember that

10

or who and who)

The distance is
more much than all
of timely space
(was and be will)
from beautiful

obvious to

Mere but one small
most of a rose
easily(while
will be goes was)
can travel this

or i and you

I I

so many selves(so many fiends and gods
each greedier than every)is a man
(so easily one in another hides;
yet man can,being all,escape from none)

so huge a tumult is the simplest wish:
so pitiless a massacre the hope
most innocent(so deep's the mind of flesh
and so awake what waking calls asleep)

so never is most lonely man alone
(his briefest breathing lives some planet's year,
his longest life's a heartbeat of some sun;
his least unmotion roams the youngest star)

—how should a fool that calls him "I" presume
to comprehend not numerable whom?

12

tw

o o
ld
o

nce upo

n
a(
n

o mo

re
)time
me

n

sit(l
oo
k)dre

am

13

chas sing does(who
,ins
tead,
smiles alw

ays a trifl
e
w
hile ironin

g!
nob odyknowswhos esh
?i
rt)n't

14

out of more find than seeks

thinking,swim(opening)grow
are(me wander and nows to the

power of blueness)whos(ex-
plore my unreal in

-credible true each new

self)smile.   Eyes.   & we
remember:yes;we played with a piece of when

till it rolled behind forever, we touched a shy
animal called where and she disappeared.

Out of more(fingeryhands

me and whying)seek than finds
feeling(seize)floats(only by

only)a silence only made of,bird

15

hair your a brook
(it through are gaze
the unguessed whys
by me at look)

swirls to engulf
(in which in soft)
firm who outlift
queries of self

pouring(alive
twice)and becomes
eithering dreams
the secret of

16

if the

green
opens
a little a
little
was
much and much
is

too if

the green robe
o
p
e
n
s
and two are

wildstrawberries

17

(swooning)a pillar of youngly

loveflesh topped
with danc
ing egghead strutstrolls

eager a(twice

by
Dizzying eyeplums
pun

ctured)moo

nface swimming
ly
dreamseems

(vivi

d
an O
of

milky tranceworld writhes

in
twi
nn

ingly scarlet woundsmile)

18

a(ncient)a

weigh
tless

puppet of once
man(clutched
by immense

the-seat-of-the
pants
inani
nvisible Fist)drifts

a
long conway
's

unstreet with
treadwatering

nonlegs(strictly)smiling

19

out of the mountain of his soul comes
a keen pure silence)such hands can
build a(who are like ocean patient)dream's

eternity(you feel behind this man
earth's first sunrise)and his voice
is green like growing(is miraculous like
tomorrow)all around the self of this

being are growing stones(neither awake
are goddesses nor sleeping)since he's young
with mysteries(each truly his more than
some eighty years through which that memory strolls)
and every ours for the mere worshipping

(as calmly as if aristide maillols
occurred with any ticking of a clock

20

goo-dmore-ning(en

ter)nize-aday(most
gently herculanean

my mortal)yoo

make sno eye kil
yoo(friend the laughing
grinning)we

no(smiling)strike

agains
De Big Boss
(crying)jew wop
rich poor(sing

ing)

He
    no
        care
            so
                what

yoo-gointa-doo?(ice

coal wood
man)nic
he like
wint-air

nic like ot-am

sum-air(young
old nic)
like spring yoo

un-air-stan?me

crazy
me like

evry-ting

21

jake hates
       all the girls(the
shy ones,the bold
ones;the meek
proud sloppy sleek)
all except the cold
            ones

paul scorns all
        the girls(the
bright ones,the dim
ones;the slim
plump tiny tall)
all except the
        dull ones

gus loves all the
          girls(the
warped ones,the lamed
ones;the mad
moronic maimed)
all except
      the dead ones

mike likes all the girls
           (the
fat ones,the lean
ones;the mean
kind dirty clean)
all
   except the green ones

when serpents bargain for the right to squirm
and the sun strikes to gain a living wage—
when thorns regard their roses with alarm
and rainbows are insured against old age

when every thrush may sing no new moon in
if all screech-owls have not okayed his voice
—and any wave signs on the dotted line
or else an ocean is compelled to close

when the oak begs permission of the birch
to make an acorn—valleys accuse their
mountains of having altitude—and march
denounces april as a saboteur

then we'll believe in that incredible
unanimal mankind(and not until)

23

three wealthy sisters swore they'd never part:
Soul was(i understand)
seduced by Life;whose brother married Heart,
now Mrs Death.   Poor Mind

24

one day a nigger
caught in his hand
a little star no bigger
than not to understand

"i'll never let you go
until you've made me white"
so she did and now
stars shine at night

2 5

pieces(in darker
than small is dirtiest
any city's least
street)of mirror

lying are each(why
do people say it's un
lucky to break one)
whole with sky

26

who sharpens every dull
here comes the only man
reminding with his bell
to disappear a sun

and out of houses pour
maids mothers widows wives
bringing this visitor
their very oldest lives

one pays him with a smile
another with a tear
some cannot pay at all
he never seems to care

he sharpens is to am
he sharpens say to sing
you'd almost cut your thumb
so right he sharpens wrong

and when their lives are keen
he throws the world a kiss
and slings his wheel upon
his back and off he goes

but we can hear him still
if now our sun is gone
reminding with his bell
to reappear a moon

27

"summer is over
—it's no use demanding
that lending be giving;
it's no good pretending
befriending means loving"
(sighs mind:and he's clever)
"for all,yes for all
sweet things are until"

"spring follows winter:
as clover knows,maybe"
(heart makes the suggestion)
"or even a daisy—
your thorniest question
my roses will answer"
"but dying's meanwhile"
(mind murmurs;the fool)

"truth would prove truthless
and life a mere pastime
—each joy a deceiver,
and sorrow a system—
if now than forever
could never(by breathless
one breathing)be" soul
"more" cries:with a smile

28

noone" autumnal this great lady's gaze

enters a sunset "can grow(gracefully or
otherwise)old.   Old may mean anything
which everyone would rather not become;
but growing is" erect her whole life smiled

"was and will always remain:who i am.

Look at these(each serenely welcoming
his only and illimitably his
destiny)mountains!how can each" while flame
crashed "be so am and i and who?each grows"

then in a whisper,as time turned to dream

"and poets grow;and(there—see?)children" nor
might any earth's first morning have concealed
so unimaginably young a star

29

nine birds(rising

through a gold moment)climb:
ing i

-nto
wintry
twi-

light
(all together a
manying
one

-ness)nine
souls
only alive with a single mys-

tery(liftingly
caught upon falling)silent!

ly living the dying of glory

30

snow means that

life is a black cannonadin
g into silenc
e go

lliw

og-dog)life
?
tree3ghosts

are Is A eyes

Strange
known
Face

(whylaughing!among:skydiamonds

31

infinite jukethrob smoke & swallow to dis

gorge)
        a sulky gob with entirely white
eyes of elsewhere
                    jabber while(infinite
fog & puking jukepulse hug)large less
than more magnetic pink unwhores
                                a wai
ter lugs his copious whichwhat skilfully here
&(simply infinite)there &
                    (smoke)a fair
y socked flopslump(& juke)ing shrieks Yew May
n't Dew Thiz Tew Mee
                        as somebody's almost moth
er folds(but infinite)gently up
                        the with
a carroty youth blonde whis(gorgedis reswal
lowing spewnonspew clutch)pers again & again
(jukejog mist & strict)
                & again
                        (ly infin)

It's Snowing Isn't That Perfectly Wonderful

32

blossoming are people

nimbler than Really
go whirling into gaily

white thousands return

by millions and dreaming

drift hundreds come swimming
(Each a keener secret

than silence even tells)

all the earth has turned to sky

are flowers neither why nor how
when is now and which is Who

and i am you are i am we

(pretty twinkle merry bells)

Someone has been born
everyone is noone

dance around the snowman

33

if a cheerfulest Elephantangelchild should sit

(holding a red candle over his head
by a finger of trunk,and singing out of a red

book)on a proud round cloud in a white high night

where his heartlike ears have flown adorable him
self tail and all(and his tail's red christmas bow)
—and if,when we meet again,little he(having flown
even higher)is sunning his penguinsoul in the glow

of a joy which wasn't and isn't and won't be words

while possibly not(at a guess)quite half way down
to the earth are leapandswooping tinily birds
whose magical gaiety makes your beautiful name—

i feel that(false and true are merely to know)
Love only has ever been,is,and will ever be,So

34

a thrown a

-way It
with some-
thing sil
-very

;bright,&:mys(

a thrown a-
way
X
-mas)ter-

i

-ous wisp A of glo-
ry.pr
-ettily
cl(tr)in(ee)gi-

ng

35

light's lives lurch
   a once world quickly from rises

army the gradual of unbeing(fro
on stiffening greenly air and to ghosts go
drift slippery hands tease slim float twitter faces)
only stand with me,love!against these its
until you are and until i am dreams

until comes vast dark until sink last things

(least all turns almost now;now almost swims
into a hair's width:into less?into

not)
  love,stand with me while silence sings

not into nothing and nothing into never
and never into(touch me!love)forever
—until is and shall be and was are night's

total exploding millionminded Who

quick i the death of thing
glimpsed(and on every side
swoop mountains flimsying
become if who'd)

me under a opens
(of petals of silence)
hole bigger than
never to have been

what above did was
always fall
(yes but behind yes)
without or until

no atom couldn't die
(how and am quick i
they'll all not conceive
less who than love)

37

F is for foetus(a

punkslapping
mobsucking
gravypissing poppa but
who just couldn't help it no

matter how hard he never tried)the

great pink
superme
diocri
ty of

a hyperhypocritical D

mocra
c(sing
down with the fascist beast
boom

boom)two eyes

for an eye four
teeth for a tooth
(and the wholly babble open at
blessed are the peacemuckers)

$ $ $ etc(as

the boodle's bent is the
crowd inclined it's
freedom from freedom
the common man wants)

honey swoRkey mollypants

38

why must itself up every of a park

anus stick some quote statue unquote to
prove that a hero equals any jerk
who was afraid to dare to answer "no"?

quote citizens unquote might otherwise
forget(to err is human;to forgive
divine)that if the quote state unquote says
"kill" killing is an act of christian love.

"Nothing" in 1944 A D

"can stand against the argument of mil
itary necessity"(generalissimo e)
and echo answers "there is no appeal

from reason"(freud)—you pays your money and
you doesn't take your choice.   Ain't freedom grand

39

open his head,baby
& you'll find a heart in it
(cracked)

open that heart,mabel
& you'll find a bed in it
(fact)

open this bed,sibyl
& you'll find a tart in it
(wed)

open the tart,lady
& you'll find his mind in it
(dead)

40

i'm
asking
you dear to
what else could a
no but it doesn't
of course but you don't seem
to realize i can't make
it clearer war just isn't what
we imagine but please for god's O
what the hell yes it's true that was
me but that me isn't me
can't you see now no not
any christ but you
must understand
why because
i am
dead

41

whose are these(wraith a clinging with a wraith)

ghosts drowning in supreme thunder?ours
(over you reels and me a moon;beneath,

bombed the by ocean earth bigly shudders)

never was death so alive:chaos so(hark
—that screech of space)absolute(my soul
tastes If as some world of a spark

's gulped by illimitable hell)

and never have breathed such miracle murdered we
whom cannot kill more mostful to arrive
each(futuring snowily which sprints for the
crumb of our Now)twiceuponatime wave—

put out your eyes,and touch the black skin
of an angel named imagination

42

neither awake
(there's your general
yas buy gad)
nor asleep

booted & spurred
with an apish grin
(extremely like
but quite absurd

gloved fist on hip
& the scowl of a cannibal)
there's your mineral
general animal

(five foot five)
neither dead
nor alive
(in real the rain)

43

o to be in finland
now that russia's here)

swing low
sweet ca

rr
y on

(pass the freedoms pappy or
uncle shylock not interested

44

where's Jack Was
General Was
the hero of the Battle of Because
    he's squatting
in the middle of remember
with his rotten old forgotten
full of why
    (rub–her–bub)
    bub?
    (bubs)

where's Jim Soon
Admiral Soon
the saviour of the Navy of the Moon
    he's swooning
at the bottom of the ocean
of forever with a never
in his fly
    (rub–her–bub)
    bub?
    (bubs)

where's John Big
Doughgob Big
pastmaster of the Art of Jigajig
    sitting pretty
on the top of notwithstanding
with his censored up a wench's
rock–a–bye
    (rub–her–bub)
    bub?
    (bubs)

45

when your honest redskin toma
hawked and scalped his victim ,

not to save a world for stalin
was he aiming ;

spare the child and spoil the rod
quoth the palmist .

46

a kike is the most dangerous
machine as yet invented
by even yankee ingenu
ity(out of a jew a few
dead dollars and some twisted laws)
it comes both prigged and canted

47

meet mr universe(who clean

and jerked 300 lbs)i mean
observe his these regard his that(sh)

who made the world's best one hand snatch

48

&(all during the

dropsin
king god my sic
kly a thingish o crashdis
appearing con ter fusion ror collap
sing thatthis is whichwhat yell itfulls o
f cringewiltdroolery i
mean really th
underscream of sudde
nly perishing eagerly everyw
here shutting forever&forever fol
ding int
o absolute gone &
positive quite n
ever & bi
g screeching new black perfectly isn

't)one rose opened

49

this is a rubbish of human rind
with a photograph
clutched in the half
of a hand and the word
love underlined

this is a girl who died in her mind
with a warm thick scream
and a keen cold groan
while the gadgets purred
and the gangsters dined

this is a deaf dumb church and blind
with an if in its soul
and a hole in its life
where the young bell tolled
and the old vine twined

this is a dog of no known kind
with one white eye
and one black eye
and the eyes of his eyes
are as lost as you'll find

50

no time ago
or else a life
walking in the dark
i met christ

jesus)my heart
flopped over
and lay still
while he passed(as

close as i'm to you
yes closer
made of nothing
except loneliness

51

who were so dark of heart they might not speak,
a little innocence will make them sing;
teach them to see who could not learn to look
—from the reality of all nothing

will actually lift a luminous whole;
turn sheer despairing to most perfect gay,
nowhere to here,never to beautiful:
a little innocence creates a day.

And something thought or done or wished without
a little innocence,although it were
as red as terror and as green as fate,
greyly shall fail and dully disappear—

but the proud power of himself death immense
is not so as a little innocence

52

to start,to hesitate;to stop
(kneeling in doubt:while all
skies fall)and then to slowly trust
T upon H,and smile

could anything be pleasanter
(some big dark little day
which seems a lifetime at the least)
except to add an A?

henceforth he feels his pride involved
(this i who's also you)
and nothing less than excellent
E will exactly do

next(our great problem nearly solved)
we dare adorn the whole
with a distinct grandiloquent
deep D;while all skies fall

at last perfection,now and here
—but look:not sunlight?yes!
and(plunging rapturously up)
we spill our masterpiece

53

mighty guest of merely me

—traveller from eternity;
in a single wish,receive
all i am and dream and have.

Be thou gay by dark and day:
gay as only truth is gay
(nothing's false,in earth in air
in water and in fire,but fear—

mind's a coward;lies are laws)
laugh,and make each no thy yes:
love;and give because the why

—gracious wanderer,be thou gay

54

maybe god

is a child
's hand)very carefully
bring
-ing
to you and to
me(and quite with
out crushing)the

papery weightless diminutive

world
with a hole in
it out
of which demons with wings would be streaming if
something had(maybe they couldn't
agree)not happened(and floating-
ly int

o

55

(fea
therr
ain

:dreamin
g field o
ver forest &;

wh
o could
be

so
!f!
te

r?n
oo
ne)

56

a like a
grey
rock wanderin

g
through
pasture
wom

an creature whom
than
earth hers

elf
could
silent more no
be

655

57

(im)c-a-t(mo)
b,i;l:e

FallleA
ps!fl
OattumblI

sh?dr
IftwhirlF
(Ul)(lY)
&&&

away wanders:exact
ly;as if
not
hing had,ever happ
ene

D

58

after screamgroa
ning.ish:ly;
come

  (s

gruntsqueak
,while,
idling-is-grindstone

one;what:of.thumb

stutt(er(s a)mu)ddied
bushscytheblade
"pud-dih-gud"

)S

creang
roami
ngis

59

the little horse is newlY

Born)he knows nothing,and feels
everything;all around whom is

perfectly a strange
ness(Of sun
light and of fragrance and of

Singing)is ev
erywhere(a welcom
ing dream:is amazing)
a worlD.and in

this world lies:smoothbeautifuL
ly folded;a(brea
thing and a gro

Wing)silence,who;
is:somE

oNe.

60

(nothing whichful about

thick big this
friendly
himself of
a boulder)nothing

mean in tenderly

whoms
of sizeless a
silence by noises
called people called

sunlight

(elsewhere flat the mechanical
itmaking
sickness of mind sprawls)
here

a livingly free mysterious

dreamsoul floatstands
oak by birch by maple
pine
by hemlock spruce by

tamarack(

nothing pampered puny
impatient
and nothing
ignoble

)everywhere wonder

61

if(touched by love's own secret)we,like homing
through welcoming sweet miracles of air
(and joyfully all truths of wing resuming)
selves,into infinite tomorrow steer

—souls under whom flow(mountain valley forest)
a million wheres which never may become
one(wholly strange;familiar wholly)dearest
more than reality of more than dream—

how should contented fools of fact envision
the mystery of freedom?yet,among
their loud exactitudes of imprecision,
you'll(silently alighting)and i'll sing

while at us very deafly a most stares
colossal hoax of clocks and calendars

62

in

Spring comes(no-
one
asks his name)

a mender
of things

with eager
fingers(with
patient
eyes)re

-new-

ing remaking what
other
-wise we should
have
thrown a-

way(and whose

brook
-bright flower-
soft bird
-quick voice loves

children
and sunlight and

mountains)in april(but
if he should
 Smile)comes

nobody'll know

63

honour corruption villainy holiness
riding in fragrance of sunlight(side by side
all in a singing wonder of blossoming yes
riding)to him who died that death should be dead

humblest and proudest eagerly wandering
(equally all alive in miraculous day)
merrily moving through sweet forgiveness of spring
(over the under the gift of the earth of the sky

knight and ploughman pardoner wife and nun
merchant frere clerk somnour miller and reve
and geoffrey and all)come up from the never of when
come into the now of forever come riding alive

down while crylessly drifting through vast most
nothing's own nothing children go of dust

64

the of an it ignoblest he
to nowhere from arrive
human the most catastrophe
april might make alive

filthy some past imagining
whowhich of mad rags strode
earth ignorantly blossoming
a scarecrow demongod

countless in hatred pity fear
each more exactly than
the other un good people stare
for it or he is one

65

i thank You God for most this amazing
day:for the leaping greenly spirits of trees
and a blue true dream of sky;and for everything
which is natural which is infinite which is yes

(i who have died am alive again today,
and this is the sun's birthday;this is the birth
day of life and of love and wings:and of the gay
great happening illimitably earth)

how should tasting touching hearing seeing
breathing any—lifted from the no
of all nothing—human merely being
doubt unimaginable You?

(now the ears of my ears awake and
now the eyes of my eyes are opened)

66

the great advantage of being alive
(instead of undying)is not so much
that mind no more can disprove than prove
what heart may feel and soul may touch
—the great(my darling)happens to be
that love are in we,that love are in we

and here is a secret they never will share
for whom create is less than have
or one times one than when times where—
that we are in love,that we are in love:
with us they've nothing times nothing to do
(for love are in we am in i are in you)

this world(as timorous itsters all
to call their cowardice quite agree)
shall never discover our touch and feel
—for love are in we are in love are in we;
for you are and i am and we are(above
and under all possible worlds)in love

a billion brains may coax undeath
from fancied fact and spaceful time—
no heart can leap,no soul can breathe
but by the sizeless truth of a dream
whose sleep is the sky and the earth and the sea.
For love are in you am in i are in we

67

when faces called flowers float out of the ground
and breathing is wishing and wishing is having—
but keeping is downward and doubting and never
—it's april(yes,april;my darling)it's spring!
yes the pretty birds frolic as spry as can fly
yes the little fish gambol as glad as can be
(yes the mountains are dancing together)

when every leaf opens without any sound
and wishing is having and having is giving—
but keeping is doting and nothing and nonsense
—alive;we're alive,dear:it's(kiss me now)spring!
now the pretty birds hover so she and so he
now the little fish quiver so you and so i
(now the mountains are dancing,the mountains)

when more than was lost has been found has been found
and having is giving and giving is living—
but keeping is darkness and winter and cringing
—it's spring(all our night becomes day)o,it's spring!
all the pretty birds dive to the heart of the sky
all the little fish climb through the mind of the sea
(all the mountains are dancing;are dancing)

68

love our so right
is,all(each thing
most lovely)sweet
things cannot spring
but we be they'll

some or if where
shall breathe a new
(silverly rare
goldenly so)
moon,she is you

nothing may,quite
your my(my your
and)self without,
completely dare
be beautiful

one if should sing
(at yes of day)
younger than young
bird first for joy,
he's i he's i

69

now all the fingers of this tree(darling)have
hands,and all the hands have people;and
more each particular person is(my love)
alive than every world can understand

and now you are and i am now and we're
a mystery which will never happen again,
a miracle which has never happened before—
and shining this our now must come to then

our then shall be some darkness during which
fingers are without hands;and i have no
you:and all trees are(any more than each
leafless)its silent in forevering snow

—but never fear(my own,my beautiful
my blossoming)for also then's until

70

blue the triangular why

of a dream(with
crazily
eyes of window)may

be un

less it
were(floati
ng through

never)a kite

like face of
the child who's
every

child(&

therefore invisible)anyhow you
've(whoever
we are)stepped carefully o

ver(& i)some

newer
than life(or than
death)is on

f

ilthi
es
t

sidewalk blossoming glory

71

luminous tendril of celestial wish

(whying diminutive bright deathlessness
to these my not themselves believing eyes
adventuring,enormous nowhere from)

querying affirmation;virginal

immediacy of precision:more
and perfectly more most ethereal
silence through twilight's mystery made flesh—

dreamslender exquisite white firstful flame

—new moon!as(by the miracle of your
sweet innocence refuted)clumsy some
dull cowardice called a world vanishes,

teach disappearing also me the keen
illimitable secret of begin

95 Poems

to marion

l(a

le
af
fa

ll

s)
one
l

iness

2

to stand(alone)in some

autumnal afternoon:
breathing a fatal
stillness;while

enormous this how

patient creature(who's
never by never robbed of
day)puts always on by always

dream,is to

taste
not(beyond
death and

life)imaginable mysteries

3

now air is air and thing is thing:no bliss

of heavenly earth beguiles our spirits,whose
miraculously disenchanted eyes

live the magnificent honesty of space.

Mountains are mountains now;skies now are skies—
and such a sharpening freedom lifts our blood
as if whole supreme this complete doubtless

universe we'd(and we alone had)made

—yes;or as if our souls,awakened from
summer's green trance,would not adventure soon
a deeper magic:that white sleep wherein
all human curiosity we'll spend
(gladly,as lovers must)immortal and

the courage to receive time's mightiest dream

4

this man's heart

is true to his
earth;so
anyone's world
does

-n't interest him(by the

look
feel taste smell
& sound
of a silence who can

guess

ex-
actly
what life
will do)loves

nothing

as much as
how(first
the arri
-v-

in

-g)a snowflake twi-
sts
,on
its way to now

-here

5

crazy jay blue)
demon laughshriek
ing at me
your scorn of easily

hatred of timid
& loathing for(dull all
regular righteous
comfortable)unworlds

thief crook cynic
(swimfloatdrifting
fragment of heaven)
trickstervillain

raucous rogue &
vivid voltaire
you beautiful anarchist
(i salute thee

6

spirit colossal
(& daunted by always
nothing)you darling
diminutive person

jovial ego(&
mischievous tenderly
phoebeing alter)
clown of an angel

everywhere welcome
(but chiefly at home in
snowily nowheres
of winter his silence)

give me a trillionth
part of inquisitive
merrily humble
your livingest courage

7

because you take life in your stride(instead
of scheming how to beat the noblest game
a man can proudly lose,or playing dead
and hoping death himself will do the same

because you aren't afraid to kiss the dirt
(and consequently dare to climb the sky)
because a mind no other mind should try
to fool has always failed to fool your heart

but most(without the smallest doubt)because
no best is quite so good you don't conceive
a better;and because no evil is
so worse than worst you fall in hate with love

—human one mortally immortal i
can turn immense all time's because to why

8

dominic has

a doll wired
to the radiator of his
ZOOM DOOM

icecoalwood truck a

wistful little
clown
whom somebody buried

upsidedown in an ashbarrel so

of course dominic
took him
home

& mrs dominic washed his sweet

dirty
face & mended
his bright torn trousers(quite

as if he were really her &

she
but)& so
that

's how dominic has a doll

& every now & then my
wonderful
friend dominic depaola

gives me a most tremendous hug

knowing
i feel
that

we & worlds

are
less alive
than dolls &

dream

9

both eaching come ghostlike
(inch)wraithish(by inch)grin
ning heshaped two these(stroll
more slowly than trees)

dodreamingly phantoms
(exchanging)è vero
madonna(nudge whispershout)
laugh matching onceupons

each bothing(if)creep(by
if)timelessly foundlost
glad(children of)dirtpoor
(popes emperors)undeaths

through(slapsoothed by sundark)
brightshadowfully fountaining
man's thingfulest godtown
(kissed bigly by bells)

maggie and milly and molly and may
went down to the beach(to play one day)

and maggie discovered a shell that sang
so sweetly she couldn't remember her troubles,and

milly befriended a stranded star
whose rays five languid fingers were;

and molly was chased by a horrible thing
which raced sideways while blowing bubbles:and

may came home with a smooth round stone
as small as a world and as large as alone.

For whatever we lose(like a you or a me)
it's always ourselves we find in the sea

I I

in time's a noble mercy of proportion
with generosities beyond believing
(though flesh and blood accuse him of coercion
or mind and soul convict him of deceiving)

whose ways are neither reasoned nor unreasoned,
his wisdom cancels conflict and agreement
—saharas have their centuries;ten thousand
of which are smaller than a rose's moment

there's time for laughing and there's time for crying—
for hoping for despair for peace for longing
—a time for growing and a time for dying:
a night for silence and a day for singing

but more than all(as all your more than eyes
tell me)there is a time for timelessness

12

lily has a rose
(i have none)
"don't cry dear violet
you may take mine"

"o how how how
could i ever wear it now
when the boy who gave it to
you is the tallest of the boys"

"he'll give me another
if i let him kiss me twice
but my lover has a brother
who is good and kind to all"

"o no no no
let the roses come and go
for kindness and goodness do
not make a fellow tall"

lily has a rose
no rose i've
and losing's less than winning(but
love is more than love)

13

So shy shy shy(and with a
look the very boldest man
can scarcely dare to meet no matter

how he'll try to try)

So wrong(wrong wrong)and with a
smile at which the rightest man
remembers there is such a thing

as spring and wonders why

So gay gay gay and with a
wisdom not the wisest man
will partly understand(although

the wisest man am i)

So young young young and with a
something makes the oldest man
(whoever he may be)the only

man who'll never die

14

but also dying

(as well as
to cry and sing,
my love

and wonder)is something

you have and i
've been
doing as long as to

(yes)forget(and longer

dear)our
birth's the because of a
why but our doom is

to grow(remember

this my sweet)not
only
wherever the sun and the stars and

the

moon
are we're;but
also

nowhere

15

on littlest this
the of twig three
souls sit
round with cold

three(huddling a-
gainst one immense
deep hell
-o of keen

moon)dream unthings
silent three like
your my
life and our

16

in time of daffodils(who know
the goal of living is to grow)
forgetting why,remember how

in time of lilacs who proclaim
the aim of waking is to dream,
remember so(forgetting seem)

in time of roses(who amaze
our now and here with paradise)
forgetting if,remember yes

in time of all sweet things beyond
whatever mind may comprehend,
remember seek(forgetting find)

and in a mystery to be
(when time from time shall set us free)
forgetting me,remember me

17

for prodigal read generous
—for youth read age—
read for sheer wonder mere surprise
(then turn the page)

contentment read for ecstasy
—for poem prose—
caution for curiosity
(and close your eyes)

18

once White&Gold

daisy in the Dust
(trite now and old)

lie we so must

most lily brief

(rose here&gone)
flesh all is If

all blood And When

19

un(bee)mo

vi
n(in)g
are(th
e)you(o
nly)

asl(rose)eep

20

off a pane)the
(dropp
ingspinson
his

back mad)fly(ly
who
all at)stops
(once

2 1

joys faces friends

feet terrors fate
hands silence eyes
love laughter death

(dreams hopes despairs)

Once
        happened
nowhere else
imagine
            Now

rapidly this

(a
    forest has slowly
Murdered the House)
hole swallows it
                self

while nobody

(and stars moon
sun fall rise come
go rain snow)

remembers

22

why from this her and him
did you and did i climb
(crazily kissing)till

into themselves we fell—

how have all time and space
bowed to immortal us
if in one little bed

she and he lie(undead)

23

albutnotquitemost

lost(in this br
am
bliest tangle of hi
llside)a

few dim tombstones

try to re(still u
ntumbled but slant
ing drun
kenly)mind

me of noone i ever &

someone(the others have
long ago laid
them)i never(selves
any than

every more silent

ly)heard(& how
look at it blue is the
high is
the deep is the far o my

darling)of(down

24

dim
i
nu
tiv

e this park is e
mpty(everyb
ody's elsewher
e except me 6 e

nglish sparrow
s)a
utumn & t
he rai

n
th
e
raintherain

25

that melancholy

fellow'll play
his handorgan
until you say

"i want a fortune"

.At which(smiling)he stops:
& pick
ing up a magical stick
t,a,p,s

this dingy cage:then with a ghost

's rainfaint windthin
voice-which-is
no-voice sobcries

"paw?lee"

—whereupon out(SlO
wLy)steps(to
mount the wand)a by no
means almost

white morethanPerson;who

(riding through space
to diminutive this
opened drawer)tweak

S with his brutebeak

one fatal faded(pinkish or
yellowish maybe)piece
of pitiful paper—
but now,as Mr bowing Cockatoo

proffers the meaning of the stars

14th st dis(because my tears
are full of eyes)appears.   Because
only the truest things always

are true because they can't be true

26

round a so moon could dream(i sus

pect)only god himself & as
loveless some world not any un

god manufacture might but man

kind yet in park this grim most(these

one who are)lovers cling & kiss
neither beholding a nor seen

by some that bum who's every one

27

jack's white horse(up

high in
the night
at the end
of doubleyou

4th)reminds me

in spite of his buggy of
lady godiva
& that(for no reason at
all)reminds

me the

cheerfulest goddamned
sonofabitch
i ever met
or hope to meet in

the course of a shall we say somewhat

diversified
(putting
it
quietly)

life was a blindman

28

as joe gould says in

his terrifyingly hu
man man
ner the only reason every wo
man

should

go to college is so
that she never can(kno
wledge is po
wer)say o

if i

'd
OH
n
lygawntueco

llege

29

ev erythingex Cept:

that
's what she's
got

—ex

cept what?
why
,what it

Takes.   now

you know(just as
well as i
do)what

it takes;& i don't mean It—

&
i don't
mean any

thing real

Ly what
;or ev
erythi

ng which.   but,

som
e
th

ing:Who

30

what Got him was Noth

ing & nothing's exAct
ly what any
one Living(or some
body Dead
like
even a Poet)could
hardly express what
i Mean is
what knocked him over Wasn't
(for instance)the Knowing your

whole(yes god

damned)life is a Flop or even
to
Feel how
Everything(dreamed
& hoped &
prayed for
months & weeks & days & years
& nights &
forever)is Less Than
Nothing(which would have been

Something)what got him was nothing

31

a he as o
ld as who stag
geri
ng up some streetfu

l of peopl
e lurche
s viv
idly

from ti(& d
esperate
ly)m
e to ti

me shru
gg
ing as if to say b
ut for chreyesake how ca

n
i s
ell drunk if i
be pencils

32

who(at

her nons-
elf
's unself too
-thf-
ully lee
-r-

ing)can this plati

-num fl-
oozey
begin to(a
-lm-
ost)imagi
-n-

e she is

33

a gr

eyhaire
d(m
utteri
ng)bab
yfa

ced

dr(lun
g)u
(ing)
nk g

RowL

(eyeaintu)
s
(hfraiduh

nOHw

u
n)

!

34

ADHUC SUB JUDICE LIS

when mack smacked phyllis on the snout

frank sank him with an uppercut
but everybody(i believe)

else thought lucinda looked like steve

3 5

"so you're hunting for ann well i'm looking for will"
"did you look for him down by the old swimminghole"
"i'd be worse than a fool to have never looked there"
"and you couldn't well miss willy's carroty hair"

"it seems like i just heard your annabel screech
have you hunted her round by the rasberrypatch"
"i have hunted her low i have hunted her high
and that pretty pink pinafore'd knock out your eye"

"well maybe she's up to some tricks with my bill
as long as there's haymows you never can tell"
"as long as there's ladies my annie is one
nor she wouldn't be seen with the likes of your son"

"and who but your daughter i'm asking yes who
but that sly little bitch could have showed billy how"
"your bastard boy must have learned what he knows
from his slut of a mother i rather suppose"

"will's dad never gave me one cent in his life
but he fell for a whore when he married his wife
and here is a riddle for you red says
it aint his daughter her father lays"

"black hell upon you and all filthy men
come annabel darling come annie come ann"
"she's coming right now in the rasberrypatch
and 'twas me that she asked would it hurt too much

and 'twas me that looked up at my willy and you
in the newmown hay and he telling you no"
"then look you down through the old swimminghole
there'll be slime in his eyes and a stone on his soul"

36

yes but even

4 or(&
h
ow)dinary
a

meri

can b
usiness soca
lled me
n dis

cussing "parity" in l'hô

tel nor
man(rue d
e l'échelle)
die can't

quite poison God's sunlight

37

handsome and clever and he went cruising
into a crazy dream
two were a hundred million whos
(while only himself was him)

two were the cleanest keenest bravest
killers you'd care to see
(while a stuttering ghost that maybe had shaved
three times in its life made three)

brawny and brainy they sing and they whistle
(now here is a job to be done)
while a wisp of why as thick as my fist
stuck in the throat of one

two came hurrying home to the dearest
little women alive
(but jim stood still for a thousand years
and then lay down with a smile)

38

s.ti:rst;hiso,nce;ma:n

c
ollapse
d

.i:ns;unli,gh;t:

"ah
gwonyuhdoanfool
me"

toitselfw.hispering

39

THANKSGIVING (1956)

a monstering horror swallows
this unworld me by you
as the god of our fathers' fathers bows
to a which that walks like a who

but the voice-with-a-smile of democracy
announces night & day
"all poor little peoples that want to be free
just trust in the u s a"

suddenly uprose hungary
and she gave a terrible cry
"no slave's unlife shall murder me
for i will freely die"

she cried so high thermopylae
heard her and marathon
and all prehuman history
and finally The UN

"be quiet little hungary
and do as you are bid
a good kind bear is angary
we fear for the quo pro quid"

uncle sam shrugs his pretty
pink shoulders you know how
and he twitches a liberal titty
and lisps "i'm busy right now"

so rah-rah-rah democracy
let's all be as thankful as hell
and bury the statue of liberty
(because it begins to smell)

40

silence

.is
a
looking
bird:the

turn
ing;edge,of
life

(inquiry before snow

4 ¹

Beautiful

is the
unmea
ning
of(sil

ently)fal

ling(e
ver
yw
here)s

Now

42

from spiralling ecstatically this

proud nowhere of earth's most prodigious night
blossoms a newborn babe:around him,eyes
—gifted with every keener appetite
than mere unmiracle can quite appease—
humbly in their imagined bodies kneel
(over time space doom dream while floats the whole

perhapsless mystery of paradise)

mind without soul may blast some universe
to might have been,and stop ten thousand stars
but not one heartbeat of this child;nor shall
even prevail a million questionings
against the silence of his mother's smile

—whose only secret all creation sings

43

who(is?are)who

(two faces at a dark
window)this father and his
child are watching snowflakes
(falling & falling & falling)

eyes eyes

looking(alw
ays)while
earth and sky grow
one with won

der until(see

the)with the
bigger much than biggest
(little is)now(dancing yes for)white
ly(joy!joy!joy)and whiteliest all

wonderings are silence is becom

ing each
truebeautifully
more-than-thing
(& falling &)

EverychildfatheringOne

44

—laughing to find
anyone's blind
(like me like you)
except in snow—

a whom we make
(of grin for smile
whose head's his face
with stones for eyes

for mind with none)
boy after girl
each brings a world
to build our clown

—shouting to see
what no mind knows
a mindless he
begins to guess

what no tongue tells
(such as ourselves)
begins to sing
an only grin—

dancing to feel
nots are their whys
stones become eyes
locks open keys

haven't is have
doubt and believe
(like me like you)
vanish in so

—laughing to find
a noone's more
by far than you're
alive or i'm—

crying to lose
(as down someone
who's we ungrows)
a dream in the rain

45

i love you much(most beautiful darling)

more than anyone on the earth and i
like you better than everything in the sky

—sunlight and singing welcome your coming

although winter may be everywhere
with such a silence and such a darkness
noone can quite begin to guess

(except my life)the true time of year—

and if what calls itself a world should have
the luck to hear such singing(or glimpse such
sunlight as will leap higher than high
through gayer than gayest someone's heart at your each

nearerness)everyone certainly would(my
most beautiful darling)believe in nothing but love

46

never could anyone
who simply lives to die
dream that your valentine
makes happier me than i

but always everything
which only dies to grow
can guess and as for spring
she'll be the first to know

47

out of night's almosT Floats a colour(in

-to day's bloodlight climbs the onlying
world)
      whose
silence are cries
poems children dreams &

through slowquickly opening ifless

this irre-
VocA
-ble flame

is
   lives
      breath
          es(over-

ing
   un
-derfully & a-
rounding
      death)

L

o

v

e

48

someone i am wandering a town(if its
houses turning into themselves grow

silent upon new perfectly blue)

i am any(while around him streets
taking moment off by moment day
thankfully become each other)one who

feels a world crylaughingly float away

leaving just this strolling ghostly doll
of an almost vanished me(for whom
the departure of everything real is the
arrival of everything true)and i'm

no(if deeply less conceivable than
birth or death or even than breathing shall

blossom a first star)one

49

noone and a star stand,am to am

(life to life;breathing to breathing
flaming dream to dreaming flame)

united by perfect nothing:

millionary wherewhens distant,as
reckoned by the unimmortal mind,
these immeasurable mysteries
(human one;and one celestial)stand

soul to soul:freedom to freedom

till her utmost secrecies and his
(dreaming flame by flaming dream)
merge—at not imaginable which

instant born,a(who is neither each
both and)Self adventures deathlessness

50

!

o(rounD)moon,how
do
you(rouNd
er
than roUnd)float;
who
lly &(rOunder than)
go
:ldenly(Round
est)

?

51

f

  eeble a blu
r of cr
umbli
ng m

oo

   n(
poor shadoweaten
was
of is and un of

so

)h
   ang
   s
   from

thea lmo st mor ning

52

why

do the
fingers

of the lit
tle once beau
tiful la

dy(sitting sew
ing at an o
pen window this
fine morning)fly

instead of dancing
are they possibly
afraid that life is
running away from
them(i wonder)or

isn't she a
ware that life(who
never grows old)
is always beau

tiful and
that nobod
y beauti

ful ev
er hur

ries

53

n

ot eth
eold almos
tladyf eebly
hurl ing
cr u

mb

son ebyo
neatt wothre
efourfi ve&six
engli shsp
arr ow

s

54

ardensteil–henarub–izabeth)

this noN
allgotupfittokill
She with the
& how

p-e-r-f-e-c-t-l-y-d-e-a-d

Unvoice(which frightenS
a noisy most
park's
least timorous pigeons)squ

-I-

nts(while showe
ring cigaretteash O
ver that scre
Amingfeeblyoff

s,p;r:i;n,g

55

you no

tice
nobod
y wants

Less(not to men

tion least)& i
ob
serve no

body wants Most

(not
putting it mildly
much)

may

be be
cause
ever

ybody

wants more
(& more &
still More)what the

hell are we all morticians?

56

home means that
when the certainly
roof leaks it
's our(home

means if any moon
or possibly
sun shines they are
our also my

darling)but should some im
probably
unworld crash
to 1

nonillion(& so)nothings
each(let's
kiss)means
home

57

old age sticks
up Keep
Off
signs)&

youth yanks them
down(old
age
cries No

Tres)&(pas)
youth laughs
(sing
old age

scolds Forbid
den Stop
Must
n't Don't

&)youth goes
right on
gr
owing old

730

58

a total stranger one black day
knocked living the hell out of me—

who found forgiveness hard because
my(as it happened)self he was

—but now that fiend and i are such
immortal friends the other's each

59

when any mortal(even the most odd)

can justify the ways of man to God
i'll think it strange that normal mortals can

not justify the ways of God to man

60

dive for dreams
or a slogan may topple you
(trees are their roots
and wind is wind)

trust your heart
if the seas catch fire
(and live by love
though the stars walk backward)

honour the past
but welcome the future
(and dance your death
away at this wedding)

never mind a world
with its villains or heroes
(for god likes girls
and tomorrow and the earth)

6 1

Young m
oon:be kind to olde
r this
m

ost ol
d than(a

sleep)whom and tipto
e t

hrough
his dream;dancin

g you
Star

62

your birthday comes to tell me this

—each luckiest of lucky days
i've loved,shall love,do love you,was

and will be and my birthday is

63

precisely as unbig a why as i'm
(almost too small for death's because to find)
may,given perfect mercy,live a dream
larger than alive any star goes round

—a dream sans meaning(or whatever kills)
a giving who(no taking simply which)
a marvel every breathing creature feels
(but none can think)a learning under teach—

precisely as unbig as i'm a why
(almost too small for dying's huge because)
given much mercy more than even the
mercy of perfect sunlight after days

of dark,will climb;will blossom:will sing(like
april's own april and awake's awake)

64

out of the lie of no
rises a truth of yes
(only herself and who
illimitably is)

making fools understand
(like wintry me)that not
all matterings of mind
equal one violet

65

first robin the;
you say something
(for only me)
and gone is who.

since becomes why:
old turns to young
(winter goodbye)
april hello,

66

"but why should"

the
greatest
of

living magicians(whom

you and i
some
times call

april)must often

have
wondered
"most

people be quite

so(when flowers)in
credibly
(always are beautiful)

ugly"

67

this little huge

-eyed per-
son(nea
-rly burs-

ting with the

in
-expressib-
le

num

-berlessn-
ess of her
selves)can't

u

-nderstan-
d my o
-nl-

y me

68

the(oo)is

lOOk
(aliv
e)e
yes

are(chIld)and

wh(g
o
ne)
o

w(A)a(M)s

69

over us if(as what was dusk becomes

darkness)innumerably singular
strictly immeasurable nowhere flames
—its farthest silence nearer than each our

heartbeat—believe that love(and only love)

comprehends huger easily beyonds
than timelessly alive all glories we've
agreed with nothing deeper than our minds

to call the stars.   And(darling)never fear:

love,when such marvels vanish,will include
—there by arriving magically here—
an everywhere which you've and i've agreed
and we've(with one last more than kiss)to call

most the amazing miracle of all

70

whatever's merely wilful,
and not miraculous
(be never it so skilful)
must wither fail and cease
—but better than to grow
beauty knows no

their goal(in calm and fury:
through joy and anguish)who've
made her,outglory glory
the little while they live—
unless by your thinking
forever's long

let beauty touch a blunder
(called life)we die to breathe,
itself becomes her wonder
—and wonderful is death;
but more,the older he's
the younger she's

71

stand with your lover on the ending earth—

and while a(huge which by which huger than
huge)whoing sea leaps to greenly hurl snow

suppose we could not love,dear;imagine

ourselves like living neither nor dead these
(or many thousand hearts which don't and dream
or many million minds which sleep and move)
blind sands,at pitiless the mercy of

time time time time time

—how fortunate are you and i,whose home
is timelessness:we who have wandered down
from fragrant mountains of eternal now

to frolic in such mysteries as birth
and death a day(or maybe even less)

7 2

i shall imagine life
is not worth dying,if
(and when)roses complain
their beauties are in vain

but though mankind persuades
itself that every weed's
a rose,roses(you feel
certain)will only smile

73

let's,from some loud unworld's most rightful wrong

climbing,my love(till mountains speak the truth)
enter a cloverish silence of thrushsong

(and more than every miracle's to breathe)

wounded us will becauseless ultimate
earth accept and primeval whyless sky;
healing our by immeasurable night

spirits and with illimitable day

(shrived of that nonexistence millions call
life,you and i may reverently share
the blessed eachness of all beautiful
selves wholly which and innocently are)

seeming's enough for slaves of space and time
—ours is the now and here of freedom.   Come

74

sentinel robins two
guard me and you
and little house this our
from hate from fear

a which of slim of blue
of here will who
straight up into the where
so safe we are

7 5

(hills chime with thrush)

A
hummingbird princess
FlOaTs
doll-angel-life
from

Bet:To;Bouncing,Bet

the
ruby&emerald zigging
HE
of a zagflash king
poUnc

es buzzsqueaking th

ey
tangle in twitter
y t
wofroing chino
ise

r(!)i(?)e(.)s

these from my mother's greatgrandmother's rosebush white

roses are probably the least probable roses
of her improbable world and without any doubt
of impossible ours
               —God's heaven perhaps comprises
poems(my mother's greatgrandmother surely would know)
of purest poem and glories of sheerest glory
a little more always less believably so
than(how should even omnipotent He feel sorry
while these were blossoming)roses which really are dreams
of roses—
          "and who" i asked my love "could begin
to imagine quite such eagerly innocent whoms
of merciful sweetness except Himself?"
                    —"noone
unless it's a smiling" she told me "someone"(and smiled)

"who holds Himself as the little white rose of a child"

77

i am a little church(no great cathedral)
far from the splendor and squalor of hurrying cities
—i do not worry if briefer days grow briefest,
i am not sorry when sun and rain make april

my life is the life of the reaper and the sower;
my prayers are prayers of earth's own clumsily striving
(finding and losing and laughing and crying)children
whose any sadness or joy is my grief or my gladness

around me surges a miracle of unceasing
birth and glory and death and resurrection:
over my sleeping self float flaming symbols
of hope,and i wake to a perfect patience of mountains

i am a little church(far from the frantic
world with its rapture and anguish)at peace with nature
—i do not worry if longer nights grow longest;
i am not sorry when silence becomes singing

winter by spring,i lift my diminutive spire to
merciful Him Whose only now is forever:
standing erect in the deathless truth of His presence
(welcoming humbly His light and proudly His darkness)

78

all nearness pauses,while a star can grow

all distance breathes a final dream of bells;
perfectly outlined against afterglow
are all amazing the and peaceful hills

(not where not here but neither's blue most both)

and history immeasurably is
wealthier by a single sweet day's death:
as not imagined secrecies comprise

goldenly huge whole the upfloating moon.

Time's a strange fellow;
                          more he gives than takes
(and he takes all)nor any marvel finds
quite disappearance but some keener makes
losing,gaining
                 —love! if a world ends

more than all worlds begin to(see?)begin

79

whippoorwill this

moonday into
(big with unthings)

tosses hello

whirling whose rhyme

(spilling his rings)
threeing alive

pasture and hills

80

if the Lovestar grows most big

a voice comes out of some dreaming tree
(and how i'll stand more still than still)
and what he'll sing and sing to me

and while this dream is climbing sky
(until his voice is more than bird)
and when no am was ever as i

then that Star goes under the earth

81

here's s

omething round(& so
mething lost)& som
ething like
a mind with
out a body(turn
ing silently to a
lmost)dis
appearing
how patiently be

coming some(&

merciful
ly which is
every)un(star
rain snow moon
dream wing tree
leaf bird
sun
& singing &)
thing found

one old blue wheel in a pasture

82

now comes the good rain farmers pray for(and
no sharp shrill shower bouncing up off
burned earth but a blind blissfully seething
gift wandering deeply through godthanking ground)

bluest whos of this snowy head we call
old frank go bluer still as(shifting his life
from which to which)he reaches the barn's immense
doorway and halts propped on a pitchfork(breathing)

lovers like rej and lena smile(while looming
darkly a kindness of fragrance opens around
them)and whisper their joy under entirely the coming
quitenotimaginable silenceofsound

(here is that rain awaited by leaves with all
their trees and by forests with all their mountains)

83

perished have safe small
facts of hilltop
(barn house wellsweep
forest & clearing)

gone are enormous
near far silent
truths of mountain
(strolling is there here

everywhere fairyair
feelable heavenless
warm sweet mistfully
whispering rainlife)

infinite also
ourselves exist sans
shallbe or was
(laws clocks fears hopes

beliefs compulsions
doubts & corners)
worlds are to dream now
dreams are to breathe

84

how generous is that himself the sun

—arriving truly,faithfully who goes
(never a moment ceasing to begin
the mystery of day for someone's eyes)

with silver splendors past conceiving who

comforts his children,if he disappears;
till of more much than dark most nowhere no
particle is not a universe—

but if,with goldenly his fathering

(as that himself out of all silence strolls)
nearness awakened,any bird should sing:
and our night's thousand million miracles

a million thousand hundred nothings seem
—we are himself's own self;his very him

85

here pasture ends—
this girl and boy
who're littler than
(day disappears)

their heartbeats dare
some upward world
of each more most
prodigious Selves

both now alive
creatures(bright if
by shadowy
if)swallowing

is everywhere
beginningless
a Magic of
green solitude

(go marvels come)
as littler much
than littlest they
adventure(wish

by terror)steep
not guessable
each infinite
Oblivions

found a by lost
child and a(float
through sleeping firsts
of wonder)child

unbreathingly
share(huge Perhaps
by hugest)dooms
of miracle

drift killed swim born
a dream and(through
stillness beyond
conceiving)dream

until No least
leaf almost stirs
as never(in
againless depths

of silence)and
forever touch
or until she
and he become

(on tiptoe at
the very quick
of nowhere)we
—While one thrush sings

86

this
forest pool
A so

of Black
er than est
if

Im
agines
more than life

must die to
merely
Know

87

now(more near ourselves than we)
is a bird singing in a tree,
who never sings the same thing twice
and still that singing's always his

eyes can feel but ears may see
there never lived a gayer he;
if earth and sky should break in two
he'd make them one(his song's so true)

who sings for us for you for me
for each leaf newer than can be:
and for his own(his love)his dear
he sings till everywhere is here

88

joyful your complete fearless and pure love
with one least ignorance may comprehend
more than shall ever provingly disprove
eithering vastnesses of orish mind

—nothing believable inhabits here:
overs of known descend through depths of guess,
shadows are substances and wings are birds;
unders of dream adventure truths of skies—

darling of darlings!by that miracle
which is the coming of pure joyful your
fearless and complete love,all safely small
big wickedly worlds of world disappear

all and(like any these my)words of words
turn to a silence who's the voice of voice

89

now what were motionless move(exists no

miracle mightier than this:to feel)
poor worlds must merely do,which then are done;
and whose last doing shall not quite undo
such first amazement as a leaf—here's one

more than each creature new(except your fear
to whom i give this little parasol,
so she may above people walk in the air
with almost breathing me)—look up:and we'll

(for what were less than dead)dance,i and you;
high(are become more than alive)above
anybody and fate and even Our
whisper it Selves but don't look down and to

-morrow and yesterday and everything except love

90

rosetree,rosetree
—you're a song to see:whose
all(you're a sight to sing)
poems are opening,
as if an earth was
playing at birthdays

each(a wish no
bigger than)in roguish
am of fragrance
dances a honeydunce;
whirling's a frantic
struts a pedantic

proud or humble,
equally they're welcome
—as if the humble proud
youngest bud testified
"giving(and giving
only)is living"

worlds of prose mind
utterly beyond is
brief that how infinite
(deeply immediate
fleet and profound this)
beautiful kindness

sweet such(past can's
every can't)immensest
mysteries contradict
a deathful realm of fact
—by their precision
evolving vision

dreamtree,truthtree
tree of jubilee:with
aeons of (trivial
merely)existence,all
when may not measure
a now of your treasure

blithe each shameless
gaiety of blossom
—blissfully nonchalant
wise and each ignorant
gladness—unteaches
what despair preaches

myriad wonder
people of a person;
joyful your any new
(every more only you)
most emanation
creates creation

lovetree!least the
rose alive must three,must
four and(to quite become
nothing)five times,proclaim
fate isn't fatal
—a heart her each petal

91

unlove's the heavenless hell and homeless home

of knowledgeable shadows(quick to seize
each nothing which all soulless wraiths proclaim
substance;all heartless spectres,happiness)

lovers alone wear sunlight.   The whole truth

not hid by matter;not by mind revealed
(more than all dying life,all living death)
and never which has been or will be told

sings only—and all lovers are the song.

Here(only here)is freedom:always here
no then of winter equals now of spring;
but april's day transcends november's year

(eternity being so sans until
twice i have lived forever in a smile)

92

i carry your heart with me(i carry it in
my heart)i am never without it(anywhere
i go you go,my dear;and whatever is done
by only me is your doing,my darling)
                                        i fear
no fate(for you are my fate,my sweet)i want
no world(for beautiful you are my world,my true)
and it's you are whatever a moon has always meant
and whatever a sun will always sing is you

here is the deepest secret nobody knows
(here is the root of the root and the bud of the bud
and the sky of the sky of a tree called life;which grows
higher than soul can hope or mind can hide)
and this is the wonder that's keeping the stars apart

i carry your heart(i carry it in my heart)

93

spring!may—
everywhere's here
(with a low high low
and the bird on the bough)
how?why
—we never we know
(so kiss me)shy sweet eagerly my
most dear

(die!live)
the new is the true
and to lose is to have
—we never we know—
brave!brave
(the earth and the sky
are one today)my very so gay
young love

why?how—
we never we know
(with a high low high
in the may in the spring)
live!die
(forever is now)
and dance you suddenly blossoming tree
—i'll sing

94

being to timelessness as it's to time,
love did no more begin than love will end;
where nothing is to breathe to stroll to swim
love is the air the ocean and the land

(do lovers suffer?all divinities
proudly descending put on deathful flesh:
are lovers glad?only their smallest joy's
a universe emerging from a wish)

love is the voice under all silences,
the hope which has no opposite in fear;
the strength so strong mere force is feebleness:
the truth more first than sun more last than star

—do lovers love?why then to heaven with hell.
Whatever sages say and fools,all's well

95

if up's the word;and a world grows greener
minute by second and most by more—
if death is the loser and life is the winner
(and beggars are rich but misers are poor)
—let's touch the sky:
                        with a to and a fro
(and a here there where)and away we go

in even the laziest creature among us
a wisdom no knowledge can kill is astir—
now dull eyes are keen and now keen eyes are keener
(for young is the year,for young is the year)
—let's touch the sky:
                        with a great(and a gay
and a steep)deep rush through amazing day

it's brains without hearts have set saint against sinner;
put gain over gladness and joy under care—
let's do as an earth which can never do wrong does
(minute by second and most by more)
—let's touch the sky:
                        with a strange(and a true)
and a climbing fall into far near blue

if beggars are rich(and a robin will sing his
robin a song)but misers are poor—
let's love until noone could quite be(and young is
the year,dear)as living as i'm and as you're
—let's touch the sky:
                        with a you and a me
and an every(who's any who's some)one who's we

73 Poems

I

O the sun comes up-up-up in the opening

sky(the all the
any merry every pretty each

bird sings birds sing
gay-be-gay because today's today)the
romp cries i and the me purrs

you and the gentle
who-horns says-does moo-woo
(the prance with the
three white its stimpstamps)

the grintgrunt wugglewiggle
champychumpchomps yes
the speckled strut begins to scretch and
scratch-scrutch

and scritch(while
the no-she-yes-he fluffies tittle
tattle did-he-does-she)& the

ree ray rye roh
rowster shouts

rawrOO

2

for any ruffian of the sky
your kingbird doesn't give a damn—
his royal warcry is I AM
and he's the soul of chivalry

in terror of whose furious beak
(as sweetly singing creatures know)
cringes the hugest heartless hawk
and veers the vast most crafty crow

your kingbird doesn't give a damn
for murderers of high estate
whose mongrel creed is Might Makes Right
—his royal warcry is I AM

true to his mate his chicks his friends
he loves because he cannot fear
(you see it in the way he stands
and looks and leaps upon the air)

3

seeker of truth

follow no path
all paths lead where

truth is here

4

SONG

but we've the may
(for you are in love
and i am)to sing,
my darling:while
old worlds and young
(big little and all
worlds)merely have
the must to say

and the when to do
is exactly theirs
(dull worlds or keen;
big little and all)
but lose or win
(come heaven,come hell)
precisely ours
is the now to grow

it's love by whom
(my beautiful friend)
the gift to live
is without until:
but pitiful they've
(big little and all)
no power beyond
the trick to seem

their joys turn woes
and right goes wrong
(dim worlds or bright;
big little and all)
whereas(my sweet)
our summer in fall
and in winter our spring
is the yes of yes

love was and shall
be this only truth
(a dream of a deed,
born not to die)
but worlds are made
of hello and goodbye:
glad sorry or both
(big little and all)

5

the first of all my dreams was of
a lover and his only love,
strolling slowly(mind in mind)
through some green mysterious land

until my second dream begins—
the sky is wild with leaves;which dance
and dancing swoop(and swooping whirl
over a frightened boy and girl)

but that mere fury soon became
silence:in huger always whom
two tiny selves sleep(doll by doll)
motionless under magical

foreverfully falling snow.
And then this dreamer wept:and so
she quickly dreamed a dream of spring
—how you and i are blossoming

6

fair ladies tall lovers
riding are through the
(with wonder into colours
all into singing)may

wonder a with deep
(A so wonder pure)
even than the green
the new the earth more

moving(all gay
fair brave tall young
come they)through the may
in fragrance and song

wonderingly come
(brighter than prayers)
riding through a Dream
like fire called flowers

over green the new
earth a day of may
under more a blue
than blue can be sky

always(through fragrance
and singing)come lovers
with slender their ladies
(Each youngest)in sunlight

7

it's

so damn sweet when Anybody—
yes;no

matter who,some

total(preferably
blonde
of course)

or on the other

well
your oldest
pal
for instance(or

;why

even
i
suppose
one
's wife)

—does doesn't unsays says looks smiles

or simply Is
what makes
you feel you
aren't

6 or 6

teen or sixty
000,000
anybodyelses—

but for once

(imag
-ine)

You

8

plant Magic dust

expect hope doubt
(wonder mistrust)
despair
and right
where soulless our
(with all their minds)
eyes blindly stare

life herSelf stands

9

now is a ship

which captain am
sails out of sleep

steering for dream

10

because it's

Spring
thingS

dare to do people

(& not
the other way

round)because it

's A
pril

Lives lead their own

persons(in
stead

of everybodyelse's)but

what's wholly
marvellous my

Darling

is that you &
i are more than you

& i(be

ca
us

e It's we)

11

humble one(gifted with

illimitable joy)
bird sings love's every truth

beyond all since and why

asking no favor but

(while down come blundering
proud hugenesses of hate

sometimes called world)to sing

12

Me up at does

out of the floor
quietly Stare

a poisoned mouse

still who alive

is asking What
have i done that

You wouldn't have

13

o
nly this
darkness(in
whom always i
do nothing)deepens
with wind(and hark
begins to

      Rain)a

house
like shape
stirs through(not
numerably
or as lovers a
chieve oneness)each
othering

      Selves i

sit
(hearing
the rain)un
til against my
(where three dreams live)fore
head is stumbling
someone(named

      Morning)

14

a great

man
is
gone.

Tall as the truth

was who:and
wore his(mountains
understand

how)life

like a(now
with
one sweet sun

in it,now with a

million
flaming billion kinds
of nameless

silence)sky;

15

at just 5 a
m i hear eng
(which cannot sing)
lish sparrows say

then 2 or per
(who can and do
fat pigeons coo)
haps even 4

now man's most vast
(unmind by brain)
more than machine
turns less than beast

at 6 this bell
's whisper asks(of
a world born deaf)
"heaven or hell"

16

e
cco the uglies
t

s
ub
sub

urba
n skyline on earth between whose d
owdy

hou
se
s

l
ooms an eggyellow smear of wintry sunse
t

17

n
Umb a
stree
t's wintr

y ugli
nes
s C
omprises

6
twirls of do
gsh
it m

uch f
ilt
h
Y slus

h & h
ideou
s 3 m
aybe

o
nce V
o
ices

18

nobody could
                in superhuman flights
of submoronic fancy
                            be more not

conceivably future than mrs somethingwitz

nay somethingelsestein.   Death should take his hat
off to this dame:he won't be out of work
while she can swarm.   To doubt that in whose form
less form all goodness truth and beauty lurk,
simply to her does not occur(alarm
ing notion for idealists?so what)

all politicians like the sight of vote

and politics,as everyone knows,is
wut ektyouelly metus.   Unbeside
which limps who might less frenziedly have cried

eev mahmah hadn chuzd nogged id entwhys

19

everybody happy?
WE-WE-WE
& to hell with the chappy
who doesn't agree

(if you can't dentham
comma bentham;
or 1 law for the lions &
oxen is science)

Q:how numb can an unworld get?
A:number

20

fearlessandbosomy

this
grand:gal
who

liked men horses roses

& $(in
that
order)is

      wHISpEr

it
left;at the age
of

8

ysomethi
ng
(imagine)

with,pansies

2 I

why

don't
be
sil
ly

,o no in-

deed;
money
can't do(never
did &

never will)any

damn
thing
:far
from it;you

're wrong,my friend.   But

what does
do,
has always done
;&

will do alw

-ays something
is(guess)yes
you're
right:my enemy

.   Love

annie died the other day

never was there such a lay—
whom,among her dollies,dad
first("don't tell your mother")had;
making annie slightly mad
but very wonderful in bed
—saints and satyrs,go your way

youths and maidens:let us pray

23

nite)
thatthis
crou
    ched

moangrowl-&-thin
g stirs(m
id)a
life whats wh

(un)ich(cur
ling)s
    ilentl
y are(mi

dnite also conce
als 2 ph
antoms clutch
ed in

a writhewho room)as
hows of
whi
   ne
      climbscr

e
AM
e
xploding aRe(n't

24

insu nli gh t

o
verand
o
vering

A

onc
eup
ona
tim

e ne wsp aper

25

a grin without a
face(a look
without an i)
be care

ful(touch noth
ing)or
it'll disapp
ear bangl

essly(into sweet
the earth)&
nobody
(including our

selves)
will reme
mber
(for 1 frac

tion of
a mo
ment)where
what how

when
who why
which
(or anything)

26

if seventy were young
and death uncommon
(forgiving not divine,
to err inhuman)
or any thine a mine
—dingdong:dongding—
to say would be to sing

if broken hearts were whole
and cowards heroes
(the popular the wise,
a weed a tearose)
and every minus plus
—fare ill:fare well—
a frown would be a smile

if sorrowful were gay
(today tomorrow,
doubting believing and
to lend to borrow)
or any foe a friend
—cry nay:cry yea—
november would be may

that you and i'd be quite
—come such perfection—
another i and you,
is a deduction
which(be it false or true)
disposes me to shoot
dogooding folk on sight

27

in heavenly realms of hellas dwelt
two very different sons of zeus:
one,handsome strong and born to dare
—a fighter to his eyelashes—
the other,cunning ugly lame;
but as you'll shortly comprehend
a marvellous artificer

now Ugly was the husband of
(as happens every now and then
upon a merely human plane)
someone completely beautiful;
and Beautiful,who(truth to sing)
could never quite tell right from wrong,
took brother Fearless by the eyes
and did the deed of joy with him

then Cunning forged a web so subtle
air is comparatively crude;
an indestructible occult
supersnare of resistless metal:
and(stealing toward the blissful pair)
skilfully wafted over them-
selves this implacable unthing

next,our illustrious scientist
petitions the celestial host
to scrutinize his handiwork:
they(summoned by that savage yell
from shining realms of regions dark)
laugh long at Beautiful and Brave
—wildly who rage,vainly who strive;
and being finally released
flee one another like the pest

thus did immortal jealousy
quell divine generosity,
thus reason vanquished instinct and
matter became the slave of mind;
thus virtue triumphed over vice
and beauty bowed to ugliness
and logic thwarted life:and thus—
but look around you,friends and foes

my tragic tale concludes herewith:
soldier,beware of mrs smith

28

"right here the other night something
odd occurred" charlie confessed
(halting)"a tall strong young
finelooking fellow,dressed

well but not over,stopped
me by 'could you spare three cents please'
—why guesswho nearly leaped
out of muchtheworseforwear shoes

'fair friend' we enlightened this stranger
'some people have all the luck;
since our hero is quite without change,you're
going to get one whole buck'

not a word this stranger replied—
but as one whole buck became his
(believe it or don't)by god
down this stranger went on both knees"

green turns red(the roar
of traffic collapses:through
west ninth slowly cars pour
into sixth avenue)

"then" my voice marvels "what happened"
as everywhere red goes green
—groping blank sky with a blind
stare,he whispers "i ran"

29

the greedy the people
(as if as can yes)
they sell and they buy
and they die for because
though the bell in the steeple
says Why

the chary the wary
(as all as can each)
they don't and they do
and they turn to a which
though the moon in her glory
says Who

the busy the millions
(as you're as can i'm)
they flock and they flee
through a thunder of seem
though the stars in their silence
say Be

the cunning the craven
(as think as can feel)
they when and they how
and they live for until
though the sun in his heaven
says Now

the timid the tender
(as doubt as can trust)
they work and they pray
and they bow to a must
though the earth in her splendor
says May

30

one winter afternoon

(at the magical hour
when is becomes if)

a bespangled clown
standing on eighth street
handed me a flower.

Nobody,it's safe
to say,observed him but

myself;and why?because

without any doubt he was
whatever(first and last)

mostpeople fear most:
a mystery for which i've
no word except alive

—that is,completely alert
and miraculously whole;

with not merely a mind and a heart

but unquestionably a soul—
by no means funereally hilarious

(or otherwise democratic)
but essentially poetic
or ethereally serious:

a fine not a coarse clown
(no mob,but a person)

and while never saying a word

who was anything but dumb;
since the silence of him

self sang like a bird.
Mostpeople have been heard
screaming for international

measures that render hell rational
—i thank heaven somebody's crazy

enough to give me a daisy

31

POEM(or
"the divine right of majorities,
that illegitimate offspring of the
divine right of kings" Homer Lea)

here are five simple facts no sub

human superstate ever knew
(1)we sans love equals mob
love being youamiare(2)

the holy miraculous difference between

firstrate & second implies nonth
inkable enormousness by con
trast with the tiny stumble from second to tenth

rate(3)as it was in the begin

ning it is now and always will be or
the onehundredpercentoriginal sin
cerity equals perspicuity(4)

Only The Game Fish Swims Upstream &(5)
unbeingdead isn't beingalive

32

all which isn't singing is mere talking
and all talking's talking to oneself
(whether that oneself be sought or seeking
master or disciple sheep or wolf)

gush to it as deity or devil
—toss in sobs and reasons threats and smiles
name it cruel fair or blessed evil—
it is you(né i)nobody else

drive dumb mankind dizzy with haranguing
—you are deafened every mother's son—
all is merely talk which isn't singing
and all talking's to oneself alone

but the very song of(as mountains
feel and lovers)singing is silence

33

christ but they're few

all(beyond win
or lose)good true
beautiful things

god how he sings

the robin(who
'll be silent in
a moon or two)

34

"nothing" the unjust man complained
"is just"("or un-" the just rejoined

3 5

the trick of finding what you didn't lose
(existing's tricky:but to live's a gift)
the teachable imposture of always
arriving at the place you never left

(and i refer to thinking)rests upon
a dismal misconception;namely that
some neither ape nor angel called a man
is measured by his quote eye cue unquote.

Much better than which,every woman who's
(despite the ultramachinations of
some loveless infraworld)a woman knows;
and certain men quite possibly may have

shall we say guessed?"
                        "we shall" quoth gifted she:
and played the hostess to my morethanme

36

if in beginning twilight of winter will stand

(over a snowstopped silent world)one
spirit serenely truly himself;and

alone only as greatness is alone—

one(above nevermoving all nowhere)
goldenly whole,prodigiously alive
most mercifully glorying keen star

whom she-and-he-like ifs of am perceive

(but believe scarcely may)certainly while
mute each inch of their murdered planet grows
more and enormously more less:until
her-and-his nonexistence vanishes

with also earth's
                    —"dying" the ghost of you
whispers "is very pleasant" my ghost to

37

now that,more nearest even than your fate

and mine(or any truth beyond perceive)
quivers this miracle of summer night

her trillion secrets touchably alive

—while and all mysteries which i or you
(blinded by merely things believable)
could only fancy we should never know

are unimaginably ours to feel—

how should some world(we marvel)doubt,for just
sweet terrifying the particular
moment it takes one very falling most
(there:did you see it?)star to disappear,

that hugest whole creation may be less
incalculable than a single kiss

38

silently if,out of not knowable
night's utmost nothing,wanders a little guess
(only which is this world)more my life does
not leap than with the mystery your smile

sings or if(spiralling as luminous
they climb oblivion)voices who are dreams,
less into heaven certainly earth swims
than each my deeper death becomes your kiss

losing through you what seemed myself,i find
selves unimaginably mine;beyond
sorrow's own joys and hoping's very fears

yours is the light by which my spirit's born:
yours is the darkness of my soul's return
—you are my sun,my moon,and all my stars

39

white guardians of the universe of sleep

safely may by imperishable your
glory escorted through infinite countries be
my darling(open the very secret of hope
to her eyes,not any longer blinded with
a world;and let her heart's each whisper wear

all never guessed unknowable most joy)

faithfully blossoming beyond to breathe
suns of the night,bring this beautiful
wanderer home to a dream called time:and give
herself into the mercy of that star,
if out of climbing whom begins to spill
such golden blood as makes his moon alive

sing more will wonderfully birds than are

40

your homecoming will be my homecoming—

my selves go with you,only i remain;
a shadow phantom effigy or seeming

(an almost someone always who's noone)

a noone who,till their and your returning,
spends the forever of his loneliness
dreaming their eyes have opened to your morning

feeling their stars have risen through your skies:

so,in how merciful love's own name,linger
no more than selfless i can quite endure
the absence of that moment when a stranger
takes in his arms my very life who's your

—when all fears hopes beliefs doubts disappear.
Everywhere and joy's perfect wholeness we're

41

a round face near the top of the stairs
speaks in his kind sweet big voice:
then a slender face(on the mantelpiece
of a bedroom)begins to croon

more particularly at just
midnight this hearty fellow'll exist
—whereas that delicate creature is most
herself while uttering one

a third face,away in the sky
finally faintly(higher than high
in the rain in the wind in the dark)whispers.
And i and my love are alone

42

n
OthI
n

g can

s
urPas
s

the m

y
SteR
y

of

s
tilLnes
s

43

may i be gay

like every lark
who lifts his life

from all the dark

who wings his why

beyond because
and sings an if

of day to yes

44

Now i lay(with everywhere around)
me(the great dim deep sound
of rain;and of always and of nowhere)and

what a gently welcoming darkestness—

now i lay me down(in a most steep
more than music)feeling that sunlight is
(life and day are)only loaned:whereas
night is given(night and death and the rain

are given;and given is how beautifully snow)

now i lay me down to dream of(nothing
i or any somebody or you
can begin to begin to imagine)

something which nobody may keep.
now i lay me down to dream of Spring

45

what time is it?it is by every star
a different time,and each most falsely true;
or so subhuman superminds declare

—nor all their times encompass me and you:

when are we never,but forever now
(hosts of eternity;not guests of seem)
believe me,dear,clocks have enough to do

without confusing timelessness and time.

Time cannot children,poets,lovers tell—
measure imagine,mystery,a kiss
—not though mankind would rather know than feel;

mistrusting utterly that timelessness

whose absence would make your whole life and my
(and infinite our)merely to undie

46

out of midsummer's blazing most not night
as floats a more than day whose sun is moon,
and our(from inexistence moving)sweet
earth puts on immortality again

—her murdered selves exchanging swiftly for
the deathlessness who's beauty:reoccurs
so magically,farthest becomes near
(one silent pasture,all a heartbeat dares;

that mountain,any god)while leaf twig limb
ask every question time can't answer:and
such vivid nothing as green meteors swim
signals all some world's millionary mind

never may partly guess—thus,my love,to
merely what dying must call life are you

47

without the mercy of
your eyes your
voice your
ways(o very most my shining love)

how more than dark i am,
no song(no
thing)no
silence ever told;it has no name—

but should this namelessness
(completely
fleetly)
vanish,at the infinite precise

thrill of your beauty,then
my lost my
dazed my
whereful selves they put on here again

—to livingest one star
as small these
all these
thankful(hark)birds singing wholly are

48

t,h;r:u;s,h;e:s

are
silent
now

.in silverly

notqu
-it-
eness

dre(is)ams

a
the
o

f moon

49

faithfully tinying at twilight voice
of deathless earth's innumerable doom:
againing(yes by microscopic yes)
acceptance of irrevocable time

particular pure truth of patience heard
above the everywhereing fact of fear;
and under any silence of each bird
who dares to not forsake a failing year

—now,before quite your whisper's whisper is
subtracted from my hope's own hope,receive
(undaunted guest of dark most downwardness
and marvellously self diminutive

whose universe a single leaf may be)
the more than thanks of always merest me

50

while a once world slips from
few of sun fingers numb)

with anguished each their me
brains of that this and tree
illimitably try
to seize the doom of sky

(silently all then known
things or dreamed become un-

51

but

he" i
staring

into winter twi

light(whisper)"was
my friend" reme
mbering "&

friendship

is a
miracle"
his always
not imaginably

morethanmostgenerous

spirit.   Feeling
only
(jesus)every(god)

where

(chr
ist)

what absolute nothing

52

who are you,little i

(five or six years old)
peering from some high

window;at the gold

of november sunset

(and feeling:that if day
has to become night

this is a beautiful way)

53

of all things under our
blonder than blondest star

the most mysterious
(eliena,my dear)is this

—how anyone so gay
possibly could die

54

timeless

ly this
(merely and whose
not

numerable leaves are

fall
i
ng)he

StandS

lift
ing against the
shrieking

sky such one

ness as
con
founds

all itcreating winds

55

i
never
guessed any
thing(even a
universe)might be
so not quite believab
ly smallest as perfect this
(almost invisible where of a there of a)here of a
rubythroat's home with its still
ness which really's herself
(and to think that she's
warming three worlds)
who's ama
zingly
Eye

56

"could that" i marvelled "be

you?"
and a chickadee
to all the world,but to me some
(by name
myself)one long ago
who had died

,replied

57

mi(dreamlike)st

makes
big each dim
inuti

ve turns obv

ious t
o s
trange

un

til o
urselve
s are

will be wor

(magi
c
ally)

lds

58

& sun &

sil
e
nce
e

very

w
here
noon
e

is exc

ep
t
on
t

his

b
oul
der
a

drea(chipmunk)ming

59

who is this
dai
   nty
mademoiselle

the o
    f her
luminous
se
   lf
a shy(an

if a
   whis
per a where
a hidi
     ng)est

meta
ph
  or
?la lune

60

2 little whos
(he and she)
under are this
wonderful tree

smiling stand
(all realms of where
and when beyond)
now and here

(far from a grown
-up i&you-
ful world of known)
who and who

(2 little ams
and over them this
aflame with dreams
incredible is)

6 1

one

t
hi
s

snowflake

(a
  li
    ght
  in
g)

is upon a gra

v
es
t

one

62

now does our world descend
the path to nothingness
(cruel now cancels kind;
friends turn to enemies)
therefore lament,my dream
and don a doer's doom

create is now contrive;
imagined,merely know
(freedom:what makes a slave)
therefore,my life,lie down
and more by most endure
all that you never were

hide,poor dishonoured mind
who thought yourself so wise;
and much could understand
concerning no and yes:
if they've become the same
it's time you unbecame

where climbing was and bright
is darkness and to fall
(now wrong's the only right
since brave are cowards all)
therefore despair,my heart
and die into the dirt

but from this endless end
of briefer each our bliss—
where seeing eyes go blind
(where lips forget to kiss)
where everything's nothing
—arise,my soul;and sing

63

(listen)

this a dog barks and
how crazily houses
eyes people smiles
faces streets
steeples are eagerly

tumbl

ing through wonder
ful sunlight
—look—
selves,stir:writhe
o-p-e-n-i-n-g

are(leaves;flowers)dreams

,come quickly come
run run
with me now
jump shout(laugh
dance cry

sing)for it's Spring

—irrevocably;
and in
earth sky trees
:every
where a miracle arrives

(yes)

you and i may not
hurry it with
a thousand poems
my darling
but nobody will stop it

With All The Policemen In The World

64

"o purple finch
                please tell me why
this summer world(and you and i
who love so much to live)
                                must die"

"if i
        should tell you anything"
(that eagerly sweet carolling
self answers me)
                        "i could not sing"

65

"though your sorrows not
any tongue may name,
three i'll give you sweet
joys for each of them
But it must be your"
whispers that flower

murmurs eager this
"i will give you five
hopes for any fear,
but it Must be your"
perfectly alive
blossom of a bliss

"seven heavens for
just one dying,i'll
give you" silently
cries the(whom we call
rose a)mystery
"but it must be Your"

66

D-re-A-mi-N-gl-Y

leaves
(sEe)
locked

in

gOLd
after-
gLOw

are

t
ReMbLiN
g

, ; : . . ; , ,

67

enter no(silence is the blood whose flesh
is singing)silence:but unsinging.   In
spectral such hugest how hush,one

dead leaf stirring makes a crash

—far away(as far as alive)lies
april;and i breathe-move-and-seem some
perpetually roaming whylessness—

autumn has gone:will winter never come?

o come,terrible anonymity;enfold
phantom me with the murdering minus of cold
—open this ghost with millionary knives of wind—
scatter his nothing all over what angry skies and

gently
        (very whiteness:absolute peace,
never imaginable mystery)
                        descend

68

what is
a
voyage

?

up
upup:go
ing

downdowndown

com;ing won
der
ful sun

moon stars the all,& a

(big
ger than
big

gest could even

begin to be)dream
of;a thing:of
a creature who's

O

cean
(everywhere
nothing

but light and dark;but

never forever
& when)un
til one strict

here of amazing most

now,with what
thousands of(hundreds
of)millions of

CriesWhichAreWings

69

!hope
faith!
!life
love!

bells cry bells
(the sea of the sky is
ablaze with their
voices)all

shallbe and was
are drowned by
prodigious a
now of magnificent

sound(which
makes
this
whenworld squirm

turns
houses to
people and streets
into faces and cities

to eyes)drift
bells glide
seethe
glow

(undering proudly
humbly overing)
all bright all
things swim climb minds

(down
slowly swoop wholly
up
leaping through merciful

sunlight)to
burst
in
a thunder of oneness

dream!
!joy
truth!
!soul

70

pity his how illimitable plight
who dies to be at any moment born—
some for whom crumbs of colour can create

precision more than angels fear to learn

and even fiends:or,if he paints with sound,
newly one moving cadence may release
the fragrance of a freedom which no mind

contrives(but certainly each spirit is)

and partially imagine whose despair
when every silence will not make a dream
speak;or if to no millionth metaphor
opens the simple agony of time

—small wonder such a monster's fellowmen
miscalled are happy should his now go then

71

how many moments must(amazing each
how many centuries)these more than eyes
restroll and stroll some never deepening beach

locked in foreverish time's tide at poise,

love alone understands:only for whom
i'll keep my tryst until that tide shall turn;
and from all selfsubtracting hugely doom
treasures of reeking innocence are born.

Then,with not credible the anywhere
eclipsing of a spirit's ignorance
by every wisdom knowledge fears to dare,

how the(myself's own self who's)child will dance!

and when he's plucked such mysteries as men
do not conceive—let ocean grow again

72

wild(at our first)beasts uttered human words
—our second coming made stones sing like birds—
but o the starhushed silence which our third's

73

all worlds have halfsight,seeing either with

life's eye(which is if things seem spirits)or
(if spirits in the guise of things appear)
death's:any world must always half perceive.

Only whose vision can create the whole

(being forever born a foolishwise
proudhumble citizen of ecstasies
more steep than climb can time with all his years)

he's free into the beauty of the truth;

and strolls the axis of the universe
—love.   Each believing world denies,whereas
your lover(looking through both life and death)
timelessly celebrates the merciful

wonder no world deny may or believe

Uncollected Poems

I

TO WILLIAM F. BRADBURY

Leader and teacher, we whom you have taught,
Knowing that nothing ever can repay
The friendly aid that marked your honored stay,
Arise to thank and bless you. Where we sought
For help in that with which we could do naught,
You were at hand, prepared to show the way,
And when we came to you in sore dismay
You made most clear the path with perils fraught.

Now when we find ourselves about to lose
Your leadership, whose strength will ever dwell
In us and by us to the very end,
We know no better title we can use
In wishing you a final, fond farewell,
Than that which fits you best,—our faithful friend!

From *The Cambridge Review*, February 1910.

2

THE COMING OF MAY
Ballade

We have wintered the death of the old, cold year,
We have left our tracks in the melting snow,
We have braved harsh March's biting jeer,
And April's gusty overflow.
And now, when Nature begins to grow,
And the buds are out, and the birds are gay
And all is well—above and below,—
Here's to the coming of blithesome May.

Winter was good when he met us here,
With his sharp, clear days, and his flashing snow,
But we carried Winter out on his bier,
And buried him, many a month ago.
March was not hard with all his blow,
With April, Spring seemed on her way,
But we've reached the best at last, and so
Here's to the coming of blithesome May.

Winter has ended his cold career,—
No more death, and no more woe,—
We've come at last to a different sphere,
With no more freezing, and—mistletoe.
Spring in coming was very slow,—
Altogether too much delay,—
But we've cheered her on from foe to foe:
Here's to the coming of blithesome May.

Envoi

Think of the gratitude all must owe,—
Heaven has visited earth to-day.—
All the earth's in a warm, glad glow.—
Here's to the coming of blithesome May!

From *The Cambridge Review*, May 1910.

3

BALLAD OF THE SCHOLAR'S LAMENT

When I have struggled through three hundred years
    Of Roman history, and hastened o'er
Some French play—(though I have my private fears
    Of flunking sorely when I take the floor
In class),—when I have steeped my soul in gore
    And Greek, and figured over half a ream
With Algebra, which I do (not) adore,
    How shall I manage to compose a theme?

It's well enough to talk of poor and peers,
    And munch the golden apples' shiny core,
And lay a lot of heroes on their biers;—
    While the great Alec, knocking down a score,
Takes out his handkerchief, boohoo-ing, "More!"—
    But harshly I awaken from my dream,
To find a new,—er,—privilege,—in store:
    How shall I manage to compose a theme?

After I've swallowed prophecies of seers,
    And trailed Aeneas from the Trojan shore,
Learned how Achilles, after many jeers,
    On piggy Agamemnon got to sore,
And heard how Hercules, Esq., tore
    Around, and swept and dusted with a stream,
There's one last duty,—let's not call it bore,—
    How shall I manage to compose a theme?

Envoi

Of what avail is all my mighty lore?
    I beat my breast, I tear my hair, I scream:
"Behold, I have a Herculean chore.
    How shall I manage to compose a theme?"

From *The Cambridge Review*, [October 1910].

4

SKATING

Spring is past, and Summer's past,
    Autumn's come, and going;
Weather seems as though at last
    We might get some snowing.
Spring was good, and Summer better,
    But the best of all is waiting,—
Madame Winter—don't forget her.—
      O
          You
              Skating!

Spring we welcomed when we met,
    Summer was a blessing;
Autumn points to school, but yet
    Let's be acquiescing.
Spring had many precious pleasures;
    Winter's on a different rating;
She has greater, richer treasures,—
      O
          You
              Skating!

Gleam of ice, and glint of steel,
    Jolly, snappy weather;
Glide on ice and joy of zeal,
    All, alone, together.
Fickle Spring!   Who can imprint her?—
    Faithless while she's captivating;
Here's to trusty Madame Winter.—
      O
          You
              Skating!

From *The Cambridge Review*, December [1910].

5

METAMORPHOSIS

We've plodded through a weird and weary time,
  Called Winter by the calendar alone;
We have beheld an earth pool-deep in slime,
  Image a heaven of stone.

We've found life hid between the folds of mire,
  Sensed life in every place, heard life in tune.
The earth-shell cracks with underneath desire;
  Spring crawls from the cocoon.

Her puny wings vibrant with will to grow,
  She clings, expanding like an opening eye;
More large, more able, more developed, lo,
  The perfect butterfly.

From *The Cambridge Review*, March [1911].

6

VISION

The dim deep of a yellow evening slides
Across the green, and mingles with the elms.
A faint beam totters feebly in the west,
Trembles, and all the earth is wild with light,
Stumbles, and all the world is in the dark.

The huge black sleep above;—lo, two white stars.

Harvard, your shadow-walls, and ghost-toned tower,
Dim, ancient-moulded, vague, and faint, and far,
Is gone!   And through the flesh I see the soul:
Colouring iron in red leaping flame,
The thunder-strokes of mighty, sweating men,
Furious hammers clashing fierce and high,—
And in a corner of the smithy coiled,
Black, brutal, massive-linked, the toil-wrought chain
Which is to bind God's right hand to the world.

From *The Harvard Monthly*, November 1911.

7

MIST

Earth is become the seat of a new sea;
Above our heads the splendid surges roll,
Only each mountain, like a steadfast soul,
Up through the strangling billows towers free.
Huge finny forms of phosphorescence flee—
Weird shadows—through the deeps, or caracole
With the sea-horses on some eye-less shoal,
Quickening the leafage of a wave-tombed tree.
As a great miser, morbid with his gain,
Pricked by unhealthy frettings, drowns dismay
In gorging on his plunders, one by one,—
Sudden—out of the vault of Heaven, the Sun
Unlocks the rainbow's glory, and the day.
The air is strange with rare birds after rain.

From *The Harvard Monthly*, February 1913.

8

WATER-LILIES

Behold—a mere like a madonna's head
Black-locked, enchapleted with lilies white;
By Him the Prince of Artists in Earth's sight,
Eons ere her most ancient master wed
With Immortality.   Such lustre, spread
So livingly before our starting sight,
Cries in the accents of its primal might:
"This artist and his art were never dead!"
See, when Dawn paints still water with the skies,
The wreath of consecrated faces rise,
With parted lips in fragrancy of prayer;
Look, while the ripening Night bends Heaven's bough,
Upon the mere—each spiritual brow
Sleeps in the floating halo of its hair.

From *The Harvard Monthly*, February 1913.

9

MUSIC

Music is sweet from the thrush's throat!
   Oh little thrush
   With the holy note,
Like a footstep of God in a sick-room's hush
   My soul you crush.

Unstopped organ, from earth you break
   To knock at the skies,
   And I can but shake
My fragile fetters, and with you rise
   Into Paradise.

But Love, your music requires not wings.
   To the common breed
   It clings, and sings:
"Heaven on earth is Heaven indeed.
   This is my creed."

From *The Harvard Monthly*, March 1913.

10

SUMMER SILENCE
(Spenserian Stanza)

Eruptive lightnings flutter to and fro
Above the heights of immemorial hills;
Thirst-stricken air, dumb-throated, in its woe
Limply down-sagging, its limp body spills
Upon the earth.   A panting silence fills
The empty vault of Night with shimmering bars
Of sullen silver, where the lake distils
Its misered bounty.—Hark!   No whisper mars
The utter silence of the untranslated stars.

From *The Harvard Advocate*, March 7, 1913.

II

SUNSET

Great carnal mountains crouching in the cloud
That marrieth the young earth with a ring,
Yet still its thought builds heavenward, whence spring
Wee villages of vapor, sunset-proud.—
And to the meanest door hastes one pure-browed
White-fingered star, and little, childish thing,
The busy needle of her light to bring,
And stitch, and stitch, upon the dead day's shroud.
Poises the sun upon his west, a spark
Superlative,—and dives beneath the world;
From the day's fillets Night shakes out her locks;
List!   One pure trembling drop of cadence purled—
"Summer!"—a meek thrush whispers to the dark.
Hark! the cold ripple sneering on the rocks!

From *The Harvard Advocate*, March 21, 1913.

12

BALLADE

The white night roared with a huge north-wind,
And he sat before his thundering flame,
    Quaffing holly-crowned wine.
"Say me, who is she, and whence came
The snow-white maid with the hair of Inde?
    For I will have her mine!"

"She was crouched in snow by the threshold, lord,
And we took her in (for the storm is loud),
    But who, we may not know.
For, poorly-clad, she is strangely proud,
And will not sit at the servants' board,
    But saith she comes of the snow."

"She shall sit by me," he sware amain;
"Go, ere another ash-stick chars,
    Ask of her whom she loves."
"We ask her, lord, and she saith, 'The stars.'"
And he sware, "I will kiss with kisses twain
    Those cheeks which are two white doves."

The wind had tucked in bed her earth,
And tiptoed over valley and hill,
    Humming a slumber-croon;
And all the shining night lay still,
And the rude trees dropped their hollow mirth;
    Silently came the moon.

He rose from the table, red with wine;
He put one hand against the wall,
    Swaying as he did stand;
Three steps took he in the breathless hall,
Said, "You shall love me, for you are mine."
    And touched her with his hand.

White stretched the north-land, white the south...
She was gone like a spark from the ash that chars;
    And "After her!" he sware...
They found the maid.   And her eyes were stars,
A starry smile was upon her mouth,
    And the snow-flowers in her hair.

From *The Harvard Advocate*, April 25, 1913.

13

SONNET

A rain-drop on the eyelids of the earth,
That wakes the clod in flowers, and the skies
In depthless sunlight, and that mortifies
The soul, and drives it far from home and hearth
To seek the music of the Naiad's mirth
That laughs in falling waters, or surprise
The green tree—spirits with their dreaming eyes,—
The rosy baby of the May hath birth.

Delicious dark the hive of heaven drips;
Now in the firmament all shining crowd
The trembling, yearning stars, that cannot speak
For perfect joy; now steals a shadowy cloud,
A radiant tear, across the moon's pale cheek.
Dumbly the glorious sky yields up her lips.

From *The Harvard Monthly*, May 1913.

14

SONNET

Long since, the flicker brushed with shameless wing
The pale earth crucified, and to all lands
Bore the death-cry; uplifting her frail hands,
You aged maple, bowed with sorrowing,
Caught the red life.   New skies new seasons bring.
Wee red men build their lodge of yellow sands
In the primeval grass; the willow stands
Donned in her ermine, to be crowned with Spring.

How high the sky's vast purple palace towers!
And lo, the pride of majesty beguiled,
With playful hands, King Winter's laughing child,
Sweet April Heaven, from that royal brow
Hath plucked the snowy wreath of cloud, and now
Flings from her lap the million fluttering flowers.

15

Do you remember when the fluttering dusk,
Beating the west with faint wild wings, through space
Sank, with Night's arrow in her heart?   The face
Of heaven clouded with the Day's red doom
Was veiled in silent darkness, and the musk
Of summer's glorious rose breathed in the gloom.

Then from the world's harsh voice and glittering eyes,
The awful rant and roar of men and things,
Forth fared we into Silence.   The strong wings
Of Nature shut us from the common crowd;
On high, the stars like sleeping butterflies
Hung from the great grey drowsy flowers of cloud.

From *The Harvard Monthly*, June 1913.

16

NOCTURNE

When the lithe moonlight silently
Leaped like a satyr to the grass,
Filling the night with nakedness,
All silently I loved my love
    In gardens of white ivory.

Three fragrant trees which guard the gates,
Three perfume-trees which sweeten nights,
Rise upon heaven, full of stars
And dripping with white radiance.
    Her body is more white than trees.

Five founts of Bacchus, honey-cold,
Five showers making drunk the lawns,
Spout up a dark delicious rain
Filling the earth with sleep and tears.
    Her tresses are more sweet than wine.

Seven flowers which breathe divinity,
Seven wondering blossoms of embrace,
Open their glory to the moon,
Kissing white immortality.
    Her mouth is chaster than a flower.

When the fleet moonlight silently
Fled like a white nymph down the grass,
Leaving the night to loneliness,
All songfully I loved my love
    In gardens of white ivory.

The strings are silver to my harp,
And all the frame is ebony
I think the moon is blossoming—
My hungry fingers bite the strings—
    My harp becomes a flower, and blooms.

The strings are golden to my harp,
And all the frame is as a rose.
I think the moon is quivering—
My longing fingers search the chords—
    My harp becomes a heart, and breaks.

When the first day-beam silently
Broke like an arrow from the east,
Quivering unto the heights of dawn,
All silently I left my love
    In gardens of white ivory.

There are three trees which stand like dreams
Before the gates of ivory;
The moon has withered in the west—
My harp has withered—Hail the day!
    (Wherefore this dagger at my thighs.)

There are five founts which play like sleep
Upon the gates of ivory;
The moon is songless in the west—
My harp is songless—Hail the day!
    (Wherefore this dagger at my hands.)

There are seven flowers which smile like death
Within the gates of ivory;
The moon is broken in the west—
My harp is broken—Hail the day!
    (Wherefore this dagger at my heart.)

From *The Harvard Monthly*, March 1914.

17

SONNET

For that I have forgot the world these days,
To enter at the smokeless lodge, and take
Life naked at primeval hands, to make
Clean comrades of large things in mighty ways;
That I have wrestled with the huge dismays
Which make the high head bow, the strong heart quake,
That I have battled for a golden stake,
Richer by every terror and amaze,—

For that I have forgot the world her cries
In the vast painted silences, that men
Have meant me nothing, under the great skies,
Over the high hills of God's caress,—
Ye pitying elements!—be with me when
I kiss the little feet of foolishness.

From *The Harvard Monthly*, May 1914.

18

NIGHT

Night, with sunset hauntings;
A red cloud under the moon.
Here will I meet my love
Beneath hushed trees.

Over the silver meadows
Of flower-folded grass,
Shall come unto me
Her feet like arrows of moonlight.

Under the magic forest
Mute with shadow,
I will utterly greet
The blown star of her face.

By white waters
Sheathed in rippling silence,
Shall I behold her hands
Hurting the dark with lilies.

Hush thee to worship, soul!
Now is thy movement of love.
Night; and a red cloud
Under the moon.

From *The Harvard Monthly*, November 1914.

19

SONNET

No sunset, but a grey, great, struggling sky
Full of strong silence.   In green cloisters throng
Shy nuns of evening, telling beads of song.
Swallows, like winged prayers, soar steadily by,
Hallowing twilight.   From the faint and high,
Night waves her misting censers, and along
The world, the singing rises into strong,
Pure peace.   Now earth and heaven twain raptures die.

I knew your presence in the twilight mist,
In the world-filling darkness, in the rain
That spoke in whispers,—for the world was kissed
And laid in sleep.—These wild, sweet, perfect things
Are little miracles your memory sings,
Till heart on heart makes us one music again.

From *The Harvard Monthly*, Christmas 1914.

20

LONGING

I miss you in the dawn, of gradual flowering lights
And prayer-pale stars that pass the drowsing-incensed hymns,
When early earth through all her greenly-sleeping limbs
Puts on the exquisite gold day.   The Christlike sun
Moves to his resurrection in rejoicing heights,
And priestly hills partake of morning one by one.

I look for you when comes the beautiful blue moon,
When earth is as a queen whose soul hath taken flight,
Embalmed in the entire strength of perfect light.
The immense heaven, a vase of utter silence, towers
Vastward, beyond where dreams the unawakened moon,
Holding infinity and her invisible flowers.

The hours drum up to sunset; now the west awakes
To armies.   Suddenly across the firmament
Couriers of light spur forth their captain's high intent.
Now devout legions, mustering heavenward without cease,
Face the hushed hordes of night.   A trumpet-radiance breaks—
I see the young ranked glories marching down to peace.

Twilight, and great with silence of beginning dreams,
Yet haunted still by broken hosts in brave retreat,
Of blameless cohorts whelmed into sublime defeat,
Which, darkly under world their ragged spears withdraw,
Shall rise to fire the night in far victorious gleams,
When over the towered east leaps the white sword of dawn.

So do I want you, when in heavenly spaces God
Slips His white wonders on the silent trail of time;
When out the smoking eve begins to slowly climb
A great, red, fearsome flower, about whose fatal face
The faint moths gather and die—till withered pale, she nod
Far in the west, and morn the little dreams shall chase.

Now is the world at peace; Heaven unto her heart
Holdeth sublimities afar from touch of day,
Presents divine the fates shall never take away,
Unfaded memories, immortal ponderings,
The little knock of prayer whereby are thrown apart
Those inner doors which lead into all priceless things.

O night, mother divine of poetry and stars!
O thou whose patient face is nearest unto God,
Thou of chaste feet with beautiful oblivion shod,
Having the dear, swift-winged dark within thy hands,—
The prison invisible of souls thy peace unbars,
And love and I rise up into unspoken lands.

From *The Harvard Monthly*, April 1915.

21

BALLAD OF LOVE

Where is my love! I cried.
Life, I bid thee to say.
Who hath taken away
Her who sate at my side.
For whiter is she than any pearl;
But the nights be lonely and dread.
Life, what hast thou done with thy loveliest girl?
    Look to the wood, She said.
For the white bird, O, the white bird,
Sleep he toucheth the white bird,
The white bird and the red.

Give me her eyes! I cried.
For I would kiss them asleep,
That are so cool and deep,
So soft and wondering wide.
Bluer are they than ponds of dream;
But the skies be grey o'erhead.
Life, where may the eyes of thy fairest gleam?
    Look to the field, She said.
For the blue flower, O, the blue flower,
Night he stilleth the blue flower,
The blue flower and the red.

O, for her hair! I cried.
Her young and wonderful hair,
To hide my sorrow there,
In the heart of a shining tide.
For her hair is more yellow than Heaven's dawn;
But the world's last leaves be shed.
Life, where is thy youngest angel gone?
    Look to the west, She said.
For the yellow light, O, the yellow light,
Death he moweth the yellow light,
The yellow light and the red.

From *The Harvard Monthly*, May 1915.

22

BALLADE OF SOUL

Not for the naked make I this my prayer,
That up and down the streets of life do go,
Having, save rags, no pleasant thing to wear,
Albeit the timid ways have put on snow
Against such wind as only God can blow:
Well 'ware art Thou that these have no redress,
For always in Thine eyes is all distress
Of bodies that without due raiment be;
But are there Souls in winter garmentless,
Be with them, God! and pity also me.

Not for the hungry has my spirit care,
Whether their bodies shall be filled or no,
With whom the world her bounty will not share,
Wherefore they move on feeble feet and slow,
Feeling dear Death within their bodies grow:
Thou knowest these at pain beyond confess,
For sorrow never may Thy ears transgress,
Though lips be locked and pain shall hold the key;
But are there Souls whom hunger doth oppress.
Be with them, God! and pity also me.

Not for the homeless do I ask, where e'er
The lights of Hell their haunting faces show,
The legion undesired anywhere,
Whose hearts Love shall not build in,—who shall sow
And reap such loneliness as murder's woe:
Thy gracious mouth to these shall acquiesce,
Which is so very wonderful to bless
The plundered heart with joy held long in fee;
But are there Souls that know not Love's caress,
Be with them God! and pity also me.

Envoi

Father, for this we thank Thee without cesse:
Death is the body's birthright, as I guess,
But are there Souls that walk in hopelessness,
Be with them God! and pity also me.

From *The Harvard Monthly*, July 1915.

23

SAPPHICS

When my life his pillar has raised to heaven,
When my soul has bleeded and builded wonders,
When my love of earth has begot fair poems,
    Let me not linger.

Ere my day be troubled of coming darkness,
While the huge whole sky is elate with glory,
Let me rise, and making my salutation,
    Stride into sunset.

From *The Harvard Monthly*, January 1916.

24

SONNET

I dreamed I was among the conquerors,
Among those shadows, wonderfully tall,
Which splendidly inhabit the hymned hall
Whereof is "Fame" writ on its glorious doors.
Cloaked in green thunder are the sudden shores
Guarding the lintel's gold, whence of the wall
Leaps the white echo; and within, the fall
Is heard of the eternal feet of wars.

Here, at high ease, saw I those purple lords,
Sipping the wine of unforgetfulness,
Upon thrones intimate with all the skies:
Roland, and Richard, 'mid the shining press;
Leonidas, belted with living swords;
And Albert, with the lions in his eyes.

From *The Harvard Monthly*, March 1916.

25

HOKKU

I care not greatly
Should the world remember me
In some tomorrow.

There is a journey,
And who is for the long road
Loves not to linger.

For him the night calls,
Out of the dawn and sunset
Who has made poems.

From *The Harvard Monthly*, April 1916.

26

BELGIUM

Oh thou that liftest up thy hands in prayer,
Robed in the sudden ruin of glad homes,
And trampled fields which from green dreaming woke
To bring forth ruin and the fruit of death,
Thou pitiful, we turn our hearts to thee.

Oh thou that mournest thy heroic dead
Fallen in youth and promise gloriously,
In the deep meadows of their motherland
Turning the silver blossoms into gold,
The valor of thy children comfort thee.

Oh thou that bowest thy ecstatic face,
Thy perfect sorrows are the world's to keep!
Wherefore unto thy knees come we with prayer,
Mother heroic, mother glorious,
Beholding in thy eyes immortal tears.

From *The New York Evening Post*, May 20, 1916.

27

W.H.W., JR.
In Memory of "A House of Pomegranates"

Speak to me friend! Or is the world so wide
That souls may easily forget their speech,
And the strong love that binds us each to each
Who have stood together watching God's white tide
Pouring, and those bright shapes of dreams which ride
Through darkness; we who have walked the silent beach
Strown with strange wonders out of ocean's reach
Which the next flood in her great heart shall hide?

Do not forget me, though the sands should fall,
And many things be swept away in deep,
And a new vision uttered to the shore,—
If after days bespeak me not at all,
Nor other's praise awake my song from sleep,
Nor Poetry remember, anymore.

From *The Harvard Monthly*, June 1916.

28

FINIS

Over silent waters
                  day descending
                                   night ascending
floods the gentle glory of the sunset
In a golden greeting
                          splendidly to westward
as pale twilight
              trem-
                  bles
                        into
                              Darkness
comes the last light's gracious exhortation
                                     Lifting up to peace
so when life shall falter
                          standing on the shores of the
eternal
god
        May i behold my sunset
Flooding
            over silent waters

From *Eight Harvard Poets*, New York 1917.

29

because
an obstreperous grin minutely floats
out of this onelegged flower—
girl's eyes and
bounding timorously
caroms against quickly taxis

or a chiselled god's
Mother hugs carefully against her
stone dull little breast the
with rain streaked Boy,quietly whose
mutilated eyes remember flowers

these clouds
imitate curiously
a 1st judgment lightening
on top of the large bold soft noisy

world
       filling me promptly
         up:
in order that i may be sharply
emptied into Silence(which is

nothing;but whom we call,darkness)

From *The Little Review*, Spring 1923.

Louis Aragon

FRONT ROUGE

Une douceur pour mon chien
Un doigt de champagne Bien Madame
Nous sommes chez Maxim's l'an mille
Neuf cent trente
On met des tapis sous les bouteilles
Pour que leur cul d'aristocrate
ne se heurte pas aux difficultés de la vie
des tapis pour cacher la terre
des tapis pour éteindre
le bruit de la semelle des chaussures des garcons
Les boissons se prennent avec des pailles
qu'on tire d'un petit habit de précaution
Délicatesse
Il y a des fume-cigarettes entre la cigarette et l'homme
des silencieux aux voitures
des escaliers de service pour ceux
qui portent les paquets
et du papier de soie autour des paquets
et du papier autour du papier de soie
du papier tant qu'on veut cela ne coûte
rien le papier ni le papier de soie ni les pailles
ni le champagne ou si peu
ni le cendrier réclame ni le buvard
réclame ni le calendrier
réclame ni les lumières
réclame ni les images sur les murs
réclame ni les fourrures sur Madame
réclame réclame les cure-dents
réclame l'éventail et réclame le vent
rien ne coûte rien et pour rien
des serviteurs vivants vous tendent dans la rue des prospectus
Prenez c'est gratis
le prospectus et la main qui le tend
Ne fermez pas la porte
le Blount s'en chargera Tendresse
Jusqu'aux escaliers qui savent monter seuls
dans les grands magasins
Les journées sont de feutre
les hommes de brouillard Monde ouaté
sans heurt
Vous n'êtes pas fous Des haricots Mon chien
n'a pas encore eu la maladie

30

THE RED FRONT

A gentleness for my dog
A finger of Champagne Very well Madame
We are at Maxim's A.D. one thousand
nine hundred thirty
Carpets have been put under the bottles
so that their aristocratic arses
may not collide with life's difficulties
there are carpets to hide the earth
there are carpets to extinguish
the noise of the soles of the waiters' shoes
Drinks are sipped through straws
which you pull out of a little safety-dress
Delicacy
There are cigaretteholders between cigarette and man
there are silent people at the cars
there are service-stairs for those
who carry packages
and there's tissue paper around the packages
and there's paper around the tissue paper
there's all the paper you want that doesn't cost
anything paper nor tissue paper nor straws
nor champagne or so little
nor the advertisement-ashtray, nor the
advertisement-blotter nor the
advertisement-calendar nor the
advertisement-lights nor the
advertisement-pictures on the walls nor the
advertisement-furs on Madame the
advertisement-toothpicks the advertisement-fan and the advertisement wind
nothing costs anything and for nothing
real live servitors, tender you prospectuses in the street
Take it, it's free
the prospectus and the hand which tenders it
Don't close the door
the Blount will take care of that Tenderness
Up to the very stairs which know how to ascend by themselves
in the department stores
Days are made of felt
Men are made of fog The world is padded
without collision
You aren't crazy Some beans My dog
hasn't been sick yet

O pendulettes pendulettes
avez-vous assex fait rêver les fiancés sur les grands boulevards
et le lit Louis XVI avec un an de crédit
Dans les cimetières les gens de ce pays si bien huilé
se tiennent avec la décence du marbre
leurs petites maisons ressemblent
à des dessus de cheminée

Combien coûtent les chrysanthèmes cette année

Fleurs aux morts fleurs aux grandes artistes
L'argent se dépense aussi pour l'idéal
Et puis les bonnes œuvres font traîner des robes noires
dans des escaliers je ne vous dis que ca
La princesse est vraiment trop bonne
Pour la reconnaissance qu'on vous en a
A peine s'ils vous remercient
C'est l'exemple des bolchéviques
Malheureuse Russie
L'U. R. S. S.
L'U. R. S. S. ou comme ils disent S. S. S. R.
S. S. comment est-ce S. S.
S. S. R. S. S. R. S. S. S. R. oh ma chère
Pensez donc S. S. S. R.
Vous avez vu
les grèves du Nord
Je connais Berck et Paris-plage
Mais non les grèves SSSR
SSSR SSSR SSSR

Quand les hommes descendaient des faubourgs
et que Place de la République
le flot noir se formait comme un poing qui se ferme
les boutiques portaient leurs volets à leurs yeux
pour ne pas voir passer l'éclair
Je me souviens du premier mai mil neuf cent sept
quand régnait la terreur dans les salons dorés
On avait interdit aux enfants d'aller à l'école
dans cette banlieue occidentale où ne parvenait qu'affaibli
l'écho lointain de la colère
Je me souviens de la manifestation Ferrer
quand sur l'ambassade espagnole s'écrasa
la fleur d'encre de l'infamie
Paris il n'y a pas si longtemps
que tu as vu le cortège fait à Jaurés
et le torrent Sacco-Vanzetti

O little clocks little clocks
have you given enough dreams to the lovers on the great boulevards
and the Louis XVI bed with a year's credit
In the cemeteries the people of this so-well-oiled country
hold themselves with the decency of the marble
Their little houses resemble
chimneypots

How much are chrysanthemums this year

Flowers for the dead flowers for the great artistes
Money is also spent for ideals
And besides good deeds wear long black trailing gowns
on the stairs I only tell you that
The princess is really too kind
for the gratitude which is owed you
Scarcely if they thank you
It's the bolsheviks' example
Unhappy Russia
The URSS
The URSS or as they say SSSR
SS how is it SS
SSR SSR SSR oh my dear
just think SSSR
You have seen
the strikes in the North
I know Berck and Paris-plage
But not the strikes in the SSSR
SSSR SSSR SSSR

When men came down from the suburbs
and at the Place de la République
the black wave formed like a shutting fist
the shops wore their shutters over their eyes
so as not to see the lightning pass
I remember the first of May nine hundred seven
when terror reigned in the gilded drawingrooms
The children had been forbidden to go to school
in that occidental district which was reached by only a feeble
distant echo of wrath
I remember the Ferrer manifestation
when on the Spanish embassy was crushed
the ink-flower of infamy
Paris not so long ago
thou hast seen the procession made for Jaurés
and the Sacco–Vanzetti torrent

Paris tes carrefours frémissent encore de toutes leurs narines
Tes pavés sont toujours prêts à jaillir en l'air
Tes arbres à barrer la route aux soldats
Retourne-toi grand corps appelé
Belleville
Ohé Belleville et toi Saint-Denis
où les rois sont prisonniers des rouges
Ivry Javel et Malakoff
Appelle-les tous avec leurs outils
les enfants galopeurs apportant les nouvelles
les femmes aux chignons alourdis les hommes
qui sortent de leur travail comme d'un cauchemar
le pied encore chancelant mais les yeux clairs
Il y a toujours des armuriers dans la ville
des autos aux portes des bourgeois
Pliez les réverbères comme des fétus de paille
faites valser les kiosques les bancs les fontaines Wallace
Descendez les flics
camarades
Descendez les flics
Plus loin plus loin vers l'ouest où dorment
Les enfants riches et les putains de previère classe
Dépasse la Madeleine Prolétariat
que ta fureur balaye l'Elysée
Tu as bien droit au bois de Boulogne en semaine
Un jour tu feras sauter l'arc de Triomphe
Prolétariat connais ta force
Connais ta force et déchaîne-la
Il prépare son jour Sachez mieux voir
Entendez cette rumeur qui vient des prisons
Il attend son jour attend son heure
sa minute la seconde
où le coup porté sera mortel
et la balle à ce point sûre que tous les médecins social-fascistes
penchés sur le corps de la victime
auront beau promener leurs doigts chercheurs sous la chemise de dentelles
ausculter avec des appareils de précision son cœur déjà pourrissant
ils ne trouveront pas le remède habituel
et tomberont aux mains des émeutiers qui les colleront au mur
Feu sur Léon Blum
Feu sur Boncour Frossard Déat
Feu sur les ours savants de la social-démocratie
Feu Feu j'entends passer
la mort qui se jette sur Garchery Feu vous dis-je
Sous la conduite du Parti communiste
SFIC

Paris thy crossroads shudder still with all their nostrils
Thy pavements are always ready to leap in air
Thy trees to bar the way to soldiers
Turn back great body called
Belleville
Ohé Belleville and thou Saint-Denis
where the kings are prisoners of the reds
Ivry Javel and Malakoff
Call them all with their tools
the errandboys bringing news
the women with their heavy chignons the men
who come out of their work as if out of a nightmare
their feet still tottering but their eyes clear
There are always gunsmiths in the city
and autos at the bourgeois' doors
Fold the reflectors like wisps of straw
make the kiosks benches Wallace fountains waltz
Bring down the cops
Comrades
Bring down the cops
On on toward the west where sleep
rich children and first-class tarts
Go beyond the Madeleine, Proletariat
let thy fury sweep the Elysée
Thou hast good right to the bois de Boulogne on weekdays
Some day thou wilt blow up the Arc de Triomphe
Proletariat know thy force
Know thy force and unchain it
It prepares its day Know how to see better
Hear that rumour which comes from prisons
It prepares its day it awaits its hour
its minute its second
when the mortal blow shall be struck
and the bullet so sure that all the social-fascist doctors
bent over the victim's body
will have a time making their searching fingers wander under the lace-chemise
sounding with instruments of precision its already rotting heart
They won't find the usual remedy
and will fall into the hands of the rioters who will glue them to the wall
Fire on Léon Blum
Fire on Boncour Frossard Déat
Fire on the trained bears of the social-democracy
Fire Fire I hear pass by
the death which throws itself on Garchery Fire I tell you
Under the guidance of the Communist Party
SFIC

vous attendez le doigt sur la gâchette
Feu
mais Lénine
le Lénine du juste moment
De Clairvaux s'élève une voix que rien n'arrête
C'est le journal parlé
la chanson du mur
la vérité révolutionnaire en marche
Salut à Marty le glorieux mutin de la Mer Noire
Il sera livré encore ce symbole inutilement enfermé
Yen-Bay
Quel est ce vocable qui rappelle qu'on ne bâillonne
pas un peuple qu'on ne le
mâte pas avec le sabre courbe du bourreau
Yen-Bay
A vous frères jaunes ce serment
Pour chaque goutte de votre vie
Coulera le sang d'un Varenne

Ecoutez le cri des Syriens tués à coups de fléchettes
par les aviateurs de la Troisième République
Entendez les hurlements des Marocains morts
sans qu'on ait mentionné leur âge ni leur sexe

Ceux qui attendent les dents serrées
d'exercer enfin leur vengeance
sifflent un air qui en dit long
un air un air UR
SS un air joyeux comme le fer SS
SR un air brûlant c'est l'es-
pérance c'est l'air SSSR c'est la chanson c'est la chanson d'octobre aux
fruits éclatants
Sifflez sifflez SSSR SSSR la patience
n'aura qu'un temps SSSR SSSR SSSR

Dans les plâtras croûlants
parmi les fleurs fanées des décorations anciennes
les derniers napperons et les dernières étagères
soulignent la vie étrange des bibelots
Le ver de la bourgeoisie
essaye en vain de joindre ses tronçons épars
Ici convulsivement agonise une classe
les souvenirs de famille s'en vont en lambeaux
Mettez votre talon sur ces vipères qui se réveillent
Secouez ces maisons que les petites cuillères
En tombent avec les punaises la poussière les vieillards

you are waiting finger on trigger
Fire
but Lenin
the Lenin of the right moment
From Clairvaux rises a voice which nothing stops
It's the talking-newspaper
the song of the wall
the revolutionary truth on the march
Hail to Marty the glorious mutineer of the Black Sea
He shall yet be free that symbol in vain imprisoned
Yen-Bay
What is this word which reminds us that a people can't be
gagged, that it can't be
subdued with the curving sword of the executioner
Yen-Bay
To you yellow brothers this pledge
For every drop of your life
shall flow the blood of a Varenne

Listen to the cry of the Syrians killed with darts
by the aviators of the third Republic
Hear the groans of the dead Moroccans
who died without a mention of their age or sex

Those who await with shut teeth
to practise at last their vengeance
whistle a tune which carries far
a tune a tune UR
SS a joyous tune like iron SS
SR a burning tune it's
hope it's the SSSR tune it's the song
it's the song of October with bursting fruit
whistle whistle SSSR SSSR patience
won't wait forever SSSR SSSR SSSR

In crumbling plaster
among the faded flowers of old decorations
the last clothes and the last whatnots
underline the strange survival of knick-knacks
The worm of the bourgeoisie
vainly tries to join its scattered fragments
Here a class convulsively agonizes
family memories disappear in fragments
Put your heel on these vipers which are awaking
Shake the houses so that the teaspoons
will fall out of them with the bedbugs the dust the old men

qu'il est doux qu'il est doux le gémissement qui sort des ruines.

J'assiste à l'écrasement d'un monde hors d'usage
J'assiste avec enivrement au pilonnage des bourgeois
Y a-t-il jamais eu plus belle chasse que l'on donne
à cette vermine qui se tapit dans tous les recoins des villes
Je chante la comination violente du Prolétariat sur la bourgeoisie
pour l'anéantissement de cette bourgeoisie
pour l'anéantissement total de cette bourgeoisie

Le plus beau monument qu'on puisse élever sur une place
la plus surprenante de toutes les statues
la colonne la plus audacieuse et la plus fine
l'arche qui se compare au prisme même de la pluie
ne valent pas l'amas splendide et chaotique
Essayez pour voir
qu'on produit aisément avec une église et de la dynamite

La pioche fait une trouée au cœur des docilités anciennes
les écroulements sont des chansons où tournent des soleils
Hommes et murs d'autrefois tombent frappés de la même foudre
L'éclat des fusillades ajoute au paysage
une gaieté jusqu'alors inconnue
Ce sont des ingénieurs des médecins qu'on exécute
Mort à ceux qui mettent en danger les conquêtes d'octobre
Mort aux saboteurs du Plan Quinquennal

A vous Jeunesses Communistes
Balayez les débris humains où s'attarde
l'araignée incantatoire du signe de croix
Volontaires de la construction socialiste
Chassez devant vous jadis comme un chien dangereux

Dressez-vous contre vox mères
Abandonnez la nuit la peste et la famille
Vous tenez dans vos mains un enfant rieur
un enfant comme on n'en a jamais vu
Il sait avant de parler toutes les chansons de la nouvelle vie
Il va vous échapper courir il rit déjà
les astres descendent familièrement sur la terre
C'est bien le moins qu'ils brûlent en se posant
la charogne noire des égoïstes

Les fleurs de ciment et de pierre
les longues lianes du fer les rubans bleus de l'acier
n'ont jamais rêvé d'un printemps pareil

How sweet how sweet is the groan which comes out of the ruins.

I am a witness to the crushing of a world out of date
I am a witness drunkenly to the stampingout of the bourgeois
Was there ever a finer chase than the chase we give
to that vermin which flattens itself in every nook of the cities
I sing the violent domination of the bourgeoisie by the proletariat
for the annihilation of the bourgeoisie
for the total annihilation of that bourgeoisie

The fairest monument which can be erected
the most astonishing of all statues
the finest and most audacious column
the arch which is like the very prism of the rain
are not worth the splendid and chaotic heap
which is easily produced with a church and some dynamite
Try it and see

The pickaxe makes a hole in the heart of ancient docilities
crumblings are songs wherein suns revolve
Men and walls of yesterday fall struck with the same thunder bolt
The bursting of gunfire adds to the landscape
a hitherto unknown gaiety
Those are engineers, doctors that are being executed
Death to those who endanger the conquest of October
Death to the traitors to the Fiveyearplan

To you Young Communists
Sweep out the human debris where lingers
the magical spider of the sign of the cross
Volunteers for socialist construction
Chase the old days before you like a dangerous dog

Stand up against your mothers
Abandon night pestilence and the family
You hold in your hands a laughing child
a child such as has never been seen
He knows before he can talk all the songs of the new life
He will get away from you to run he laughs already
the stars descend familiarly upon the earth
it's indeed the least which they burn in assuming
the black carrion of the egoists

The flowers of cement and of stone
the long creepers of iron the blue ribbons of steel
have never dreamed of such a spring

Les collines se couvrent de primevères gigantesques
Ce sont des crèches des cuisines pour vingt mille dîneurs
des maisons des maisons des clubs
pareils à des tournesols à des trèfles à quatre feuilles
Les routes se nouent comme des cravates
Il se lève une aurore au-dessus des salles de bains
Le mai socialiste est annoncé par mille hirondelles
Dans les champs une grande lutte est ouverte
la lutte des fourmis et des loups
on ne peut pas se servir comme on voudrait des mitrailleuses
contre la routine et l'obstination
mais déjà 80% du pain cette année
provient des blés marxistes des Kolkhozes...
Les coquelicots sont devenus des drapeaux rouges
et des monstres nouveaux mâchonnent les épis

On ne sait plus ici ce que c'était que le chômage
Le bruit du marteau le bruit de la faucille
montent de la terre est-ce
bien la faucille est-ce est-ce
bien le marteau l'air est plein de criquets
Crécelles et caresses
URSS
Coups de feu Coups de couets Clameurs
C'est la jeunesse héroïque
Céréales aciéries SSSR SSSR
Les yeux bleus de la Révolution
brillent d'une cruauté nécessaire
SSSR SSSR SSSR
SSSR
Pour ceux qui prétendent que ce n'est pas un poème
pour ceux qui regrettant les lys ou le savon Palmolive
détourneront de moi leurs têtes de nuée
pour les Halte-là les Vous Voulez Rire
pour les dégoûtés les ricaneurs
pour ceux qui ne manqueront pas de percer à jour
les desseins sordides de l'auteur l'auteur
Ajoutera ces quelques mots bien simples

L'intervention devait débuter par l'entrée en scène de la Roumanie sous le prétexte, par exemple, d'un incident de frontière, entraînant la déclaration officielle de la guerre par la Pologne, et la solidarisation des Etats limitrophes. A cette intervention se seraient jointes les troupes de Wrangle qui auraient traversé la Roumanie...A leur retour de la conférence énergétique de Londres, se rendant en U. R. S. S. par Paris, Ramzine et Leritchev ont organisé la liaison avec le Torgprom par l'inter-

the hills are covered with gigantic primroses
they are homes for children kitchens for twenty thousand diners
houses houses clubs
like sunflowers like fourleafclovers
the roads are knotted like neckties
a dawn comes up over the bathhouses
The socialist May is announced by a thousand swallows
In the fields a great struggle opens
the struggle of ants and wolves
there aren't as many machineguns as we'd like
to use against routine and obstinacy
But already 80% of this year's bread
comes from the marxian wheat of the collective farms
the poppies have become redflags
the new monsters munch the ears of grain

Nobody knows here what unemployment was like
the noise of the hammer the noise of the sickle
mount from the earth is it
really the sickle is it is it
really the hammer the air is full of locusts
rattles and caresses
URSS
Gunshots cracking of whips clamours
It's the heroic youth
Steeled cereals SSSR SSSR
The blue eyes of the Revolution
shine with a necessary cruelty
SSSR SSSR SSSR
SSSR
For those who pretend that this is not a poem
for those who regret the lilies or the Palmolive soap
they will turn away from me their clouded heads
for the stop—there people the You're-joking people
for the disgusted people for the sneering people
for those who will not fail to put holes in
the sordid drawings of the author the author
Will add these few very simple words

Intervention should begin with the appearance of Rumania on
the scene, on the pretext, for instance, of some trouble on the fron-
tier involving an official declaration of war by Poland and the joining
together of the troops of Wrangel which would have traversed
Rumania...On their return from the energetic conference of
London, entering the URSS from Paris, Ramzine and Leritchev
have organized communication with the Torgprom through the in-

médiaire de Riabouchinski qui entretenait des rapports avec le Gouverne-
ment français en la personne de Loucheur...Dans l'organisation de
l'intervention le rôle directeur appartient à la France qui en a conduit la
préparation avec l'aide active du Gouvernement anglais...

Les chiens les chiens les chiens conspirent
et comme le tréponème pâle échappe au microscope
Poincaré se flatte d'être un virus filtrant
La race des danseurs de poignards des maquereaux tzaristes
les grands ducs mannequins des casinos qu'on lance
Les délateurs à 25 francs la lettre
la grande pourriture de l'émigration
lentement dans le bidet français se cristallise
La morve polonaise et la bave roumaine
la vomissure du monde entier
s'amassent à tous les horizons du pays où se construit le socialisme
et les têtards se réjouissent
se voient déjà crapauds
décorés
députés qui sait ministres
Eaux sales suspendez votre écume
Eaux sales vous n'êtes pas le déluge
Eaux sales vous retomberez dans le bourbier occidental
Eaux sales vous ne couvrirez pas les plaines où pousse le blé pur du devenir
Eaux sales Eaux sales vous ne dissoudrez pas l'oseille de l'avenir
Vous ne souillerez pas les marches de la collectivisation
Vous mourrez au seuil brûlant de la dialectique
de la dialectique aux cent tours porteuses de flammes écarlates
aux cent mille tours qui crachent le feu de mille et mille canons
Il faut que l'univers entende
une voix hurler la gloire de la dialectique matérialiste
qui marche sur ses pieds sur ses millions de pieds
chaussés de bottes militaires
sur ses pieds magnifiques comme la violence
tendant sa multitude de bras armés
vers l'image du Communisme vainqueur
Gloire à la dialectique matérialiste
et gloire à son incarnation
l'armée
Rouge
Gloire à
l'armée
Rouge
Une étoile est née de la terre
Une étoile aujourd'hui mène vers une bûche de feu
les soldats de Boudenny

termediary of Riabouchinski, who was keeping up relations with the
French government personified by Loucheur...In the organization
of the intervention the chief role belongs to France which has pre-
pared it with the active aid of the English government...

The dogs the dogs the dogs are conspiring
and as the pale tréponème escapes the microscope
Poincaré flatters himself that he's a filtering poison
The race of the daggerdancers of the tzarist pimps
the dummy grand-dukes of the casinos which we lance
the informers who charge 25 francs a letter
the huge rottenness of emigration
slowly crystallizes in the French bidet
The Polish snot and the Rumanian drivel
the puke of the whole world
are massed on the horizons of the country where socialism builds itself
and the tadpoles rejoice
see themselves already as frogs
with decorations
deputies who knows ministers
Foul waters suspend your foam
Foul waters you are not the deluge
Foul waters you will fall again in the occidental slough
Foul waters you will not cover the plains where sprouts the pure wheat of the
Foul waters Foul waters you will not dissolve the sorrel of the future   [future
You will not soil the steps of collectivization
You will die at the burning threshold of a dialectic
of a dialectic with a hundred turnings which carry scarlet flames
with a hundred thousand turnings which spit the fire of thousands and
The universe must hear   [thousands of canons
a voice yelling the glory of materialistic dialectic
marching on its feet on its millions of feet
booted with army boots
on feet magnificent like violence
outstretching its multitudinous warrior-arms
toward the image of triumphant Communism
Hail to materialistic dialectic
and hail to its incarnation
the Red
army
Hail to
the Red
army
A star is born on earth
A star today leads toward a fiery breach
the soldiers of Budenny

En marche soldats de Boudenny
Vous êtes la conscience en armes du Prolétariat
Vous savez en portant la mort
à quelle vie admirable vous faites une route
Chacun de vos corps est un diamant qui tombe
Chacun de vos vers un feu qui purifie
L'éclair de vos fusils fait reculer l'ordure
France en tête
N'épargnez rien soldats de Boudenny
Chacun de vos cris porte au loin l'Haleine embrasée
de la Révolution Universelle
Chacune de nos respirations propage
Marx et Lénine dans le ciel
Vous êtes rouges comme l'aurore
rouges comme la colére
rouges comme le sang
Vous vengez Babeuf et Liebknecht
Prolétaires de tous les pays unissez-vous
Voix Appelez-les préparez leur la
voie à ces libérateurs qui joindront aux vôtres
leurs armes Prolétaires de tous les pays
Voici la catastrophe apprivoisée
Voici docile enfin la bondissante panthère
L'Histoire menée en laisse par la troisième Internationale
le train rouge s'ébranle et rien ne l'arrêtera
U R
S S
U R
S S
U R
S S
Il n'y a personne qui reste en arrière
agitant des mouchoirs Tout le monde est en marche
U R
S S
U R
S S
Inconscients oppositionnels
Il n'y a pas de frein sur la machine
Hurle écrasé mais le vent chante
U R
SS SS
SR UR
SS SSSR
Debout les damnés de la terre
S R

March on soldiers of Budenny
You are the armed conscience of the Proletariat
You know while you carry death
to what admirable life you are making a road
Each of your blows is a diamond which falls
Each of your steps a fire which purifies
The lightning of your guns makes ordure recoil
France at the head
Spare nothing soldiers of Budenny
Each of your cries carries afar the firefilled Breath
of Universal Revolution
Each of your breathings begets
Marx and Lenin in the sky
You are red like the dawn
red like anger
red like blood
You avenge Babeuf and Liebknecht
Proletarians of all countries unite your
Voices Call them prepare for them the
way to those liberators who shall join with yours
their weapons Proletarians of all countries
Behold the tamed catastrophy
Behold docile at last the bounding panther
History led on leash by the third International
The red train starts and nothing shall stop it
UR
SS
UR
SS
UR
SS
No one remains behind
waving handkerchiefs Everyone is going
UR
SS
UR
SS
Unconscious opposers
There are no brakes on the engine
Howl crushed but the wind sings
UR
SS SS
SS UR
SS SSSR
Up you damned of earth
SS

S S
S R
S S
Le passé meurt l'instant embraye
SSSR SSSR
les roues s'élancent le rail chauffe SSSR
Le train s'emballe vers demain
SSSR toujours plus vite SSSR
En quatre ans le plan quinquennal
SSSR à bas l'exploitation de l'homme par l'homme
SSSR à bas l'ancien servage à bas le capital
à bas l'impérialisme à bas
SSSR SSSR SSSR

Ce qui grandit comme un cri dans les montagnes
Quand l'aigle frappé relâche soudainement ses serres
SSSR SSSR SSSR
C'est le chant de l'homme et son rire
C'est le train de l'étoile rouge
qui brûle les gares les signaux les airs
SSSR octobre octobre c'est l'express
octobre à travers l'univers SS
SR SSSR SSSR
SSSR SSSR

SR
SS
SR
The past dies the moment is thrown into gear
SSSR SSSR
the roads spring the rail warms SSSR
the train plunges toward tomorrow
SSSR ever faster SSSR
In four years the fiveyearplan
SSSR down with the exploiting of man by man
SSSR down with the old bondage down with capital
down with imperialism down with it!
SSSR SSSR SSSR

That which swells like a cry in the mountains
When the stricken eagle suddenly lets go with its talons
SSSR SSSR SSSR
It's the song of man and his laughter
It's the train of the red star
which burns the stations the signals the skies
SSSR October October it's the express
October across the universe SS
SR SSSR SSSR
SSSR SSSR

From *Literature of the World Revolution*, August 1931,
and *Contempo*, III.5, February 1, 1933.

31

if(you are i why certainly

the hour softly is
in all;places which move
seriously

Together.

let)us fold wholly ourselves smil-
ing because we love,
as doomed few alert(flowers and

excellently upon whom Night
wanders and wanders and)wanders
Or since,in air

like bubbles Faces
occur(shyly

to
one by bright
brief
one be)punc

-tured:the,green
nameless caterpillar of evening nib,ble,s
Solemnly a whitish leaf of sky.

From *Broom*, January 1924.

32

BALLAD OF AN INTELLECTUAL

Listen,you morons great and small
to the tale of an intellectuall
(and if you don't profit by his career
don't ever say Hoover gave nobody beer).

'Tis frequently stated out where he was born
that a rose is as weak as its shortest thorn:
they spit like quarters and sleep in their boots
and anyone dies when somebody shoots
and the sheriff arrives after everyone's went;
which isn't,perhaps,an environment
where you would(and I should)expect to find
overwhelming devotion to things of the mind.
But when it rains chickens we'll all catch larks
—to borrow a phrase from Karl the Marks.

As a child he was puny;shrank from noise
hated the girls and mistrusted the boise,
didn't like whisky,learned to spell
and generally seemed to be going to hell;
so his parents,encouraged by desperation,
gave him a classical education
(and went to sleep in their boots again
out in the land where women are main).

You know the rest:a critic of note,
a serious thinker,a lyrical pote,
lectured on Art from west to east
—did sass-seyeity fall for it? Cheast!
if a dowager balked at our hero's verse
he'd knock her cold with a page from Jerse;
why,he used to say to his friends,he used
"for getting a debutante give me Prused"
and many's the heiress who's up and swooned
after one canto by Ezra Pooned
(or—to borrow a cadence from Karl the Marx—
a biting chipmunk never barx).

But every bathtub will have its gin
and one man's sister's another man's sin
and a hand in the bush is a stitch in time
and Aint It All A Bloody Shime
and he suffered a fate which is worse than death
and I don't allude to unpleasant breath.

Our blooming hero awoke,one day,
to find he had nothing whatever to say:
which I might interpret(just for fun)
as meaning the es of a be was dun
and I mightn't think(and you mightn't,too)
that a Five Year Plan's worth a Gay Pay Oo
and both of us might irretrievably pause
ere believing that Stalin is Santa Clause:
which happily proves that neither of us
is really an intellectual cus.

For what did our intellectual do,
when he found himself so empty and blo?
he pondered a while and he said,said he
"It's the social system,it isn't me!
Not I am a fake,but America's phoney!
Not I am no artist,but Art's bologney!
Or—briefly to paraphrase Karl the Marx—
'The first law of nature is,trees will be parx.' "

Now all you morons of sundry classes
(who read the Times and who buy the Masses)
if you don't profit by his career
don't ever say Hoover gave nobody beer.

For whoso conniveth at Lenin his dream
shall dine upon bayonets,isn't and seam
and a miss is as good as a mile is best
for if you're not bourgeois you're Eddie Gest
and wastelands live and waistlines die,
which I very much hope it won't happen to eye;
or as comrade Shakespeare remarked of old
All that Glisters Is Mike Gold

(but a rolling snowball gathers no sparks
—and the same hold true of Karl the Marks).

From *Americana*, December 1932.

33

american critic ad 1935

alias faggoty slob with a sob in whose cot
tony onceaweek whisper winsomely pul

ling their wool over 120 mil
lion goats each and every one a spot
less lamb
            :nothing in any way sugge

stive
       ;nothing to which anyone might possibly obje

ct
   .& you know all he's got to do is just men
tion something & it sells ten ooo copies.won

derful.isn't it that poor man must read all the time.

read why i'd read in my sleep for half that mon
ey.you don't mean he.did i say anything again

st.wasn't that a.wasn't it.by what was the.such a funny name)

into which world is noone born alive

From *Townsman*, January 1938.

34

guilt is the cause of more disauders
than history's most obscene marorders

From *58 poèmes*, Paris 1958.

35

M   in a vicious world—to love virtue
A   in a craven world—to have courage
R   in a treacherous world—to prove loyal
I   in a wavering world—to stand firm

A   in a cruel world—to show mercy
N   in a biased world—to act justly
N   in a shameless world—to live nobly
E   in a hateful world—to forgive

M   in a venal world—to be honest
O   in a heartless world—to be human
O   in a killing world—to create
R   in a sick world—to be whole

E   in an epoch of UNself—to be ONEself

From *Adventures in Value*, New York 1962.

36

DOVEGLION

he isn't looking at anything
he isn't looking for something
he isn't looking
he is seeing

what

not something outside himself
not anything inside himself
but himself

himself how

not as some anyone
not as any someone

only as a noone(who is everyone)

From *Adventures in Value*, New York 1962.

Etcetera

The Harvard Years, 1911–16

EARLY POEMS

I

SEMI-SPRING

A thin, foul scattering of grim, grey snow,
Reaching out scrawny limbs, deep digs its nails
Into the bleeding face of suppliant earth,
And grins with all its broken, yellow teeth.

A warm, serene, soft heaven gazes down
With dreamy eyes upon the fiend-cramped world.
The rosy eastern glow, the sun's I Come,
Patters about the sky, and coos, and smiles—
Sweet babe with tender, rose-begetting feet.

From a black corpse of tree, the hideous rasp
Of staring grackles, clucking and bowing each
In drivelling salute, splits the soft air
To inharmonious fragments; everywhere
A nervous, endless, hoarse, incessant chirp
Of sparrows telling all the evil news.

Ah, God—for the flower-air of Spring!   To see
The world in bud!   To press with eager feet
The dear, soft, thrilling green again!   To be
Once more in touch with heaven upon earth!
One soul-toned thrush's perfect harmony,
One little warbler's huge felicity,
One buttercup!   One perfect butterfly!

II

THE PAPER PALACE

A clan of imps—morose and ugly things,
   Brown-bodies,evil-headed,slayers all,—
Has climbed the shuddering air with embryo wings
   And from my porch's beam slowly let fall
With toil unspeakable,a fairy ball,
A palace hung in either!   Fine as cloth
   Moon-spun on elfin loom,each filmy wall,
Light as a buoyant cloudlet's feathery froth,
Frail as a lily's face,soft as a silver moth.

III

Night shall eat these girls and boys.
Time makes his meal of thee and me.
Love a broken doll shall be;
the moon and sun like tired toys

(with all whereat joined hearts rejoice)
shall drop softly into the sea.
Night shall eat these girls and boys.
Time makes his meal of thee and me.

Love,lady,prizeth wisely thee;
whose white and little hand annoys
the universal death,pardi:
whose most white body is his voice.
Night shall eat these girls and boys.

LITERARY TRIBUTES

I

CHAUCER

Kind is his mouth and smiling are his eyes,
Who rideth on that sunny pilgrimage,
And tears and laughter be his golden wage,
And that sweet carolling which never dies.
O Pilgrim of green springtide and blue skies,
Thy heart is dear to men of every age,
All sympathy is in thy withered page,
Whose soul was singing ere thy hand was wise.

'Tis not in marble that we worship thee,
But rather when the first white flower is come
To naked gardens, and immortal youth
Leaps to the world,—there shall thy worship be
In perfect simpleness and perfect truth,—
O singing soul no dying can make dumb!

II

Great Dante stands in Florence, looking down
In marble on the centuries.   Ye spell,
Beaneath his feet who walked in Heaven and Hell,
"L'Italia."   Here no longer lord and clown
Cringe, as of yore, to the immortal frown
Of him who loved his Italy too well:
Silent he stands, and like a sentinel
Stares from beneath those brows of dread renown.

Terrible, beautiful face, from whose pale lip
Anathema hurtled upon the world,
Stern mask, we read thee as an open scroll:
What if this mouth Hate's bitter smile has curled?
These eyes have known Love's starry fellowship;
Behind which trembles the tremendous soul.

III

FAME SPEAKS

Stand forth, John Keats!   On earth thou knew'st me not;
Steadfast through all the storms of passion, thou,
True to thy muse, and virgin to thy vow;
Resigned, if name with ashes were forgot,
So thou one arrow in the gold had'st shot!
I never placed my laurel on thy brow,
But on thy name I come to lay it now,
When thy bones wither in the earthly plot.
Fame is my name.   I dwell among the clouds,
Being immortal, and the wreath I bring
Itself is Immortality.   The sweets
Of earth I know not, more the pains, but wing
In mine own ether, with the crownéd crowds
Born of the centuries.—Stand forth, John Keats!

IV

HELEN

Only thou livest.   Centuries wheel and pass,
And generations wither into dust;
Royalty is the vulgar food of rust,
Valor and fame, their days be as the grass;

What of today?   vanitas, vanitas...
These treasures of rare love and costing lust
Shall the tomorrow reckon mold and must,
Ere, stricken of time, itself shall cry alas.

Sole sits majestic Death, high lord of change;
And Life, a little pinch of frankincense,
Sweetens the certain passing...from some sty

Leers even now the immanent face strange,
That leaned upon immortal battlements
To watch the beautiful young heroes die.

LOVE POEMS

I

I have looked upon thee—and I have loved thee,
Loved thy mouth, whose curve is the moon's young crescent,
Loved thy beauty-blossoming eyes, and eyelids
    Petal-like, perfect;
I would brush the dew in a flashing rainbow
From thy face's twain mysterious flowers,
And, supremely throned on the lips' full luna,
    Soar into Heaven.

II

REVERIE
(A translation from Sophocles's *Electra*)

This love of ours, you of my heart, is no light thing;
For I have seen it in the east and in the west,
And I have found it in the cloud and in the clear.
Are you not with me at all times, faithfully standing,
The soul of that golden prelude which is the childhood of day,
By each imperishable stanza called a moment,
Unto the splendid close, glory and light, envoi,
Followed with stars?
                          Verily you were near to me,
To watch the strong boy-swallows carolling in sunset,
To barter day and thought for night and ecstasy,
To dream great dreams, you of my heart; to live great lives.

You are the sunset.   You are the long night of peace.
And dawn is of you, a thrilling glory frightening stars.

III

Thy face is a still white house of holy things,
Graced with the quiet glory of thy hair.
Upon thy perfect forehead the sweet air
Hath laid her beauty where girlhood clings.
Thine eyes are quivering celestial springs
Of naked immortality, and there
God hath Hope, where those twin angels stare,
That sometimes sleep beneath their sheltering wings.
The seals of love on those strong lips of thine
Are perfect still; thy cheeks await their kiss.
Thou art all virginal; God made thee His.
Lost in the unreal life, the deathful din,
Man bows himself before the Only Shrine—
Who shall go in, O God—who shall go in?

IV

What is thy mouth to me?
A cup of sorrowful incense,
A tree of keen leaves,
An eager high ship,
A quiver of superb arrows.

What is thy breast to me?
A flower of new prayer,
A poem of firm light,
A well of cool birds,
A drawn bow trembling.

What is thy body to me?
A theatre of perfect silence,
A chariot of red speed;
And O, the dim feet
Of white-maned desires!

V

DEDICATION

The white rose my soul
Is blown upon the ways.
Over the high earth
Valleys bring it forth,
And it is found upon mountains.

The white rose my soul
Knoweth all winds and wings,
All nests, all songs,
With each smiling star,
And every graceful day.

The white rose my soul
Is under the world's feet.
(Only thou dost hold,
In that how little hand,
The red rose my heart.)

VI

I love you
For your little,startled,thoughtless ways,
For your ponderings,like soft dark birds,
And when you speak 'tis a sudden sunlight.

I love you
For your wide child eyes,and fluttering hands,
For the little divinities your wrists,
And the beautiful mysteries your fingers.

I love you.
Does the blossom study her day of life?
Is the butterfly vexed with an hour of soul?
I had rather a rose than live forever.

VII

After your poppied hair inaugurates
Twilight, with earnest of what pleading pearls;
After the carnal vine your beauty curls
Upon me, with such tingling opiates
As immobile my literal flesh awaits;
Ere the attent wind spiritual whirls
Upward the murdered throstles and the merles
Of that prompt forest which your smile creates;

Pausing, I lift my eyes as best I can,
Where twain frail candles close their single arc
Upon a water-colour by Cézanne.
But you, love thirsty, breathe across the gleam;
For total terror of the actual dark
Changing the shy equivalents of dream.

VIII

Moon-in-the-Trees,
The old canoe awaits you.
He is not, as you know, afraid of the dark,
And has unaided captured many stars.

The same tent expects your coming,
Moon-in-the-Trees.
You remember how the spruce smelled sweet
When the dawn was full of little birds?

In the ears of my days
Is a thunder of accomplished rivers;
In the nostrils of my nights
An incense of irrevocable mountains.

IX

When thou art dead,dead,and far from the splendid sin,
And the fleshless soul whines at the steep of the last abyss
To leave forever its heart acold in an earthy bed,

When,forth of the body which loved my body,the soul-within
Comes,naked from the pitiless metamorphosis,
What shall it say to mine,when we are dead,dead?

(When I am dead,dead, and they have laid thee in,
The body my lips so loved given to worms to kiss,
And the cool smooth throat,and bright hair of the head—).

X

You are tired,
(I think)
Of the always puzzle of living and doing;
And so am I.

Come with me, then,
And we'll leave it far and far away—
(Only you and I, understand!)

You have played,
(I think)
And broke the toys you were fondest of,
And are a little tired now;
Tired of things that break, and—
Just tired.
So am I.

But I come with a dream in my eyes tonight,
And I knock with a rose at the hopeless gate of your heart—
Open to me!
For I will show you the places Nobody knows,
And, if you like,
The perfect places of Sleep.

Ah, come with me!
I'll blow you that wonderful bubble, the moon,
That floats forever and a day;
I'll sing you the jacinth song
Of the probable stars;
I will attempt the unstartled steppes of dream,
Until I find the Only Flower,
Which shall keep (I think) your little heart
While the moon comes out of the sea.

XI

Let us lie here in the disturbing grass,
And slowly grow together under the sky
Sucked frail by Spring,whose meat is thou,and I,
This hurrying tree,and yonder pausing mass
Hitched to time scarcely,eager to surpass
Space:for the day decides;O let us lie
Receiving deepness,
Hearing,over

The poised,rushing night ring in the brim
Of Heaven;then,perpendicular odors stealing
Through curtains of new loosened dark;and one—
As the unaccountable bright sun
Becomes the horizon—
Bird,nearly lost,lost;wheeling,wheeling.

FRIENDS

I

T.A.M.
Sailed July, 1914

Auf wiedersehen!   We part a little while,
Friends alway, till what time we meet again.
Of this our life, the hours of sun and rain,
No palest flower the future can beguile;
Then let him frown his frown or smile his smile!
There are some things which have not lived in vain,
These which have made us men and which remain,
Tho' tide and time be lost 'twixt mile and mile.

Fear not, for thou shalt speak with me, my friend,
Who care not if this little journey's end
Lie past so great a gulf as never yields
One smallest murmur.—When the world's in sleep,
I will go out where God's white legions keep
A shining bivouac in celestial fields.

II

S.F.D.
In Memory of Claude o'Dreams

Behold, I have taken at thy hands immortal wine
The fume whereof is ecstasy of perfect pain,
Which is more sweet than flowers unknown uttered of rain,
More potent than the fumbling might of the brute of brine.
Lo, my pale soul is blown upon far peaks with thine,
Steeped in star-terrible silence, at whose feet the plain
Murmurs of thought and time's illimitable refrain,
Upon whose brows eternity setteth high sign.

This thing hath been, by grace; one music in our souls,
One fane beyond the world, whence riseth sacrifice
Unto that god whom gifts invisible appease.
So be it when sunset's golden diapaison rolls.
Over our life—then shalt thou, smiling, touch the keys,
And draw me softly with thee into Paradise.

III

Softly from its still lair in Plympton Street
It stole on silent pads, and, raping space,
Shot onward in a fierce infernal race,
And shivered townward on revolving feet,
Skidded, fortuitously indiscreet;
And now a lady doth its bosom grace,
And now the 'phone, tingling its wild disgrace,
Telleth that hearts be broke and time is fleet.

O Watson, born beneath a generous star,
Oft have I seen thee draped upon a bar;
Thou might'st have slain us with a bloody couteau
And,

    O Watson, moriturus te saluto,

Infinite in thy fair beatitude;
But you could not do anything so rude.

IV

S.T.

O friend, who hast attained thyself in her,
Thy wife, the almost woman whose tresses are
The stranger part of sunlight, in the far
Nearness of whose frail eyes instantly stir

Unchristian perfumes more remote than myrrh,
Whose smiling is the swiftly singular
Adventure of one inadvertent star,
With angels previously a loiterer,

Friend, who dost thy unfearing soul pervert
From the perfection of its constancy
To that unspeakable fellowship of Art—

Receive the complete pardon of my heart,
Who dost thy friend a little while desert
For the sensation of eternity.

LATE POEMS

I

They have hung the sky with arrows,
Targes of jubilant flame, and helms of splendor,
Knives and daggers of hissing light, and furious swords.

They have hung the lake with moth-wings,
Blurs of purple, and shaggy warmths of gold,
Lazy curious wines, and curving curds of silver.

They have hung my heart with a sunset,
Lilting flowers, and feathered cageless flames,
Death and love: ashes of roses, ashes of angels.

II

A painted wind has sprung
Clean of the rotten dark,
Lancing the glutted wolves of rain.

The sky is carried by a blue assault.
Strident with sun the heights swarm,
The vasts bulge with banners.

Working angels
Shovel light in heaven.

To carnival, to carnival,
In ribbons of red fire,
With spokes of golden laughter,
God drives the jingling world.

III

You shall sing my songs, O earth.
With tilted lips and dancing throat shall you sing them,
The songs my poems.

You shall dream my dreams, O world.
Locked in the shining house of beautiful sleep,
Of the dreams my poems.

You shall smile my smile, love.
My eyes, my eyes have stroked the bird of your soul,
The bird my poems.

IV

In Healey's Palace I was sitting—
Joe at the ivories, Irene spitting
Rag into the stinking dizzy
Misbegotten Hall, while Lizzie,
Like a she-demon in a rift
Of Hell-smoke, toured the booths, half-piffed.

I saw two rah-rahs—caps, soft shirts,
Match-legs, the kind of face that hurts,
The walk that makes death sweet—Ted Gore
And Alec Ross; they had that whore
Mary between them.   Don't know which,
One looked; and May said: "The old bitch
Lulu, as I'm a virgin, boys!"
And I yelled back over the noise:
"Did that three-legged baby croak
That you got off the salesman-bloke?"

The beer-glass missed.   It broke instead
On old man Davenport's bald head.
I picked a platter up, one-handed.
Right on her new straw lid it landed.
Cheest, what a crash!
                          Before you knew,
Ted slipped the management a new
Crisp five, and everyone sat down
But May, that said I'd spoiled her gown,
And me, that blubbered on her shoulder,
And kissed her shiny nose, and told her
I didn't mean to smash her...Crowst,
But I was beautifully soused!
I think Al called me "good old sport,"
And three smokes lugged out Davenport.

Experiments, 1916–17

I

The awful darkness of the town
crushes;in rows
houses every one a different shade of brown
(unity in variety,I suppose).
It almost snows:
inside,the silly people are teaing with bread-and-butter sandwiches

talking of the weather,and who
married whom
(the sons of b--s)
—thin smiles glue
the pasteboard faces,and prevent
sawdust from pouring out of this
chink or that.
The gloom
is flat,
as a poor pancake is
flat;"My dear,our church sent
three thousand bandages only last week
to those poor soldiers"—Whew!
how they reel

those sweet people.   But I'm
going into the Parthenon
to lap yaoorti with my eyes shut
tight.   Goodbye
Cambridge.   I'm going

in to see Nichol,and devour shishkabob(what
's the time?
Five? I must be moving on,
leaving the houses-all-alike
thank God)and I guess I'll drop in and get Mike
to give me a high.

II

A GIRL'S RING

the round of gold
tells me slenderly
twinkling
fauns pinkly

leapingassembled
to pipe-sob
and grappling
cymbals lunge thwart vistas

buxom
swaggering satyrs
from thousand
coverts smooth dryads

peek
eyes
trail
with merriment of spiraea

III

logeorge
              lo
                       wellifitisn't eddy   how's the boy
grandhave youheard
                              shoot

                                      you knowjim
goodscout   well

     married

     the hellyousay
                    whoto

          'member ritagail
     do i remember rita   what'sthejoke

                                        well

                                                              goddam

          don'ttakeit too hard old boy

sayare you kidding   me   because   ifyouare   byhell
     easyall george   watchyourstep old fellow

     christ

              that   that

mut

IV

wee people
            dwelling
between serene
                day-
light
and

    god

      o make room for
my coming which shall be
                    as
the sky comes

            down into those valleys

                        cocks cheer softly
                            a cow-bell

                            occassional
                            invisible

                            tamps
                            twilight

                    V

                the sky
                was   can dy
            lu   mi
                nous   ed
                                i
                ble
                    spry   pinks
                    shy   lem
                ons

                                        greens
            cool
        choco   lates
                un   der
        a   lo
            co
            mo   tive   s pout
                            ing
                vi
            o   lets

938

VI

beyond the stolid iron pond
soldered with complete silence
the huge timorous hills
squat like permanent vegetables

the judging sun pinches smiling
here and there some huddling vastness
claps the fattest finally
and tags it with his supreme blue

whereat the just adjacent valley
rolls proudly his belligerent bosom
deepens his greens inflates his ochres
and in the pool doubles his winnings

VII

mr. smith
is reading
his letter
by the fire-
light

    tea-time

        smiles friend smith

no type   bold o's
           d's gloat
           droll l's twine
           r's rove

        haha

           sweet-hearts
           part   fellow
           like   darl- write
           i dream my try ned ma
           thinks
           right thing   will be still
           till death
           thine

blows ring

strokes nose   P
toasts toes   S
              kiss

VIII

don't get me wrong oblivion
I never loved you kiddo
you that was always sticking around

                spoiling me for everyone else
                telling me how it would make
                you nutty if I didn't let you
                go the distance

and I gave you my breasts to feel
didn't I
      and my mouth to kiss

O I was too good to you oblivion old kid   that's all
and when I might have told you

                to go ahead and croak yourselflike
                you was always threatening you was
                going to do
                      I didn't
                      I said   go on you inter-
                      est me
                      I let you hang around
                      and whimper

and I've been getting mine
Listen

there's a fellow I love like I never loved anyone else that's six
    foot two tall with a face any girl would die to kiss and a skin
    like a little kitten's
that's asked me to go to Murray's tonight with him and see the cab-
    aret and dance   you know
well
if he asks me to take another I'm going to and if he asks me to take
another after that I'm going to do that and if he puts me into a taxi
and tells the driver to take her easy and steer for the morning I'm
going to let him and if he starts in right away putting it to me in
the cab
    I'm not going to whisper
    oblivion
do you get me
    not that I'm tired of automats and Childs's and handing out ribbon to
    old ladies that ain't got three teeth and being followed home by pimps

and stewed guys and sleeping lonely in a whitewashed room three thou-
sand below Zero   oh no
                              I could stand that
but it's that I'm O Gawd how tired
                              of seeing the white face of you and
                              feeling the old hands of you and
                              being teased and jollied about you
                              and being prayed and implored and
                              bribed and threatened
to give you my beautiful white body
    kiddo
              that's why

IX

wanta
spendsix

dollars Kid
      2 for the room
and
          four   for the girl
thewoman wasnot

quite Fourteen   till she smiled
                    then

Centuries   she
          soft ly
repeated
well   whadyas ay
      dear
      wan
      taspend

six

Dollars

X

maker of many mouths

earth

why yet once more pronounce
                    for the poor entertainment of
                    eternity

this old impertinence
   of the always unimportant

                         poet
                         death

   tree capable of spring

how does consent the genius of thy beauty
                                   haggard with re-
                                   hearsal

unprotestingly to take
   these uninspired lines

                  for whom

   unto what god acceptable

dost thou pronounce
indifferently
               o prompted sky

      mechanical gold

Reflections, 1918

I

along the justexisting road to Roupy
little in moonlight
go silently by men
(who will be damned if they know why)

où va-tu,Than-Time-Older with
wish-bones legs & the five bidons?
women in your eyes,
death on your shoulder

c'est madame de la guerre
with love-slovenly
mouth,
who has turned his mouth from
the crisp bright mouths of girls

the arms of wives are crying
& crying:you have taken the arms
which held us roughly and gently
madame de la Mort,we do not know you
and we hate you!

whither goest thou
Might Be Older
(death on your shoulder
women in your eyes?)

II

through the tasteless minute efficient room
march hexameters of unpleasant
twilight,a twilight smelling of Vergil,
as me bang(to and from)
the huggering rags of white Latin flesh
which her body sometimes isn't
(all night,always,a warm incessant gush
of furious Paris flutters up the hill,
cries somethings laughters loves nothings float
upward,beautifully,forces crazily rhyme,
Montmartre s'amuse!obscure eyes hotly dote
....as awkwardly toward me for the millionth time
sidles the ruddy rubbish of her kiss
i taste upon her mouth cabs and taxis.

III

my deathly body's deadly lady

smoothly-foolish exquisitely,tooled
(becoming exactly passionate Gladly

grips with chuckles of supreme sex

my mute-articulate protrusion)
Inviting my gorgeous bullet to vex

the fooling groove intuitive...

And the sharp ripples-of-her-brain bite
fondly into mine,
                    as the slow give-

of-hot-flesh Takes,me;in crazier waves of light
sweetsmelling
                    fragrant:
                              unspeakable chips
Hacked,
          from the immense sun(whose day is drooled
on night—)and the abrupt ship-of-her lips

disintegrates,with a coy!explosion

IV

first she like a piece of ill-oiled
machinery does a few naked tricks

next into unwhiteness,clumsily
lustful,plunges—covering the soiled
pillows with her violent hair
(eagerly then the huge greedily

Bed swallows easily our antics,
like smooth deep sweet ooze where
two guns lie,smile,grunting.)

"C'est la guerre"i probably suppose,
c'est la guerre busily hunting
for the valve which will stop this.
as i push aside roughly her nose

Hearing the large mouth mutter kiss pleece

V

The moon falls thru the autumn   Behind prisons she grins,
where people by huge whistles scooped from sleep land breathless
on their two feet, and look at her between bars.   She stands
greenly over the flat pasteboard hill with a little pink road
like a stand of spilled saw-dust.   The sentinel who walks asle
ep under apple-trees yawns.   The moon regards little whores
running down the prison yard into the dawn to shit, and she is
tickled too.   (Trees in morning are like strengths of young
men poised to sprint.)   There's another sentinel wanders al
ong besides a wall perhaps as old as he.   The little moon
pinks into insignificance:a grouch of sun gobbles the east—
She is a white shadow asleep in the reddishness of
Day.

VI

The moon-lit snow is falling like strange candy into the big eyes of the
little people with smiling bodies and wooden feet

hard thick feet full of toes

left-handed kiss

I think Berthe is the snow,and comes down into all corners of the city with a
smelling sound.   The moon shines all green in the snow.

then saw I 1 Star cold in the nearness of sunset. the face of this star was a
woman's and had worked hard.   the cheeks were high and hard,it powdered them
in a little mirror before everybody saying always nothing at all   The lips
were small and warped,it reddened them.   Then one cried to it & it cried Je
viens and went on looking at itself in the little mirror saying always nothing
—Then I ask the crowding orange—how is that star called? she answers Berthe,
changing into a violet very stealthily
O with whom I lay
Whose flesh is stallions
Then I knew my youth trampled with thy hooves of nakedness

23years lying with thee in the bed in the little street off the Faubourg Mon
martre

        tongue's cold wad knocks

VII

Perhaps it was Myself sits down in this chair.   There were two chairs,in fact.
My fur-coat on.   Light one cigarette.   You
came her stalking straw-coloured body,cached with longness of kimona.

Myself got up out of a chair(there are two)say "Berthe" or something else.
Her Nudity seats Itself sharply beside.   New person. —The champagne is ex-
cellent sir.— so we are drinking a little,and talked gradually of the war
France death my prison,all pleasant things.   "Je m'occuperai tout particu-
lierement de vos colis".   and send one to The Zulu,as i want, one to mon
camarade   "vous n'avez pas trop chaud avec la pelisse?"no...I decline more
champagne anyway "Vous partez—?demain matin?""le train part a huit heures
un quart"

I watched her Flesh graciously destroy its cruel posture   "alors:il faut
bien dormir
".then is to be noticed...plural darkness spanked with singular light over
the pink
bed

To Undress—laughably mechanical   how my great ludicrous silent boots thrown
off Eye each other,really
As she lay:the body a flapping rag of life;I see pale whim of suppressed face
framed in the indignant hair,a jiggling rope of smile hung between painted
cheeks. and the furry rug of tongue where her Few teeth dance slowly like
bad women
My thumb smashes the world—
frot of furied eyes on brain!heart knotted with A suddenly nakedness—.

VIII

NOISE

thugs of clumsy mutter shove upward leaving fat
            feet-prints,rumbles poke buzzing thumbs
            in eye of world

stovelike emotion rapidly scrambles toots and
            scurry nibbling screams and sleek
            whistles which sprint ribbons of
            white shriek!   clatters limp,

from svelt blubbering tubes Big dins fuzzily
            lumber rub-bing their eyes

thin very chimney lips wallow gushing cubes
            of unhasty delirium,chunks of
            indolence waddle slowly.

bangs punch.

explosion after

explosion: from black lips sail chrome
            cries extra extra whatisit no?   Yes!
            no! yea: extra wheel! oh hear it
            what no-yes (extra! extra) who, said
            Yea? what! yea! yes.

PEACE Joy's right boot squashes disciplined
            fragilities by slobber of,patient
            timidities undermined skyscrapers,
            Krash;it (explodes in a) plastic Meeow
            —with uncouth snarl of sculptural
            fur through which Claws

neatly

leap Wall Street wriggles choked with gesturing
            human swill squirms gagged with
            a sprouting filth of faces extra!
            PEACE millions like crabs about a

prosperous penis of bigness the woolworth
building,slowly waving

factories-stores-houses-burstcrack—people!
through,doorswindows,Tears a
vomit of supernatural buttons

PEACE

biffing sky battles huge city which escapes
niftily through slit-of-sunset
Broadway.
dumb signs ripe

pustules of unhealth.   squEEzed:spatter
pop-p-ings of mad

colour reveal,

canyons of superb nonsense.   Vistas of
neatness bunged with a wagging
humanity poised;In the bathing,

instant   a reek-of electric daintiness PEACE

all night from timetotime the city's accurate
face peeks from smothering blanket
of occult pandemonium

PEACE all night!   into dawn-dingy dimness:
of almost

streets; capers a trickle of mucus
shapes equals girls men.

IX

a Woman
        of bronze
unhappy
                stands
at the mouth
an oldish woman
                        in a night-gown
            Boosting a

torch
Always
        a tired woman
        she has had children
                        and They have forgotten
        Standing

                looking out
to sea

X

hips lOOsest OOping shoulders blonde& pastoral hair,strong,
arms and smelling of HAY
woman in a carotcoloured skin yellow face chipsofanger splayed
from GriNDing-mouth waist pulledup on oneside SHOWED her
sweaty corset.
         eyeslike   smoky   idols

girl,iceblue hair huGe lips like orangepeels,waV ingagreat
tricolour
      yelling silently
                cheery-nose square pash eyes splut
tering warench ofscarlet on right-breast legs
monumentally aPart
(Girl)flagstuck in her breasts. she bent her neck and bit It
jam mingIt deeper—pink—complexion tooth gone left side red
we epingeye s CHUBBY

their grey   hands tired of making   Death Probable

hairycheeks faces like hugestrawberries
                  they pass a funeral in
silence and their branches had a terrible greenness

                La Grève the Goddess
                        tooth less
witches from Whose.gumsBurs !tthe
            Cry

leather faces,crinkling with Ideal,the common,people
let-out of darkNess

XI

this cigarette is extremely long,
i get them by the indigo box of 10.
And then, you were sitting across from me:
and my blood silkily telling i was, how wrong!
(i thinking to have remembered how
you were beautiful) this cigarette, when
inhaled, produces a mystery
like scented angels joking in a sharp soft row
(i buy 10 of them in an indigo box.)
Wrists. Elbows, Shoulders. Fingers.
the minute amorous stirs
of flesh invisibly visible (this
cigarette, exhaled in musical shocks
of kiss-coloured silence) by Christ kiss me. One kiss

XII

love was—entire excellently steep

therefore(most deftly as tall dreams unleash
pale wish,between mirrors thoughts blundering
merge;softly thing forgets its name:
memories descending open—time reverses)
the million poets of our single flesh

gradually prepare to enter sleep

Around worldfully whom noises pour
carefully(exploding faintly)while(humbling

faintestly)among unminds go stumbling
cries bright whip-crash leaps lunge thundering
wheels and striving(are now faintestly)come
strutting such(wonderfully how through our

deepestly hearts immensely strolling)horses.

Poems for Elaine Orr, 1918–19

I

let us suspect,chérie,this not very big
box completely mysterious,on whose shut
lid in large letters but neatly is
inscribed "Immortality".   And not
go too near it,however people brag
of the wonderful things inside
which are altogether too good to miss—
but we'll go by,together,giving it a wide
berth.   Silently.   Making our feet
think.   Holding our breath—
if we look at it we will want to touch it.
And we mustn't because(something tells me)
ever so very carefully if we
begin to handle it

        out jumps Jack Death

II

sometime,perhaps in Paris we will
have the enormous bright hour of evening
when lazily the prostitutes are taking
thither and hither their bright slender voices
along the boulevards,among the sitting
people in cafés
                    "the world is,you feel
(I just saw a man in a taxi who looked like God)
a little sudden whore skilfully dying
in Somebody's arms,on the way to the theatre."—"Did
you?"—"And just suppose it were.   Wouldn't poor Royce's
hair tremble?   What would Old Man Emerson
say?"—"Emerson would probably say 'I went to Paris
and found myself.'"—"Probably."—"And think of this one:
'Godal Mighty and Myself,by Frank Harris'!"

III

chérie
      the very,picturesque,last Day
(when all the clocks have lost their jobs and god
sits up quickly to judge the Big Sinners)
he will have something large and fluffy to say
to me.   All the pale grumbling wings

of his greater angels will cease:as that Curse

bounds neat-ly from the angry wad

of his forehead(then fiends with pitchforkthings
will catch and toss me lovingly to
and fro.)   Last,should you look,you
'll find me prone upon a greatest flame,

which seethes in a beautiful way
upward;with someone by the name
of Paolo passing the time of day.

IV

my little heart is so wonderfully sorry
lady,to have seen you on its threshold
smiling,to have experienced the glory

of your slender and bright going, and it is so cold
(nothing being able to comfort its grief)
without you,that it would like i guess to die.
Also my lady do i feel as if
perhaps the newly darkening texture of my
upon nothing a little clumsily closing
mind will keep always something who has

fallen,who being beautiful is gone
and suddenly.   As if you will point at the evening

"in this particular place,my lover,the moon
unspeakably slender and bright was"

V

the spring has been exquisite and the
summer may be beautiful.   But,
tell me with eyes quiteshut
did you love me,will you love me

and perfectly so forth;i see,
kissing you—only kissing
you(it is still spring
and summer may be beautiful)shall we

say years?   O let us say it,girl
to boy smiling while the moments kill
us gently and infinitely.

And believe(do not believe)there'll
be a time when even these leaves will

crawl expensively away.   My lady.

VI

willing pitifully to bewitch
the nude worm of my reaching mind,to tease
its gropings curiously i remark these
frivolous slowlywinking lives which
(like four or three pretty flies)the
very and tremulous architecture
of frail light suddenly will capture.
And i think
                    (as if perhaps a tree
should remember how Spring touched it)of your
deep kiss which constructs faintly
in me an upward country(on whose new shores
the first day has not come,but it is quaintly
always morning and silence)always where

hang,in the morning,wistful corpses of stars.

VII

as
we lie side by side
my little breasts become two sharp delightful strutting towers and
i shove hotly the lovingness of my belly against you

your arms are
young;
your arms will convince me,in the complete silence speaking
upon my body
their ultimate slender language.

do not laugh at my thighs.

there is between my big legs a crisp city.
when you touch me
it is Spring in the city;the streets beautifully writhe,
it is for you;do not frighten them,
all the houses terribly tighten
upon your coming:
and they are glad
as you fill the streets of my city with children.

my love you are a bright mountain which feels.
you are a keen mountain and an eager island whose
lively slopes are based always in the me which is shrugging,which is
under you and around you and forever:i am the hugging sea.
O mountain you cannot escape me
your roots are anchored in my silence;therefore O mountain
skilfully murder my breasts,still and always

i will hug you solemnly into me.

VIII

my lady is an ivory garden,
who is filled with flowers.

under the silent and great blossom
of subtle colour which is her hair
her ear is a frail and mysterious flower
her nostrils
are timid and exquisite
flowers skilfully moving
with the least caress of breathing,her
eyes and her mouth are three flowers.   My lady

is an ivory garden
her shoulders are smooth and shining
flowers
beneath which are the sharp and new
flowers of her little breasts tilting upward with love
her hand is five flowers
upon her whitest belly there is a clever dreamshaped flower
and her wrists are the merest most wonderful flowers   my

lady is filled
with flowers
her feet are slenderest
each is five flowers her ankle
is a minute flower
my lady's knees are two flowers
Her thighs are huge and firm flowers of night
and perfectly between
them eagerly sleeping
is

the sudden flower of complete amazement

my lady who is filled with flowers
is an ivory garden.

And the moon is a young man

who i see regularly,about twilight,
enter the garden smiling to
himself.

IX

if you like my poems let them
walk in the evening,a little behind you

then people will say
"Along this road i saw a princess pass
on her way to meet her lover(it was
toward nightfall)with tall and ignorant servants."

Poems from The Dial Papers, 1919–20

I

the comedian stands on a corner,the sky is
ve   ry   soF.   t   Ly. Fal,   Ling   (snow

with a limousines the and whisk of swiftly taxis God

knows howmany mouths eyes bodies
fleetly going into nothing,

verysky the and.of all is,slow-
Ly.faLLing
                    ,f all in g)FaLlInG   odd
....which will. swiftly Hug   kiss   or

a drunken Man bangs silentl Y   into the moo
                                                        n
the comedian is standing.   On a corner   in-a-dream
of.(sn)ow,
                    in the nib; bling tune
OF
      "nextwehave the famous dancing team
swiftness & nothing
                              ,letergo
                                    Professor!

II

like most godhouses this particular house
of god utters a chilly smell....
Within,the rector's talking normal face
like a cat who plays with a dead mouse
skilfully mumbles about Hell,
pretending it's alive,knowing it is
not.   That head which(you'll confess)
looks like the apple whereby Adam fell
belongingly adorns the fat demure
hairless man sitting heavily with what
is obviously his wife,his small unthrilled
circular ears winking to the word of God
his large unclever mind carefully filled
with inexpensive christian funiture.

III

This is the vase,   Here

is the crisp and the only and the very sudden garden in
which the little princes strut,taller than
flowers

(here are,a thousand erect and bright
princes tenderly smiling and smiling forever)

this is the vase.
Here are a million alwaysmoving ladies
always moving,and moving slenderly
around a keen and little princess

taller than a day,

This
is the vase   here are a billion
warriors with furious and supple
faces like white nouns.   With
bodies like smiling and gigantic verbs

If we turn the
vase,slowly the little and
keen princess will come slender
-ly out of a million ladies.   The
bright and erect princes suddenly will strut
in the garden.   the soldiers
who are supple and who
are furious will become,
not only and crisply,
                    Gigantic and Smiling.
They will step from the
                    vase:

                    tearless,
                    together.
taller than Tomorrow

IV

my humorous ghost precisely will
stray from the others on the hill
if only to hear someone say
exactly what someone has said.

Straying as softly as a puma,
it will come to Boston
and sit in the Howard Atheneum
up under the non si fuma,

(up in the ceiling with the old men.
With the wrinkles and eyes and tumours.)
Precisely straying like a leopard
or a music,will my ghost

visit queerly the naked girls who
wiggle at the end of second avenue
in the Burlesque As You
Like it,or gliding most

softly into Hassan's will see
them all dancing together,a turk
and one girl and three greeks
with the cousin of the old Man In The Moon playing

the kanoon.   (After that,
precisely i will float into Moskowitz's
where there's himself at the zimbalon,and
Raisin tight with Jack Shargel at a table in the

spidery music,ordering Bosca
singing oona vaap and gesturing like a Petrouska.
And i'll gesture as well as i am able in the
transparent condition which ghosts

are afflicted with,
my gestures will be in the past tense
and bright and small and ridiculous.)
And after all i'll go to a certain

house where the window is open
i will go in between the curtains
silently,like a cat or a tune.   I will find
softly and precisely a particular room where

you are perfectly asleep in your hair,
and you will kiss my ghost thinking
that it's a dream,until i leap from you
suddenly out into the morning

V

dawn

and now.begins
f e e l i n g
roofs
a cool-
ness-Before-light,(hush
) it's the indescribable minute

(noises
happen
Bigly!   a milk-wagon
totters(by,its sleepy horses step-
ping like clockwork,a driver scarcely alive.)bAnGiNgLy
along which The little a street absurdly new
      :Houses
are,with firm
light   wonderful,but and

suddenly)

hear?do you birds begin which all to talk,loudly
in the disappearing air

VI

Above a between-the-acts prattling of
the orchestra conducted by memory and behind this
justfallen curtain of uneasy flesh
which is a girl

certain things shout and curse
turning on lights setting up walls amid
a very efficient confusion as certain
other things i dare say take their
proper places wiping their mouths adjusting a cravat and
settling one's vest or smoothing
the hair
and one immaculately tailored
thing inhales a cigarette un-
clenching and clench
-ing plump fingers
and peeping at the audience

Because these to me wholly i
confess impertinent
noises are better than the politeness of
silence or that is to say when the curtain
rises   and to all the other people who
are my multitudinous cleansmelling selves
who are sitting waiting to be thrilled

Illusion!

makes its rubber gesture,

decidedly i refuse my lady your beautifully
imbecile invitation to hasten the play

VII

when time delicately is sponging sum after
sum memory after memory
from the neatening blackness
of my mind

and i am not exactly old,

(but Spring is

Plunging in the big absurd world with
a difference)and when the mauled

flower of your mouth
is old and cold,and bold....

i think(excuse me if i
speak the truth)you will be yellow & sick
for me(your
mouth and the rest of you whatever
that is,i suppose

breasts and throat,legs and hands.)   Lady
in that
day i think
(it's only thinking.   Your pardon if i err.)
i think you will be tired of telling
me & my dreams to go to hell

VIII

sometimes i am alive because with
me her alert treelike body sleeps
which i will feel slowly sharpening
becoming distinct with love slowly,
who in my shoulder sinks sweetly teeth
until we shall attain the Springsmelling
intense large togethercoloured instant

the moment pleasantly frightful

when,her mouth suddenly rising,wholly
begins with mine fiercely to fool
(and from my thighs which shrug and pant
a murdering rain leapingly reaches the
upward singular deepest flower which she
carries in a gesture of her hips)

IX

o my wholly unwise and definite
lady of the wistful dollish hands

(whose nudity hurriedly extends
its final gesture lewd and exquisite,
with a certain agreeable and wee
decorum)o my wholly made for loving
lady
    (and what is left of me
your kissing breasts timidly complicate)

only always your kiss will grasp me quite.

Always only my arms completely press
through the hideous and bright night
your crazed and interesting nakedness

—from you always i only rise from something

slovenly beautiful gestureless

X

my youthful lady will have other lovers
yet none with hearts more motionless than i
when to my lust she pleasantly uncovers
the thrilling hunger of her possible body.

Noone can be whose arms more hugely cry
whose lips more singularly starve to press her—
noone shall ever do unto my lady
what my blood does,when i hold and kiss her

(or if sometime she nakedly invite
me all her nakedness deeply to win
her flesh is like all the 'cellos of night
against the morning's single violin)

more far a thing than ships or flowers tell us,
her kiss furiously me understands
like a bright forest of fleet and huge trees
—then what if she shall have an hundred fellows?

she will remember,as i think,my hands

(it were not well to be in this thing jealous.)
My youthful lust will have no further ladies.

XI

lady you have written me a letter
which i will never keep in a foolish vermilion
box glad with possible dragons

but in a surer place,and in a better
place and in a richer(and
if sometimes i will take it out,to see
how it is,perhaps you will understand
perhaps you will know that a million

things happen richly in me.)
And where i will put it away my lady
you will understand,only if once
(if leaning and with little breasts apart
you quickly will look into the

dark box of my shutting heart

XII

but   turning a corner   ,i
(Of)was am aware a talkative
huge.ness moo.vingOne(tree   a huge,talking of rain;squabb
-ling leaves the.high   .a)
tree!Is or
(is it leaves)the   are.filled
with moving.the colour
of,night the is it col,our of the
isColoured   mobile&supreme
dark,
Ness.
colour of rain.
Ness. dark,ness.   colour of the.   colour Of of

i
am a therefore
little unsorry   for our
bodies,bodies of.you & me and
unsorry because you   and   me are is
one,tree   unsorry;that
(youandme,the)bodies!of,first singular
Am strong and moving & answerable to oblivion.

XIII

you said Is
there anything which
is dead or alive more beautiful
than my body,to have in your fingers
(trembling ever so little)?
                              Looking into
your eyes Nothing,i said,except the
air of spring smelling of never and forever.

....and through the lattice which moved as
if a hand is touched by a
hand(which
moved as though
fingers touch a girl's
breast,
lightly)
          Do you believe in always,the wind
said to the rain
I am too busy with
my flowers to believe,the rain answered

XIV

is
it

because there struts a distinct silver lady

(we being passionate O yes)upon
the carpet of evening which thrills
with the minuteness of her
walking,for she walks

upon the evening
                    shy and luxurious   .and because

we
being

passionate perceive o Yes where(immensely
near)
simply,

but with a colour like the ending of the world
rises

        slow
              ly

balloonlike

            the huge foetus of The Moon   ?

—with our gestures we pry
and our mouths battle into distinctness.   It
is this kiss which builds in us ever so softly

the coarse and terrible structure of the night.

XV

as one who(having written
late)sees his light
silenced.

    and going to his window
    a little while he
             watches
    the inevitable city's

reborn enormous whisperless

               Body
               (and

sees
      over & between the roofs

                  the lifted streets
                  un-

                  speak.
                  -ing

                      and he does not
speak.)But perhaps
inhaling a possible.cigarette
he is sorry and
pitiful.and he quietly repeats to
himself
    something peculiar and small and dead

And goes to sleep miserable & tall.

                —so,my
                lady is
                    your lover

when he a little closes his eyes
thinking "tonight i did not lie in her bed." and the Light

The
tall
extraordinary   Light   ,It

goes rapidly over the perhaps world(over
the possible Now & the lilies.over

  Whoever & me?)

  nouns and

              violets   !

                   ships,   &   countries

XVI

in front of your house i

stopped for a second in the
rain,in the Spring.
At the window
            only your hands

            beautifully,
            were

(and the green bird perched carefully upon

                        a gesture

knew me.)

XVII

Lady,i will touch you with my mind.
Touch you and touch and touch
until you give
me suddenly a smile,shyly obscene

(lady i will
touch you with my mind.)Touch
you,that is all,

lightly and you utterly will become
with infinite ease

the poem which i do not write.

Poems from the 1920's

I

1.

the newly

cued
motif smites truly to beautifully
retire through its english

the forwardflung backwardspinning top returns fasterishly
whipped the top leaps bounding upon other tops to caroming
off persist displacing its own and their lives who
grow slowly and first into different deaths

concentric arithmetics of transparency slightly
joggled sink through algebras of proud

inwardlyness to collide spirally with iron geometries
and mesh with
which when both

march outward into the freezing fire of thickness

everywhere is updownwardishly
found nowherecoloured curvecorners
gush silently into solids
more fluid than gas

2.

now two old ladies sit peacefully knitting,
and their names are sometimes and always

"i can't understand what life could have seen in him" stitch
-counting always severely remarks;and her sister(suppress-
ing a yawn)counters "o i don't know;death's rather attractive"
—"attractive!why how can you say such a thing?when i think
of my poor dear husband"—"now don't be absurd:what i said was
'rather attractive',my dear;and you know very well that
never was very much more than attractive,never was

stunning"(a crash.   Both jump)"good
heavens!" always exclaims "what
was that?"—"well here comes your daughter"
soothes sometimes;at which

death's pretty young wife enters;wringing her hands,and wailing
"that terrible child!"—"what"(sometimes and always together
cry)"now?"—"my doll:my beautiful doll;the very
first doll you gave me,mother(when i could scarcely
walk)with the eyes that opened and shut(you remember:
don't you,auntie;we called her love)and i've treasured
her all these years,and today i went through a closet
looking for something;and opened a box,and there she
lay:and when he saw her,he begged me to let him
hold her;just once:and i told him 'mankind,be careful;
she's terribly fragile:don't break her,or mother'll be angry' "

and then(except for
the clicking of needles)there was silence

3.

"out of the pants which cover me
frostbitten limbs from pole to pole
I thank whatever tailors be
for this unconquerable hole.
A little Porter tingaling
is pleasant even for Sweeney in the Spring."

And at these words a sullen murmur ran
out of the University of Pennsylvania.
"However which may be;
I grow old,I grow old,

I shall tell the tailor what he should be told."—
And as he spake Lars Porcelain
struck his bathtub
exclaiming,in words of one syllable,Eheu fugaces Postume.
(and nobody knew what daisy knew

for all men kill the thing they love:

Some does it with a turn of the screw....
and go wilde afterwards he adding settled
his frustrated celluloid collar.

4.

pound pound pound
on thy cold grey corona oh P.

but I would that my tongue could utter
the silence of Alfred Noise.

Speak speak thou Fearful guest;tell me,immediate
child of Homer—when you wrote The Dial Cantos did you know
of the organ and the monkey?

Tears,idle Tears!   I know not what you mean....
dear little Sweeney,child of fate,
how dost thou?—And the stiff dishonoured nightingales:

fled is that music.   (I perceive
a with undubitably clotted hinderparts in obviously

compatriot;let us step into this metaphor.)

5.

2 shes

both not quite
young perfectly

respectable obviously married

women each a you
know soup son more
a(with of course their well
above their showing)

sit Sat LOOK

ing and lookanding andlookingand at
what That)then i
start
ed
laughing obvicouldn't

ouslyhelp itwhy be

cause the
he can you sitting
on that very bench in perfectly
bright obviously sunlight Right
before Every
one the yes Hole

WORLD was(praying chin up eyes

tightshut locked
hands pray)ing unbeliev
able he real
(was young was
niceyeslooking but some

Yes

how weak sort of or i doano)the
atrical now you
got me laughing but we shooden eye
can't helpid omygod hehehemygodhegodmy

god.   Allatonce the apparition

arose and
looking straightahead
offwalked

dis(

appea)ring a
mong treestreestrees

greennewlying

II

I.

When parsing warmths of dusk construe
The moon a noun of personal blood
Subject to that veteran verb
Of imperative vacancy

The velvet tiger of my soul
Washing in fundamental mind
Ellided chaos hating
Leases sensation absolute

Then clustering to the average green
Slants the huge ship of total lust
Footed with foam and clewed with stars
Into my gaunt uneating heart

2.

Lady,since your footstep
is more frail than everything
which lives,than everything which breathes
in the earth and in the sea
because your body is more new,

a dream(skilfully who mimics,entirely who pictures
yourself a skilfully and entirely moving dream
with fingers,a dream with lifted little breasts
and with feet)touches

me through the day scarcely,timidly;

whereas,beside me through the long night and upon
me,always i feel the crisply and deeply moving
you which is so glad to be alive—

the you with hot big inward stealing
thighs,perfectly who steal me;or as the wise

sea steals entirely and skilfully the ignorant earth.

3.

being(just a little)
too tired from kissing
for thinking or anything
except dreaming,
let us suppose

O my lady:at dusk
between the earth and the sea

ourselves,you and i together mysteriously and always floating,

moving;absorbing mysteriously(or as desire absorbs
a dream)and(as if we were dream or dreams)mysteriously
engulfed by fatal immensities of twilight—O imagine(softly as
we,our minds,mysteriously together moving float always

between the ocean and the world)that,smiling,i remark to
you:of these five waves the wave

which waits is most great;

(of these nine roses,you
reply seriously,she who chiefly hides
herself is deepest)

4.

Lady

i pray to what is unimaginable,
to your smile
which will not even allow even my pencil
nearer than a thousand miles.

i pray to your eyes
whose niceness decides my pen
it is a thick fool.

my brushes go big and stupid
and their colour(s)turns to paint before
your laughter,to which i kneel.

i worship at your tears
i approach your tears with my best chisels
(but in your least tear there is nothing
conceivable)
              my chisels stutter and wobble.

But chiefly i entreat your timidity
(i mean that aspect of you which so easily can
explore completely and enjoy the occult textures,
consult wholly and continually the invisible edges,of that and this:
distinguish swiftly and exquisitely

in all things what entirely is alive.)

III

I.

THE RAIN IS A HANDSOME ANIMAL

Whereupon i seize a train and suddenly i am in Paris toward night,in Mai.
Along the river trees are letting go scarcely and silently wisps,parcels
of incense,which drop floatingly through a vista of talking moving people;
timidly which caress hats and shoulders,wrists and dresses;which unspeak-
ingly alight upon the laughter of men and children,girls and soldiers.
In twilight these ridiculous and exquisite things descendingly move among
the people,gently and imperishably.   People are not sorry to be alive.
People are not ashamed.   People smile,moving gaily and irrevocably moving
through twilight to The Gingerbread Fair.   I am alive,I go along too,I
slowly go up the vista among the hats and soldiers,among the smiles and
neckties,the kisses and old men,wrists and laughter.   We all together ir-
revocably are moving,are moving slowly and gaily moving.   Intricately the
shoulders of us and our hats timidly are touched by a million absurd hint-
ing things;by wisps and by women and by laughter and by forever:while,
upon our minds,fasten beautifully and close the warm tentacles of evening.

2.

AFTER SEEING FRENCH FUNERAL

in front of the cathedral hovered a mumbling nobody:its greenish fumbling
flesh swathed with crumbling alive rags,its trunk topped abruptly by a
slouch hat under which carefully existed the deep filthy face and out of
which sprouted wisely a decayed yellowish width of beard.

he came out just at noon:the little Place Saint Michel banged and tooted
in shallow hard sunlight;from all which upreaching through white fog the
boulevard hung,in a maze of sticky colour punched here and here at inter-
vals by black blunt shapes or where some hobgoblin trees poking sprouted
amputated hands.

3.

taxis toot whirl people moving perhaps laugh into the slowly
millions and finally O it is spring since at all windows
microscopic birds sing fiercely two ragged men and a
filthiest woman busily are mending three wholly broken somehow
bowls or somethings by the web curb and carefully spring is
somehow skilfully everywhere mending smashed minds
O
the massacred gigantic world
again,into keen sunlight who lifts
glittering selfish new
limbs
and my heart stirs in his rags shaking from his armpits the
abundant lice of dreams laughing
rising sweetly out of the alive new mud my old
man heart striding shouts whimpers screams breathing into
his folded belly acres of sticky sunlight chatters bellows
swallowing globs of big life pricks wickedly his
mangled ears blinks into worlds of colour shrieking
O begins
            the mutilated huge earth
again,up through darkness leaping
who sprints weirdly from its deep prison
groaning with perception and suddenly in all filthy alert things
which jumps mightily out of death
muscular,stinking,erect,entirely born.

4.

long ago,between a dream and a dream

(when monsieur matal directed la reine blanche
opposite cluny's gladly miraculous most
vierge et l'enfant)someone was morethanalive
with love;with love:with love—love of whom?
love:paris;la france,une fille and at least

(while every night was a day and a day was dimanche)
seven or—not to exaggerate—certainly five

selves beyond every human imagining my;
whereas,in this epoch of mindandsoul,to feel
you're not two billion other unselves is enough
to scare any no one nearly-if-not-quite stiff
—how did(i often ask me)that someone die?

but just as often the answer's only a smile

5.

them which despair
do we despise,being seated
in the cave's oblong darkness
having commanded our minute glasses
of colourless fire.
Nothing is better than this
except which has not happened,thence
i bid you(as very deeply you near the gates of
Hell)cast like Euridyce one brief look behind
yourself.
               Voilà Monsieur Le Patron,
excuse me:I was talking.   He pours
quickly skilfully just.
It.   Glistens.

Voilà—the waterhued extract of Is

believe:sipping,enter my arms;let us invade sumptuously
the hurrying extravagant instant....come mon amie
let us investigate suddenly
our lives,let us drink calvados,

let us shut ourselves into the garret of Now
and swallow the key.

6.

Paris,thou art not
merely these streets trees silence
twilight,nor even this single star jotting
nothing busily upon the green edges of evening;
nor the faces which sit and drink on the boulevards,laughing
which converse smoke smile,thou art
not only a million little ladies fluttering merely upon darkness—

these things thou art and thou art all which is alert perishable
alive:thou art the sublimation of our
lives eyes voices
thou art the gesture by which we express to one another all
which we hold more dear and fragile than death,
thou art the dark dear fragile
gesture which we use

Life 's—let us not too much protest—not clumsy
more than another thing.   Nor ungainly
but(after all)of a convenient size:
not too minute to die about
nor too big to lie about.

softly above everything the strolling
upward ghost of le tour Eiffel quietly wonderfully
hangs;haunting the mai.

7.

Perfectly a year,we watched Together les enfants jumping and
cry Prenez garde Monsieur c'est Le Diable and.punch jerk

bonnes giggled-background slope,Erect

...under grEEnoftrees;shadowily

  sof   tness

            mon ami
                  hoary
goldfish pluc k ing
at bread
        2balloons   red&blue   tiedtogethergo   Up.bumP ingand
HOpPinG

the merrygoround
             (eternal)
boats,
  leaping with wind comingin SatisFiedor st:uck   under the
  central fountain

              and;spherical chestnut-trees
soldiers,Le Jardin

and(still)in the louvre the knight sleeps 8 monksbear Him with
bent?heads his   feet rest,on his Dog

     paris
      paris
      paris
  it was about to rain and,a thousand girls came-marching into
the same garden flinging their marching Spurting youth
                     on the
grass
    green
   things branches in Their hands red on their Breasts crowns
of fleur d'oranger on brown heads

as if they had torn upthe World bytheroots
all seeking the sunlight-Bridegroom

                              large mouth of Jean little

a young Place soldier chucks de la half a dozen of oranges
République uptothe sitters on the Monument
                                        the women cry
                                        vive le poilu

voilà deux sous
he's forced to take their money;

8.

look
my fingers,which
touched you
and your warmth and crisp
littleness
—see?do not resemble my
fingers.   My wrists hands
which held carefully the soft silence
of you(and your body
smile eyes feet hands)
are different
from what they were.   My arms
in which all of you lay folded
quietly,like a
leaf or some flower
newly made by Spring
Herself,are not my
arms.   I do not recognise
as myself this which i find before
me in a mirror.   i do
not believe
i have ever seen these things;
someone whom you love
and who is slenderer
taller than
myself has entered and become such
lips as i use to talk with,
a new person is alive and
gestures with my
or it is perhaps you who
with my voice
are
playing.

9.

when of your eyes one smile entirely brings down
the night in rain over the shy town of my mind
when upon my heart lives the loud alive darkness
and in my blood beating and beating with love
the chuckling big night puzzles asquirm with sound
when all my reaching towers and roofs are drenched with love
my streets whispering bulge my trembling houses yearn
my walls throb and writhe my spires curl with darkness

then in me hands light lamps against this darkness(hands here
and there hands go thither and hither in my town)

carefully close windows shut doors

10.

this fear is no longer dear.   You are not going to America and
i but that doesn't in the least matter.   The big
fear Who had us deeply in his fist is
no longer,can you imagine it
i can't which doesn't matter
and what does is possibly this dear,that we
may resume impact with the inutile,collide
once more with the imagined,love,and eat sunlight(do
you believe it?   i begin to and that doesn't matter)which i
suggest teach us a new terror whereby shall always brighten
carefully those things we consider life

IV

1.

                    the other guineahen
died of a broken heart and we came to New York.
I used to sit at a table,drawing wings
with a pencil that kept breaking and i kept

remembering how your mind looked when it slept
for several years,to wake up asking why.
So then you turned into a photograph

of somebody who's trying not to laugh
at somebody who's trying not to cry

2.

love's absence is illusion,alias time

(a shadowy hell whose inmates war to seize
each nothing which all greedy wraiths proclaim
substance;all frenzied spectres,happiness)

lovers alone wear sunlight.   The whole truth

(not hid by matter;not by mind revealed)
which never was by any living death
or dying life(and never will be)told

sings only—and all lovers are the song.

Here(only here)is freedom;always here
no then of winter equals now of spring
but april's day transcends november's year

(eternity being so sans until,
twice i have lived forever in a smile)

3.

Float

ing
ly)
   i
    (in Khoury's warm

ish
)look

ing at thousands of
winter afternoons,through a
sometimes
a window In khoury
's

womB

for Ladies and Gents
like Restaurant
(always in Whom faces)
o ra mi

(sleep tick
s clock and
occasionally upon the)

perdreamhapsing
(floor cats drift)

4.

birds meet above the new Moon
an instant:drooping,describe suddenly
arcs of craziness;chasing each
other,disappear wisely into the texture of twilight....

She is as slender as an accident
and seems to notice nothing—
perhaps
what is worthy of her comprehension
does not exist
(or else

in her mute way this portion of a circumference
understands all mysteries)

—birds crying to each other
faintly whirl and
pivot in thickening air;now is the melted moment of terror and of
dreams but the earth rising imperceptibly merging with the
lost sea bends inward and
entirely,subtly vanishes.

5.

tonight the moon is round golden entire.   It
is satisfied and fragile,it does not
ask questions

such as "do you earn your living?   And if
not why not" or "how,under the circumstances,will
you support yourself?"   The moon is
round,not interested in
conduct
yellow
and complete.   Before proceeding
anywhere she takes care to surround her keen and
punctual circumference with an opaque
nimbus of perfectly safe colour,having
done which the moon
strides patiently along the wide quiet sky

like an intense disinterested virgin.

Who(finding herself with child)is peculiarly
careful not to lose the luminous smile which
has broken more than a handful of hearts,sent
a good many bright eyes into the dirt
hurried several big words into worms:

O poor moon
you will have a morning,
but you will be eventually slender
and noone will know unless perhaps the blind
force who laughs behind the sky.

the profound clown,Spring

Late Poems 1930–62

I

1.

this(a up green hugestness who and climbs)

alive this crumb(infinitesimal
this chip of being)jump does twenty times
easily unitself
                making my soul
wholly rejoice(and my only heart so full
of amazing god,each every bounce of blood
perfectly equals several trillion ams)

this(now rewandering one grassblade)how

occult particle of vitality did
totally transform the—and i mean
(sans blague)totally—universe with one
gesture.
                Thanks,colossal acrobat!
stupendous artist,feeble i salute

spontaneous insuperable you

2.

    cont)-
in
  this
      crazily
per
c
  hedtown(screams a
& screams
)&
screams
A
n(about to
bring for
       t)hW
omb
an
  -(in
u,
all;
y:

3.

mary green
cheerful & generous
flew to america
(just like a dream)

fearless & loyal
(honest & strong)
utterly irish
& realer than sunlight

it's lucky the man is
herself will make happy
(though poor he'll be rich &
if old he'll grow young)

4.

lively and loathesome moe's respectably dead

via(the papers are prudent)a heartattack:
dead is the whiteeyed face of,absurdly stuck
to its perfumed piglike body,a shark;and gone

"thiz-iz-un a chuf-tran-zish n" he frequently said

(married a nice gal who'd slaved in a buttonhole fac
tory:did odd jobs;ran errands like crazy,read black
stone every night;and landed skyhigh)no down
and out poor sonofabitch could possibly fail

to get a dollar from moe("meye sel-veye-wuz poor")

but nobody doublecrossed him and lived.   Somehow
it's devilish hard to realize we won't any more
hear his "sew-lawn-gooi eyel bih-seen-gyoo"

which maybe
                    (and Only A Just Judge knows)
                                        he will

5.

"think of it:not so long ago
this was a village"
                    "yes;i know"

"of human beings who prayed and sang:
or am i wrong?"
                    "no,you're not wrong"

"and worked like hell six days out of seven"
"to die as they lived:in the hope of heaven"

"didn't two roads meet here?"
                              "they did;
and over yonder a schoolhouse stood"

"do i remember a girl with blue-
sky eyes and sun-yellow hair?"
                        "do you?"

"absolutely"
          "that's very odd,
for i've never forgotten one frecklefaced lad"

"what could have happened to her and him?"
"maybe they waked and called it a dream"

"in this dream were there green and gold
meadows?"
          "through which a lazy brook strolled"

"wonder if clover still smells that way;
up in the mow"
              "full of newmown hay"

"and the shadows and sounds and silences"
"yes,a barn could be a magical place"

"nothing's the same:is it"
                        "something still
remains,my friend;and always will"

"namely?"
        "if any woman knows,
one man in a million ought to guess"

"what of the dreams that never die?"
"turn to your left at the end of the sky"

"where are the girls whose breasts begin?"
"under the boys who fish with a pin"

6.

out of bigg

est the knownun
barn
's
on tiptoe darkne

ss

boyandgirl
come
into a s
unwor

ld 2 to

be blessed by
floating
are
shadows of ove

r us-you-me a

n
g
e
l

s

II

1.

the phonograph may(if it likes)be prophe
tic:for instance let me recount to you,in
Sapphics quite dissimilar unto A.Swin
burne's the adventure

of Our Ezra,delver in mines strictly aes
thetic(short aes long as it happens by ex
ception)subjects,per what is loosely called a
Victor Victrola

—then right doggishly cocking one ear(bowwow)
our hero heard suddenly His Master's Voice:
"O Ezra, dear Ezra,come home to us now
for the clock in the(yes)steeple strikes(Yes)Joyce"

2.

in hammamet did camping queers et al)
with caverns measureless to man and how
lest which your worships deem apocryphal
o get a load of yonder arab now

bowed by the gaze of pederasts he queens
upon his toe and minces at the sand
the sorrows of young werther in his teens
and in his pants the urging of the hand

near and more near their draping selves redrape
lascivious hips against insisting sky
can there be no asylum no escape?
(his donkey looks mohammed in the eye

3.

bud(spiggy nuvduh fienus

cundry unduh fuggnwurl Who
Ray)this do

odling u
th with one muddy fu
t parked on yon polished readingru

mtable is a foo
llfledged soo
perstoo
dent of what was harvard yoo

niversity until a few
late unpleasantnesses made edew
cation trew

ly you
niversal by simply&silently substitou

ting for A(not C but)Bminus

4.

April"
    this letter's dated
            "23,
1946" and if anything
could prove the unprovable coming of such a spring
as nobody every imagined(including me)

Joe(for it's he)Gould's final remark would more
than execute perform achieve and do
the socalled trick with a universe to spare
(a universe far from excluding you)

so let us now pay strict attention "Af
ter all our genial friend the atomic bomb
is merely the transmutation of metal dream
ed of by mediaeval alchemists."   Paragraph

(who sighed "a rose,By any other name
would smell as"?
            Juliet)
                "Hoping you're the same

5.

come from his gal's
alf whistle song
meet frankiegang
"join us or else"
"what for i should"
alf drop like dead

gang grow&grow
grab all the dough
everyone give
who want to live
we small it strong
it right we wrong

so goodbye alf
you just a bum
go fug yoseself
because freedumb
means no one can
dare to be man

6.

"she had that softness which is falsity"
he frowned "plus budding strictly chasms of
uninnocence for eyes:and slippery
a pseudomind,not quite which could believe

in anything except most far from so
itself(with deep roots hugging fear's sweet mud
she floated on a silly nonworld's how
precarious inexistence like some dead

provocatively person of a thing
mancurious and manicured)i gave
the wandering stem a vivid(being young)
yank;and then vanished.   Seeing which,you dove

and brought me to the surface' smiling "by
my dick,which since has served me handily"

7.

says ol man no body—
datz woty say
yez,honey
But
we don't care an
we'll just sing:O
Sumpn
ter Sumpn an
lipster
lips ahmindy
OuterCo
ro
naofyohr
SolarE
clipse

8.

I'm very fond of
black bean
soup(O i'm
very
fond of black
bean soup
Yes i'm very fond
of black bean soup)But
i don't disdain
a beef-
steak

Gimme gin&bitters to
open my
eyes(O gimme
gin&
bitters to open
my eyes
Yes gimme gin&bitters
to open my eyes)But
i'll take straight rum as
a night-
cap

Nothing like a blonde for
ruining the
blues(O nothing
like a
blonde for ruining
the blues
Yes nothing like a blonde
for ruining the blues)But
i use redheads for
the tooth-
ache

Parson says a sinner will
perish in the
flames(O parson
says a
sinner will perish
in the flames
Yes Parson says a sinner
will perish in the flames)But
i reckon that's better
than freez-
ing

Everybody's dying to be
someone
else(O every
body's
dying to be some
one else
Yes everybody's dying
to be someone else)But
i'll live my life if
it kills
me

9.

devil crept in eden wood
(grope me wonderful grope me good)
and he saw two humans roaming
—hear that tree agroaning

woman chewed and man he chewed
(open beautiful open good)
and their eyes were wet and shining
—feel that snake aclimbing

lord he called and angel stood
(poke me darling o poke me good)
with a big thick sword all flaming
—o my god i'm coming

III

I.

love's the i guess most only verb that lives
(her tense beginning,and her mood unend)
from brightly which arise all adjectives
and all into whom darkly nouns descend

2.

love is a guess
that deepens
(time is a rose
which opens)
               your eyes,my
darling,are two
young worlds of dew

never yet named
a stillness
(wholly undreamed
what frailness)
                 not quite may
twilight's until
rival your smile

truer how much
than yearning
(newer to touch
than morning)
               your life is
only like one
star after rain

3.

we being not each other:without love
separate,smileless—only suppose your

spirit a certain reckoning demands...

wondering what ever is become of
with his acute gradual lusting glance
an illdressed wellmoving foolishwise

(tracking the beast Tomorrow by her spoor)
over the earth wandering hunter whom you
knew once?

what if(only suppose)

mine should overhear and answer Who
with the useless flanks and cringing feet
is this(shivering blond naked very poor
indeed)person that in the first light

standing washes my nightmare from his eyes?

4.

skies may be blue;yes
(when gone are hail and sleet and snow)
but bluer than my darling's eyes,
spring skies are no

hearts may be true;yes
(by night or day in joy or woe)
but truer than your lover's is,
hearts do not grow

nows may be new;yes
(as new as april's first hello)
but new as this our thousandth kiss,
no now is so

5.

she,straddling my lap,
hinges(wherewith I tongue each eager pap)
and,reaching down,by merely fingertips
the hungry Visitor steers to love's lips
Whom(justly as she now begins to sit,
almost by almost giving her sweet weight)
O,how those hot thighs juicily embrace!
and (instant by deep instant)as her face
watches,scarcely alive,that magic Feast
greedily disappearing least by least—
through what a dizzily palpitating host
(sharp inch by inch)swoons sternly my huge Guest!
until(quite when our touching bellies dream)
unvisibly love's furthest secrets rhyme.

6.

n w
O
h
S
LoW
h
myGODye
s s

7.

b
et
wee
n no
w dis
appear
ing mou
ntains a
re drifti
ng christi
an how swee
tliest bell
s and we'l
l be you'
ll be i'
ll be ?
? ther
efore
let'
s k
is
s

8.

when
     (day's amazing murder with)
                    perhaps

those mountains turn into these dreams who are
becauselessly themselves;alive and steps

one if(precisely nowhere from)of star,

what more than mere most spaceless and untimed
actual perfectly existences
through me have you eternally and roamed

—but still our you and i resemble us!

being without attempt each miracle
more isful than believe,how should we try
(like fictional poor minds whom fact can fool)
to live so ludicrous as death a lie?

only some silence called a thrush dares sing
(ours is a truth so beautifully young)

9.

there are so many tictoc
clocks everywhere telling people
what toctic time it is for
tictic instance five toc minutes toc
past six tic

Spring is not regulated and does
not get out of order nor do
its hands a little jerking move
over numbers slowly

                        we do not
wind it up it has no weights
springs wheels inside of
its slender self no indeed dear
nothing of the kind.

(So,when kiss Spring comes
we'll kiss each kiss other on kiss the kiss
lips because tic clocks toc don't make
a toctic difference
to kisskiss you and to
kiss me)

10.

time,be kind;herself and i
know that you must have your way

have it gently with ma belle—

but for beauty,understand,
life(and also you)would end

—time,she's very beautiful

II.

Us if therefore must forget ourselves)
or?if because more
than sleep like sleep are
they move who cannot be(never may

live have pain grow joy)alive
(therefore and or
if should night what open beyond all
memories a tomorrow of descending

brightful undeath)make
we why prayer for how things which do
not move and stern or with proudly
and peace

or only(and if because
we shall into silent go)into whitely
i shall?
go(into snow you will Go

12.

now winging selves sing sweetly,while ghosts(there
and here)of snow cringe;dazed an earth shakes sleep
out of her brightening mind:now everywhere
space tastes of the amazement which is hope

gone are those hugest hours of dark and cold
when blood and flesh to inexistence bow
(all that was doubtful's certain,timid's bold;
old's youthful and reluctant's eager now)

anywhere upward somethings yearn and stir
piercing a tangled wrack of wishless known:
nothing is like this keen(who breathes us)air
immortal with the fragrance of begin

winter is over—now(for me and you,
darling!)life's star prances the blinding blue

13.

every one of the red roses opened
(each in wholly her own amazing way
just as nobody else could ever have happened)"
up light spirits of mr and mrs dey

"well you know you said it was for a lady's",
michael's eyebrows "birthday" climbing "so"
(up light mrs and mr dey their bodies)
"naturally we're glad for her and you"

naturally(i sing to myself)imagine
that;imagine generous,gay,alive,
human:imag(and past their flowers a pigeon
swoops alighting on chaos of 10th)ine brave

"she's" proudly "so"(rose adds)"beautiful" and
dante(too)knew why the stars go round

IV

1.

ringed

with monstrous
a doomed
world's huge how

thunders are

(s
lowl
y

but certainly)crum

bl
i
ng

each more silent than each

remind
ers of this or
of that

once(who knows)maybe

fearless
him or
beautiful

possibly her

and
even lov
ing

est youme

2.

G
　ra
　　D
　　　ua
lLy &

　　as(through waiting simplicities of

space)arrived　　is
& suddenly Come makingly

silent descend,ingly creative(The

every
-Where
the from no-
where)The(silvery yesclowns

tumble!are made per!form

Featherish-nows-of-whiS

p
　e
　　r
　　)s

　　　N
　　o

　W

3.

ance)danc

-ing millions all
whispers are

blossoms of touc-
h
-able everywhere

Is
(leap who
flow dive
a-

light
&
O)
such made of
yes whiter

than wonders come
kissingly creatures
of dreaming how skilfulest
Floatingl

-y every-
thing perfectly shining
are(angels)and

a ar are ar a
-n-

d(d

4.

Cri
   C
k

et
in
-visible every
whereish;faint.ly shrill Most

(keen)
bell Of,shy a

spirit
:twisting
cry!ex
     transparent
           or

-din-

arywish;quick-
liest universal whis

per(Wis
      p
       Like un

              thing
)hearable

oar in a such tre

men
dous Sea
     who

our
s e l v e s be
ing,Call "

         t
I
M
e

  " SometimeS

5.

leastlessly

out
of this
more steep of
that most noisy muchful

colour

a(silent and
beginning)how
impossibly

fragrance

swims
is(who

the

little

who)floating a silently wanders
and very carefully smiling
how shyly to
herself moon-
childdoll

-dream

6.

s(

these out of in
finite no
where,who;arrive s
trollingly

:alight whitely and.

)now
flakes:are;guests,of t
wi
ligh

t

7.

rainsweet

s
tillnes
s

&

farnearf
uling
a thrush

's

v
oi
c

e

8.

life
    shuts &)opens the world
goes upward
         ,Spring every
where beginningly
.breathes(feels with men girls
trees lakes birds cities are bright
crisp which new)slowly most out of a more slovenly
of out most a of darkness

        rise
        things,
            move. MOVE. my

"life" in-ward-and-un-der-neath Its
ideas glides:whistling;naked:
strides,among
the clean hugeness of wind(leaps
tumbles a
foal)struts,

(erect
slim—.)
Born

9.

like a little bear twilight
climbs clumsily and beautifully the
ladder of the sky(a whipped and very little
bear who goes through his
tricks awkwardly and rapidly at
some fair,fearful of the cracking
whip)and
rungs of
cloud bend one by one under the hustling hairy
body of twilight
of
a little bear helplessly who wipes
his eyes with his
paw when the lash flicks his face,

gallops wincing

into his cage
              & a pale single
star(the performance being
concluded)bows solemnly to you & me

V

I.

BALLADE

does something lie who'd rather stand;
but if which tries to try to,the
universe opens like a wound:
spreadeagling on this bowery
dump's filthy floor a former e.
g. gentleman?—not my hands pry
fiercely that stinker from his pee
(because the poor sonofabitch is i)

do blood and flesh which danced and grinned
and skin more black than white are we
climb,jumping;at thick this rope's end:
to become such an itlike he
as,through space turning like a key,
unlocks all horror with one why?—
not my face screams in idiot glee
(because the poor sonofabitch is i)

on august sixth,let me remind
you,nineteen fortyfive a.d.
did a greengrocer from the land
of freedom and democracy
hurl out of relativity
some hundred thousand souls?—not my
life loathes that soulless s.o.b.
(because the poor sonofabitch is i)

illimitable Mystery
whom worlds must always crucify—
thanks be to God that You are me
because the poor sonofabitch is i

2.

for him alone life's worse than worst
is better than a mere world's best
whose any twilight is his last
and every sunrise is his first

3.

all stars are(and not one star only)love

—but if a day climbs from the mountain of
myself,each bird alive will sing for joy

in some no longer darkness who am i

4.

should far this from mankind's unmysteries
all nothing knowing particle who's i

look up,into not something called the sky

but(wild with midnight's millionary is)
a seething fearfully infinitude
of gladly glorying immortalities;

illimitable each transcending proud

most mind's diminutive how deathly guess

5.

thing no is(of
all things which are
who)so alive
quite as one star

kneeling whom to
(which disappear
will in a now)
i say my here

6.

should this fool die

let someone fond
of living lay

in his left hand

a flower whose

glory by no   .
mind ever was

taught how to grow

Appendices

A. FROM THE POET'S FIRST COLLECTION, 1904–5

1.

DEDICATED TO DEAR NANA CLARKE

When looking at that picture, all the past
Life of the sweet one cometh back to me;
And with emotion deep, I think when last
I saw her, in this world of vanity.

2.

As rooms are separated by a curtain,
So are our lives; yes, like those rooms; the first
One is our present life; the second is
Our life to come,—our better life in Heaven;
The separating curtain,—it is death.

3.

OUR FLAG

O flag of the nation! O Red,White and Blue!
O symbol of liberty,waving anew!
All through our lives may we reverence thee,
The nation's bright ensign for liberty!

Dear flag,thou art sacred in peace and in war,
Where many have died for the stripe and the star,
Where many have died that the slave may be free,
Have died for the nation and liberty!

Thou has seen the great battles,thou hast witnessed the strife
And the din of the conflicts,death struggling with life,
And thy bright,waving banner,the dying could see
Who had fought for the nation and liberty.

So whenever we meet thee,it matters not where;
Be thou waving at home or on battlement bare,
May we stop and salute thee,whenever we see
The nation's bright banner for liberty.

4.

GOD

Great, good, just, kind and loving God,
Oh! tell us how we can ever
Thank Thee enough for what Thou hast done!
For the bond that none can sever,
That binds us mortals close to Thee,
And gives us wisdom and eyes to see.

For it is Thou who gives us strength
To try to be like Thee.
And working, pushing toward the goal
Of purity;
We let our better nature shine
Illumined by Thy light divine.

5.

THE RIVER OF MIST

Stretching away to westward the great river lies quiet beneath me. So still it lies, that it seems as if it had not yet awakened from the delicious sleep brought on by the silence of night. A little distance from the shore a boat is moored on its glassy surface,—perfect to every detail the reflection glimmers below it. All is still and sombre and wonderful, as dawn gives way to daylight and night to morning.

As I stand leaning over the rail of the old wooden bridge that spans it, I give full play to my imagination, and gaze ahead into the morning fog that rests above its polished surface. And as I gaze, gaze into the deep white mist, my thoughts turn from earth to heaven, from mankind to my God. Far away, beyond the limits of that stream that fades into the atmosphere, I can see a great celestial river and a great celestial land. Ah! How my fancy pictures it,—how vivid and how real it seems! How plainly I can see the inestimable future! And how I doubly worship the Great Power that has created all this. How wonderful and how marvellous it all is! How sweet is this unconscious dreaming of the soul!

A slight sound from the waking city brings me back to ugly reality. I turn my head backward. In an instant, all the beauteous castles of the future which my imagination so vividly builded, vanish from my mind. All is gone! Gone in a moment! And nothing is left me but this world as I turn away from the wonderful river of mist.

B. FROM THE CAMBRIDGE LATIN SCHOOL YEARS, 1908–11

1.

The world is very big, and we
Are very small and ignorant,
But, till our Father doth transplant,
Into the garden we forsee—
Fragrant upon a far off lee—
Each frail and quickly withered plant,
He doth to each a duty grant,
And He hath given one to me!

To all the work that doth relate
To aiding these my fellow men,
To peace, to nation, and to state,
To noblest thought & impulse, when
The impulse comes—I dedicate
This heart, this soul, this mind, this pen!

2.

A chilly,murky night;
The street lamps flicker low,
A hail-like,whispering rain
Beats 'gainst the streaked,bleak pane;
The sickly,ghostly glow
Of the blurred,blinking,wavering,flickering light
Shines on the muddy streets in sombre gleams
Like a wierd lamp post on a road of dreams.

A dreary,heavy darkness;
In quivering folds it creeps
Over the shrouded world;
The leaves are dry and curl'd,
The soul of summer sleeps
In a black pall where all the world lies markless,—
And shrouded 'neath that form whose clammy breath
Chills as it clasps,he sleeps the sleep of death.

Night,thou canst not dismay!
For when,on life's dark eve,
Like flowers past their bloom,
We tenant that grim tomb,
And all behind us leave,
Know that from its cold clutch into the Day
We walk,preserved,uninjured;—comprehend
No fear,no hell,no misery,no End!

3.

THE PASSING OF THE YEAR

The world outside is dark; my fire burns low;
All's quiet, save the ticking of the clock
And rustling of the ruddy coals, that flock
Together, hot and red, to gleam and glow.
The sad old year is near his overthrow,
And all the world is waiting for the shock
That frees the new year from his dungeon lock.—
So the tense earth lies waiting in her snow.

Old year, I grieve that we should part so soon,—
The coals burn dully in the wavering light;
All sounds of joy to me seem out of tune,—
The tying embers creep from red to white,
They die. Clocks strike. Up leaps the great, glad moon!
Out peal the bells! Old year,—dear year,—good night!

4.

EARLY SUMMER SKETCH

The rain
Drips down
O'er fields
All green
With grain.

Earth's gown
Is seen
Clinging
To her
In folds
Bedraggled.

The grey
Sky yields
Great drops
Down-winging
O'er tops
Of fir
And wolds
Green-gay
With Summer,
The new-comer.

For sod
Has haggled
With sky.

The tears
Fall fast
On high.

Aghast
And Dazed
Earth stands,
And lifts
Her hands,
To see
The wrong
Which she
Has done.

The sun
Breaks out
And sears
The drifts
Of cloud
That float
Along.

The shroud
No longer
Low-lies.

The note
Of the song
Of the bird
Is heard.

The cloud
Is furled.

Earth cries
A shout
Of gladness.

O'er skies,
And trees,
And leaf,
And leas
Of bay
Breaks day.

5.

SUMMER SONG

I

Warm air throbbing with locust songs,
Warm clouds screening the heavens' blue rifts.
Warm sun shadowing over-head cloud drifts,
Warm sky straining, earth-tethered, at her cloud-thongs.

II

Far away
A thrushes' choir trills.
Far away
The murmur of a river's rills,
Drumming of the thunder fist,
Coming of the rain mist,—
Peeping,
Creeping,
Leaping,
Sweeping
O'er the weeping
Hot hills.

6.

IF

If freckles were lovely, and day was night,
And measles were nice and a lie warn't a lie,
    Life would be delight,—
    But things couldn't go right
    For in such a sad plight
I wouldn't be *I.*

If earth was heaven, and now was hence,
And past was present, and false was true,
    There might be some sense
    But I'd be in suspense
    For on such a pretense
You wouldn't be *you.*

If fear was plucky, and globes were square,
And dirt was cleanly and tears were glee
    Things *would* seem fair,—
    Yet they'd all despair,
    For if here was there
We wouldn't be *we.*

7.

THE EAGLE

I

It was one of those clear,sharp,mistless days
　　That summer and man delight in.
Never had Heaven seemed quite so high,
Never had earth seemed quite so green,
Never had world seemed quite so clean
　　　Or sky so nigh.
　　And I heard the Deity's voice in
　　　The sun's warm rays,
　　And the white cloud's intricate maze,
And the blue sky's beautiful sheen.

2

I looked to the heavens and saw him there,—
　　A black speck downward drifting.
Nearer and nearer he steadily sailed,
Nearer and nearer he slid through space,
In an unending aerial race,
　　　This sailor who hailed
　　From the Clime of the Clouds.—Ever shifting,
　　　On billows of air.
　　And the blue sky seemed never so fair;
And the rest of the world kept pace.

3

On the white of his head the sun flashed bright;
　　And he battled the wind with wide pinions,
Clearer and clearer the gale whistled loud,
Clearer and clearer he came into view,—
Bigger and blacker against the blue.
　　　Then a dragon of cloud
　　　Gathering all its minions
　　　　Rushed to the fight,
　　And swallowed him up at a bite;
And the sky lay empty clear through.

4

Long I watched.   And at last afar
    Caught sight of a speck in the vastness;
Ever smaller,ever decreasing,
Ever drifting,drifting away
Into the endless realms of day;
    Finally ceasing.
    So into Heaven's vast fastness
      Vanished that bar
Of black,as a fluttering star
Goes out while still on its way.

5

So I lost him.   But I shall always see
    In my mind
The warm,yellow sun,and the ether free;
The vista'd sky,and the white cloud trailing,
    Trailing behind.—
And below the young earth's summer-green arbors,
And on high the eagle,—sailing,sailing
    Into far skies and unknown harbors.

8.

THE BOY AND THE MAN

Once upon a time
> A boy looked to the sky
> Where big white clouds lay furled,
> And he muttered with a sigh,
> "O, would I were a man!—
> How commonplace this world!
> Would I could roam and roam,
> Where all is strange and new,
> Where there are deeds to do,
> And find a grand, new home
> Where new folks came and went"—
> Thus did the boy lament,
> Ending as he began,—
> "O, would I were a man!"

Once upon a time
> A man looked to the sky
> Where big, white clouds lay furled,
> And he cried with a sigh,
> "O, would I were a boy!—
> How dear was that old world,
> With the dear ones ever close,
> Afar from strange, new places
> Full of unknown, staring faces,
> Unfeeling, and morose.
> Give me my home, God-sent!"
> Thus did the man lament,
> Groaning, "Gone boyhood's joy!
> O, would I were a boy!"

9.

God,Thine the hand that doth extend
  The booby prize of failure,and
The victor's chaplet in the end.
  God,Thine the hand.

God,mine the power to die or live,
  To find the earth-fruit sweet or sour,
To take and keep,or take and give.
  God,mine the power.

God,keep me trying to win the prize;
  Pamper me not,though I be crying.
Though snickering worlds wink owlish eyes,
  God,keep me trying.

10.

MY PRAYER

God make me the poet of simplicity,
    Force,and clearness.   Help me to live
Ever up to ever higher standards.   Teach me to lay
    A strong,simple,big-rocked wall
    Firmly,the first of all,
And to fill in the fissures with the finer stones and clay
    Of alliteration,simile,metaphor.   Give
    Power to point out error in sorrow and in felicity.
Make me a truthful poet,ever true to the voice of my
               Call,
    Groping about in the blackest night
    For ever clearer,dearer light,
Sturdily standing firm and undismayed on a Pillar of
               Right,
    Working with heart,and soul,and a willing might,
Writing my highest Ideal large in whatsoever I write,
    Truthfully,loftily,chivalrously,and cheerfully ever,
            Fearfully,never.

II.

On souls robbed of their birth-right's better part,
Born only in one world, through life to see
This nether sphere alone—God's pity be;
Poor, purblind purchasers at life's high mart.
The Great Physician, lest the ravaged heart
Reveal itself in anguish, did decree
The Lord of Sense, Contempt, that he set free
The mangled spirit from its memory-smart.
So, deep in scorn for him of perfect sight,
The blinded soul remembereth not her scars.

——But who hath sudden felt his spirit beat,
Sped through the smoking dark with fear-shod feet,
Still hounded, haunted, hunted down the night
By all the crying beauty of the stars?

12.

DEATH'S CHIMNEY

Within,a coldly echoing floor:a terror
Of narrow,naked walls,whitened and ghastly,
Through whose grim hollowness,faint and incessant,
Is heard a murmuring horror of fires communing.
What flesh and blood,what hands and face,what beauty
Shrivels beneath the touch of flames caressing—
Becomes obliterate in this awful furnace?
What life dwelt in this formless heap of ashes
Drawn forth,—the fires subdued,the furnace opened,—
To inhabit yon dead vault of icy marble,
Under the day,dwelling in its own darkness,
Under the world,shrouded in its own silence?
What eye shall read this shadowy inscription?
What hand upon this cold thing lay its cypress?
What lip shall touch the silent vase of ashes?
The body,the human body divine,burning.

Without,warm flood of universal sunshine;
And a white butterfly,hovering,soaring,ascending...

13.

AFTER-GLOW

Blue water, and behind,
Benevolent orange sky,
And gentle sheep that troop
From their huge fields of cloud,
Hurrying, headed all
Homeward across the heaven,
Unto the western folds,
Where stands upon a hill,
Calling with gentle voice,
One cheery shepherd-star.

Stand still, O Shepherd! I,
With many other feet
And many, many flocks
From all the purple earth,
And all the yellow heaven,
Am coming, hurrying home,
Lifting mine eyes to thee,
And listening for thy call
Across the fragrant fields,
Adown the quiet world.

Grey water, yellow sky;
Alas! my star is gone,—
Departed, over the hill.
And all the flocks that heard
Their shepherd's call, and I,
Pause, midway in the rich
And honeyed middle heaven,
Sniffing the luscious sweet;—
No star, no shepherd.   Shall
We lag in the middle way?

No.   On, ye flocks!   And I,
Who heard his call, and saw
His tender, starry face,—
Down the soft, padded mead,
O'er fair, alluring fields,
Along ambrosial lands,
Away into the sun,
Will follow, follow him,
And farther, farther on,
And up, up, over the hill!

C. TRANSLATIONS FROM HORACE, 1913

I.

BOOK IV, ODE 7

Farewell,runaway snows!   For the meadow is green,and the tree stands
  Clad in her beautiful hair.
New life leavens the land!   The river,once where the lea stands,
  Hideth and huggeth his lair.
Beauty with shining limbs 'mid the Graces comes forth,and in glee stands,
  Ringed with the rythmical fair.

Hope not,mortal,to live forever,the year whispers lowly.
  Hope not,time murmurs,and flies.
Soft is the frozen sod to the Zephyr's sandal,as wholly
  Summer drives Spring from the skies,—
Dying when earth receives the fruits of Autumn,till slowly
  Forth Winter creeps,and she dies.

Yet what escapes from heaven,the fleet moons capture,retrieving;
  When through Death's dream we survey
Heroes and kings of old,in lands of infinite grieving,
  What are we?   Shadow and clay.
Say will rulers above us the fate tomorrow is weaving
  Add to the sum of today?

Hear me:whatever thou giv'st to thine own dear soul,shall not pleasure
  Hungering fingers of kin.
Once in the gloom,when the judge of Shades in pitiless measure
  Dooms thee to journey within,
Birth,nor eloquent speech,nor gift of piety's treasure
  Opens the portal of sin.

Never,goddess of chasteness,from night infernal thou freest
  One who for chastity fell.
Ever,hero of Athens,him who loved thee thou seest
  Writhe in the chainings of Hell.

2.

BOOK I, ODE 4

The fetters of winter are shattered,shattered,
And the limbs of the earth are free,—
Spring,and the breeze that loveth the lea!
And the old keels—gaping and tempest battered—
Men roll them down to the sea.

Lo,how the sweet new magic bewitcheth
The hind with his fire-side dream;
The ox in his byre stamps with desire;
No more on the meadows the white rime pitcheth
His tents of a wintry gleam.

The Graces are dancing by mountains and gorges,
Like blossoms white in the moon;
Love is their light through the spell-bound night.
Under the world in Hell's huge forges
Hammers gigantic croon.

Open thy door;death knocks,who careth
For palace and hut the same.
Why wilt thou plan with life but a span?
All feel the hand that never spareth,
The fingers that know not fame.

Tomorrow—who knows?—in her train may bring thee
The city of dim renown.
There is nought redeems from the House of Dreams—
Ne'er again shall the kind dice king thee,
Never be Pleasure thy crown.

3.

BOOK II, ODE 14

Ah, Postumus, fleet-footed are the years!
    And what is Piety's imploring glance
To Age and Death, the dauntless charioteers?

My friend, think not to buy deliverance
    With smoking centuries of hecatombs.
It shall not profit thine inheritance.

King of the City of Unnumbered Homes,
    Who doth the monster and the brute compel,
Where the blind darkness ever gropes and roams,

By that black, languorous stream that winds in Hell,
    Whereon the noble and the knave must face
A common passage—wither, who can tell!—

Great Pluto, Postumus, implores thy grace!....
    Silence....Didst think those eyes, which are two stars,
Would suffer for thy sake one tear's embrace?

Although thou locked thy portals unto Mars,
    Nor e'er bestrode,—uncurbed by bit or rein,
Old Hadria's white horses,—'scaped the scars

Of the sword-edged sirocco, 'tis in vain.
    Fate bids that journey to Cocytus' stream,
And Danaus' ill-famed race behold again,

And Sisyphus, damned unto toil supreme.
    Fate sunders wife and husband, wedded brass
And miser; all and each, as in a dream.

How treacherous the treasures we amass!
    One only hath remembrance of our care,
The hated cypress-tree.   And so we pass.

Riving an hundred locks, and laying bare
    In its ripe age rich Caecuban divine,
Purer than pontiffs quaff, a lordlier heir
    Shall paint the pavement with thy titled wine!

4.

BOOK I, ODE 24

Who chides the tears that weep so dear a head?
Sorrowful Muse,for whom the father wed
The voice of waters to a cithern string,
Teach thou my grief to sing.

Ye sisters,Right and Honor,and forsooth
Unshaken Loyalty,and naked Truth,
Quintillius the peerless ye shall weep,
Who sleeps unending sleep.

Vainly,poor Virgil,rise thy pious prayers
To heaven which took him from thee unawares;
His memory many a noble friend reveres,
Thine were the bitterest tears.

What tho' more sweet thy lyre than his of Thrace,
When listening trees joyed in the music's grace,
Would life reclaim the shade from the beyond,
Which,with his fearsome wand,

The Shepherd,harsh the doors of fate to keep,
Has gathered once unto his shadowy sheep?
'Tis hard:but when 'twere impious to rebel,
Less grows the load borne well.

5.

BOOK IV, ODE 6
(An Invocation to Apollo)

O,blessed of the gods,
Shield of the race of Rome,
Are Faith and Fame at odds?
Thy smile is Spring.—O,too long thou dost roam,
    From home.

As a fond mother stands,
Seeking with prayerful eyes
O'er sea and sinuous sands
Her long-departed son,for whom black skies
    Arise.

So doth this land of ours
Yearn for her mighty son;
All lapped in fruit and flow'rs,
While on her waves the pinioned vessels run,
    Nor shun

The pirate or his kin.
The hearths of faith are pure,
And tamed is spotted sin.
With Caesar safe,where shall the savage boor
    Endure?

The mother loves to trace
In baby eyes and brow
Gleams of the father's face.
What's war with Spain?   Who fears the Scythian now?
    O,thou,

Upon thy Roman hills
Salute the drowsy light,
And lead the vine,that fills
Thy bowls,to the chaste tree in wedlock rite.
    Requite

The Gods with prayer and wine,
And as her heroes-Greece,
So,Roman,rank divine
Thy Caesar,with a joy which shall increase,
  Nor cease.

    * * * * * *

To thee the poet drinks—
"Long life!"—ere day is done;
"Peace to thy land!"—when sinks
Under the ocean,mellow eve begun,
  The sun.

INDEX OF FIRST LINES

NOTE: All first lines are treated as single-line entries even when their physical elements have been typographically separated. A single slant (/) has been used to indicate such a separation; e.g.

for 'the/ sky/ was'
read 'the

sky

was'.

When the first lines of two or more poems are identically worded, a double slant (//) indicates the presence of a second, identifying line; e.g.

for 'why// do the'
read 'why

do the'.

a-   571
a blue woman with sticking out breasts hanging   216
A chilly,murky night;   1059
A clan of imps—morose and ugly things,   908
a clown's smirk in the skull of a baboon   361
a connotation of infinity   138
a football with white eyebrows the   465
a fragrant sag of fruit distinctly grouped.   121
A gentleness for my dog   881
a)glazed mind layed in a/ urinal   388
a gr   705
a great   786
a grin without a   797
a he as o   703
a kike is the most dangerous   644
a light Out)/& first of all foam   359
a like a   654
a man who had fallen among thieves   256
a monstering horror swallows   711
A painted wind has sprung   930
a peopleshaped toomany-ness far too   528
a politician is an arse upon   550
a pretty a day   509
A rain-drop on the eyelids of the earth,   861
a round face near the top of the stairs   813
a salesman is an it that stinks Excuse   549
A thin, foul scattering of grim, grey snow,   907
a thing most new complete fragile intense,   163
a thrown a   632
a total stranger one black day   730